ASIAN DEFENCE REVIEW 2013

ASIAN DEFENCE REVIEW 2013

Edited by

Air Marshal

Vinod Patney

SYSM, PVSM, AVSM, VrC (Retd)

KNOWLEDGE WORLD

KW Publishers Pvt Ltd

New Delhi

in association with

Centre for Air Power Studies

New Delhi

The Centre for Air Power Studies is an independent, non-profit, academic research institution established in 2002 under a registered Trust to undertake and promote policy-related research, study and discussion on the trends and developments in defence and military issues, especially air power and the aerospace arena, for civil and military purposes. Its publications seek to expand and deepen the understanding of defence, military power, air power and aerospace issues without necessarily reflecting the views of any institution or individuals except those of the authors.

Vinod Patney
Director General
Centre for Air Power Studies
P-284, Arjan Path
Subroto Park
New Delhi 110010

Tele: (91-11) 25699131

E-mail: capsnetdroff@gmail.com
website: www.capsindia.org

ISBN 978-93-83649-12-9

Published in India by Kalpana Shukla

KNOWLEDGE WORLD
KW Publishers Pvt Ltd
4676/21, First Floor, Ansari Road, Daryaganj, New Delhi 110002
✆ +91 11 23263498 / 43528107 ✉ knowledgeworld@vsnl.net • www.kwpub.com

Printed and bound in India

2011 FPBA BEST PUBLISHERS AWARD (ENGLISH)

Contents

Contributors

Air Marshal **Vinod Patney**, SYSM PVSM AVSM VrC (Retd), Director General, Centre for Air Power Studies, New Delhi.

Dr **Manpreet Sethi**, ICSSR Senior Fellow affiliated to the Centre for Air Power Studies, New Delhi.

Wing Commander **KK Nair**, Research Fellow, Centre for Air Power Studies, New Delhi.

Dr **Shalini Chawla**, ICSSR Senior Fellow affiliated to the Centre for Air Power Studies, New Delhi.

Group Captain **Ashok Kumar Chordia**, Former Senior Fellow, Centre for Air Power Studies, New Delhi.

Dr **Sitakanta Mishra**, Research Fellow, Centre for Air Power Studies, New Delhi.

Wing Commander **Nishant Gupta**, Research Fellow, Centre for Air Power Studies, New Delhi.

Wing Commander **Raj Mongia**, Research Fellow, Centre for Air Power Studies, New Delhi.

Ms **Sana Hashmi**, Associate Fellow, Centre for Air Power Studies, New Delhi.

Ms **Simrat Kaur Virk**, Research Associate, Centre for Air Power Studies, New Delhi.

Ms **Pravda P**, Non-Resident Fellow, Centre for Air Power Studies, New Delhi.

Mr **Arjun Subramaniam P**, Associate Fellow, Centre for Air Power Studies, New Delhi.

1

Air Dominance: Concept and Practice

Vinod Patney

Many years have elapsed since we witnessed a conflict where the opposing air forces were of comparable capability and it became necessary to wage a war for supremacy in the air. Possibly, the last occasion was the 1971 Indo-Pak conflict that led to the birth of Bangladesh. That was over 40 years ago! In the 1973 Arab-Israeli "Yom Kippur" War, the Israeli Air Force was challenged to start with but essentially by ground fire. There were few air battles and Israel got the upper hand in the air dominance stakes rather easily with the use of electronic jammers and good tactical flying. After that, air power played a major role in the victory that followed. In the 1982 operations in the Beka'a Valley, the Israeli Air Force outclassed the Lebanese defences to win total air superiority. Before the 1991 Gulf War, it was envisaged that an air battle could ensue but the Iraqis put up a very weak challenge, stayed on the defensive and preferred to fly their aircraft to Iran. Thereafter, in the subsequent conflicts that have occurred—in the Balkans, Kosovo, Afghanistan, Iraq, Lebanon, Gaza and more recently, in Libya, etc — there has really been no viable opposition to the North Atlantic Treaty Organisation (NATO) or 'allied' or Israeli air power. During Kargil 1999, Pakistan had a reasonably good air force but elected not to use it or was wary of the consequences of its use.

Although the military victory in the ongoing conflict in Iraq and Afghanistan was quickly achieved, peace is yet to be restored in those troubled lands. Again, there is a large and increasing number of areas on the globe where terrorism and 4th Generation Warfare are taking their toll. In these types of operations, the importance of air power, though still significant, is somewhat reduced.

The one-sided air operations over the last many years in a number of varied types of conflicts in different types of terrain has led some to question the need for the expensive weapon systems needed to win the air battle. It is argued that the nature of conflict has altered; major battles are highly unlikely in a globalised world; we must prepare for the types of conflicts that are far more likely to occur; and that defence budgets would be better utilised for procurements and training that suit the needs of the conflicts that are ongoing or those that are more likely to occur in the near future. It is also stated that in anti-insurgency and 4th Generation War, we need more manpower and far more specific to task equipment. Therefore, it is argued that we must have "more boots on the ground," and that programmes like the F-22 can, and should be, curtailed. Such sentiments are expressed in many parts of the world, and most often, presumably by military practitioners and others who have but a distant relationship with aerospace power, and a consequent lack of appreciation of what air power implies and what it can achieve.

History teaches us that whilst it would be wrong to only "prepare to fight the last war," it would be equally incorrect to forget the lessons of previous wars. Moreover, it takes a long time to develop capabilities and we cannot legislate to the enemy on the type of war to be fought. In fact, the type of war the enemy chooses to prosecute will in all likelihood take advantage of our weaknesses. Hence, we must be prepared to fight throughout the spectrum of conflict. Air dominance has a part to play, in varying degrees, in sub-conventional, conventional, even nuclear wars or even the threat of a nuclear war. Such capability would also have deterrence and coercive power. Again, there is an old and trusted adage that since the maturity of the air arm, no country has ever won a war without winning the air war, and no country that has won the air war has ever lost the war. This is a very pertinent statement and we will do well to bear it in mind.

Doubts are expressed on the need for air domination assets as, more often than not, we tend to read recent history from the point of view of the victors. The impact of air power could be better understood if we were to place ourselves in the shoes of the Kosovars, the Iraqis, the Taliban in Afghanistan, or, for that matter, the Palestinians and Lebanese who faced the wrath of Israeli air power. The lack of adequate air capability was acutely felt and a military defeat was beyond doubt.

The requirements of current conflicts and the types of conflicts that are envisaged must be met. The immediate needs demand higher priority. At the same time, the military option by itself can never bring about the desired end results, and a multi-dimensional approach is necessary. However, this article is restricted to military issues only and concentrates on the meaning of air dominance and the advisability of securing air dominance. Other equally important considerations like geopolitics, the nuclear factor, Comprehensive Test Ban Treaty (CTBT), Missile Technology Control Regime (MTCR), Fissile Material Cut-off Treaty (FMCT) and the all important consideration of international relations and diplomacy are all beyond the pale of this article. Also, in this article, the phrases "air dominance" and "air domination" are used interchangeably. It is presumed that there are degrees of air domination and air domination exists from the time one side gains the upper hand and extends to when full air dominance is achieved.

What is Air Dominance?

In simple terms, air dominance implies the dominance of the air medium. That is just a phrase but if the concept of air dominance is well understood, it will be easy to appreciate that it is the prime objective of the 'armed forces,' it supports all the armed forces, and is not only an air force task although air power will have a significant part to play in achieving it. Unquestionably, securing air dominance is the *raison d'etre* of air power. It must also be emphasised that achieving air dominance is not an end unto itself. No capability ever is. However, air dominance is a means to an end and facilitates, in no uncertain measure, the early and favourable outcome of conflict. If air dominance is only a means to an end, the question arises as to how much air effort should be devoted towards winning it? This is an important consideration but the answer is implicit in the understanding of the concept of air domination. Some will argue that almost the entire capability of air power should be used for the mission to win dominance. Others will again find fault with the air force for giving undue priority to 'fighting its own battle.' The optimum use of air assets for the air dominance battle will depend on circumstances that prevail at the time. There could also well be major differences amongst protagonists in the manner in which available assets are used. The differences will come about because of the relative strengths and capabilities, planning parameters that could vary, and the overall strategy adopted by the adversaries to bring the conflict to an early and satisfactory conclusion as seen from their own respective points of view. No hard and fast rules can be formulated. The importance and salience of air domination will be better gauged by an examination of the purpose and implications of air dominance.

Purpose and Implications of Air Dominance

The purpose of air domination is to have as near as possible full freedom of the skies. The 'freedom' has also been described as "freedom to attack and freedom from attack." Although reasonably accurate, the phrase does not fully describe the concept of air dominance. Greater elucidation is called for and the different purposes should be enumerated.

The first purpose that air dominance serves is to ensure air defence of our territory or area of interest. The area of interest could even be in enemy country. The primary objective is to inhibit enemy aircraft from attacking our sea, air or ground assets. It will be a major achievement if we can ensure that enemy aircraft cannot successfully attack any of our armed forces or centres of industry or population. The basic requirements are effective radar cover or other means so that we can ensure detection at maximum possible ranges; a sound identification system, and kill capability to engage enemy aircraft identified as hostile as far away as possible from the intended target. If we can achieve the kill in enemy territory itself, so much the better. Radar cover could be markedly augmented with the use of the Airborne Warning and Control System (AWACS) or aerostat balloons. The identification systems will involve data links and data processing, and the 'kill' systems could be aircraft armed with missiles and guns, ground-based weapon systems that will include Surface-to-Air-Missiles (SAMs) and Air Defence (AD) artillery. As and when available, lasers and directed energy weapons could also be used. Over and above these essential requirements, there must be a robust communication and control system. Air defence is a difficult operation of war. Perforce, there will be a number of vulnerable targets and it may take a few days for us to discern the enemy strategy. Again, we would not wish for our air defence assets to be spread out too thinly. Compromises will have to be made and the optimum utilisation of resources worked out and plans altered progressively, depending on the circumstances. Given the perennial scarcity of resources, it will be well nigh impossible to provide effective air defence throughout our country and other areas of interest. However, we should be able to protect defined areas over stipulated timeframes. Even then, prioritisation is essential. Such calculations and related decisions should form part of the joint planning system.

Leading on from air defence requirements, the second purpose of air dominance is to progressively move from achieving a favourable air situation to air superiority and on to air supremacy. This can be brought about by lowering the enemy air capability slowly but surely. It will involve good air defence systems as well as attacks on the air and command and control assets of the enemy. The idea is to relentlessly push the enemy onto the defensive. The degree of air superiority that we can muster is an important consideration for the prosecution of war by our surface forces and air forces. However, although the concepts of air defence and air superiority are very important considerations, they remain somewhat passive aspects with the limited objective of preventing the enemy from harming us. It is probably more important to cause harm to the enemy forces by inflicting the desired degree of damage to enemy targets and target systems.

The enemy will also try to field an effective air defence system and vie for air superiority. Hence, the third purpose of air domination is to ensure that our air operations are not hampered by enemy air or ground defences. This will involve Electronic Warfare (EW), techniques for Suppression of Enemy Air Defences (SEAD) or Destruction of Enemy Air Defences (DEAD) by hard or soft kills and, probably most importantly, by shooting down enemy air defence aircraft in air-to-air engagements. In addition, deception and other tactical considerations will also impact on this requirement.

Fourthly, and probably most importantly, air domination also encompasses the ability to hit air and surface targets effectively and speedily within the defined area where we exercise air domination. This is the essence of air domination. The previous three considerations or purposes were but a prelude to the use of air assets against enemy forces unhampered by enemy air. The same holds true for attacks on enemy economic or other targets. The success of the previous three aspects of air domination will determine the freedom to attack and, consequently, the accuracy and effectiveness of the air attacks. Enemy military assets have to be attacked to inflict damage or destruction to the required extent in order to force a military victory. At the same time, with air domination, air assets can be used against enemy forces in close vicinity of our forces with considerable impunity. Aircraft can now fly over the battle area over extended periods of time, carefully select targets and hit them. Air domination will also permit the luxury of immediate battle damage assessment and near immediate reengagements, if required. Moreover, the need for the very expensive standoff weapon systems will decrease and attacks on enemy surface forces can be carried out more cost effectively. What is stated above will apply when full air domination has been achieved. In practice, such instances will indeed be rare, particularly if the adversaries are reasonably well matched, but the effectiveness of air attacks against enemy forces will be directly dependent on the degree of air domination that we have achieved.

Fifthly, the attacks on surface forces must also include attacks on enemy missile sites and AD artillery that can target areas in our country or areas we wish to protect. The ranges of ground-to-ground missiles have increased considerably and they can be fired with effect from well within the enemy country. The option of choice to neutralise them is the use of our air assets, be they aircraft or some form of unmanned vehicles. With air domination, it will become easier to locate, acquire and destroy such targets.

Another important purpose of air domination is intelligence gathering. Gathering Intelligence with Surveillance and Reconnaissance (ISR) is a prime task for an air force. The means available could be visual reconnaissance or sensors of different types placed aboard aircraft, Unmanned Air Vehicles (UAVs) or satellites. The sensors will include those required for eavesdropping on enemy communications and interception of all types of information that is relayed from one enemy source to another. Mapping the enemy electronic Order of Battle (ORBAT) should be a priority task. Gathering intelligence is an ongoing exercise in peace and war and aerospace assets are the prime instruments for the task. In the same breath it, must also be mentioned that Human Intelligence (HUMINT) has an equally important role to play and often, the different sources complement each other and offer corroboration where needed. Air domination will also permit enhanced safety in intelligence gathering, collation, analysis and timely dissemination. Air assets can also be used as relay stations.

It will be appreciated that air dominance is a major military requirement and it represents the all embracing use of air power. Its impact on the prosecution of war is indeed significant and, for this reason alone, achieving air dominance should be a high priority task in the planning of joint military operations.

The impact of air domination would be that the side that is able to win it will be able to 'see' what it wants to see, 'hear' what it wishes to hear, discern what is necessary, hit targets at will and operate with freedom. Air domination represents the unfettered use of the air medium.

In spite of the gains that will accrue with air dominance, the question must be asked as to whether a country like India can hope to achieve it against our possible adversaries. Many would equate our quest for air dominance with chasing a mirage. It is true that fighting for air dominance will require a much stronger air force than what the adversary can bring to bear on us. However, air dominance can also be progressively achieved with better planning and optimum use of extant resources. The fundamentals should be clearly understood. Gaining air dominance will always be a worthy objective and its attainment will ease the way to military success. It must also be mentioned that although full air dominance may not be possible, any level of air dominance will be of considerable benefit. Again, much will depend on the nature of war, its likely duration and limits of action that may be placed on the armed forces. Such issues will hopefully be considered in the joint planning, and consensus reached on the desirability of maximum possible level of air dominance.

Benefits of Air Dominance

Unchallenged use of the air medium promotes obvious military advantages, some of which have been described earlier. The situation permits many options in the choice of targets, and the weapon systems to be used against them. For instance, it will not be necessary to move the battle front progressively. Parallel war can be conducted with impunity. With no, or vastly reduced, enemy air interference, planning and prosecution of military options is considerably simplified. Greater choices also become available in the weapons to be used. A smaller number of precision guided weapons would be required, as many target systems could be engaged, at reduced costs, by unguided weapons whilst retaining the ability to cause the desired degree of damage.

Our special forces are highly trained to carry out tasks in enemy country. Apart from the chance element intrinsic in such operations, a major drawback is the inherent risk in infiltration and exfiltration. With air domination, the passage to and from target areas will be safe from enemy air and the target area could also be sanitised from the air. Under the circumstances, even normal troops could be tasked for missions where otherwise the requirement would have been for special forces only. Similarly, air dropping of agents and their retrieval will be much easier and involve no detailed planning requirements. Again, air evacuation of combat casualties could be more readily carried out. Indeed, a number of operations that carry high levels of risk would be simplified beyond recognition.

Military operations involving airborne or heliborne troops are complicated and often dangerous, essentially because of high vulnerability at launch pads, air transportation to the target in machines that can be readily downed by enemy air or ground fire, problems in linking up with the main forces, if necessary, and resupply requirements. All these 'problems' are considerably eased with even a modicum of air dominance, leave alone full air dominance.

Thus, air dominance implies that the enemy territory, and the otherwise highly defended areas therein, are laid bare for attack. It would be a planner's dream if we could achieve it in full measure. However, even with reduced levels of air dominance, it would then become progressively less problematic to increase the domination quotient. In time, the enemy would be rendered incapable of offensive action. This recognition will result in the stronger adversary exercising escalation dominance and fighting the battle at intensity levels of its own choosing; and relegating the other side to either vie for peace or fight on terms dictated by the side that enjoys air domination. Air power capability is highly visible and the likelihood of one side attaining a fair degree of air domination, with consequences that will automatically follow, increases the deterrence level and, for that matter, the capability to exercise coercion as well. May be there is some substance in the claim made by an official of M/s Lockheed Martin that the F-22 aircraft is nearly as good a deterrent as a nuclear weapon! There could be some exaggeration but the import of the statement is all too clear.

Achieving Air Dominance

Achieving air dominance is not a factor of brute force alone. Considerable planning and forethought is necessary. Air power characteristics of flexibility, speed of action and reaction, etc have a major part to play. It is often mooted that air power tasks like air defence, counter-air operations, interdiction, close air support, air maintenance, etc are considered separately only for greater clarity. This is indeed true. In fact, there is a close inter-relationship and inter-dependence amongst all these tasks and others as well. In one way or the other, all air power tasks aid the battle for air dominance. In some scenarios, a major part of the entire force capability may be used to secure the essential task of air dominance. At times, surface forces must also play their part with special reference to the use of the army and naval special forces. Hence, the requirements to fight the battle for air domination will, *inter alia*, include a sufficient number of appropriate aircraft of adequate range and capability; weapons and missiles; radars and other sensors; AWACS and Air-to-Air Refuelling (AAR); data links and command and control systems; space systems; air and ground infrastructure; expertise as required; analytical systems; Electronic Warfare (EW); Information Warfare (INFOWAR); Network-Centric Warfare (NCW) capabilities; and cyber warfare assets. The increasing importance of cyber warfare cannot be overemphasised and, in the years ahead, such assets and their judicious use will significantly aid the winning of air dominance.

The quality of situational awareness is an important factor in the fight for air dominance, particularly if the opposing sides are evenly balanced. In a fluid battle environment, situational awareness will remain of concern even when air dominance has been largely won. Surprises can occur in terms of equipment fielded, tactics and possible antidotes to our strengths. We cannot let our guard down till the war is over and not even then thereafter.

Sound training schedules are also necessary to optimise the use of available systems. Very often, a well trained force used with deft planning can get the better of another force that boasts of superior equipment. Our equipment is way superior to that of our possible adversaries and we must not allow inadequate training or preparation to lower the effectiveness of the weapon systems.

The one factor that can make the difference between victory and defeat is the quality of intelligence inputs made available. Intelligence has a central role to play. Actionable intelligence that is timely, adequate and accurate will always be a force multiplier. For instance, in the battle for air dominance, the defences around the targets, enemy dispositions, definition of target systems and their exact location are inputs that will result in good and cost-effective results. Equally importantly, it will be a great help if we know the impact of our military activity not only on the battlefield but in the enemy corridors of power as well. The importance of intelligence inputs can never be overstated.

Winning the Battle for Air Domination

If there is considerable asymmetry in air power capability, adequate air dominance can be readily and quickly enforced. If the capability is more or less at par, air dominance has to be fought for. In the last conflict India was engaged in, in Kargil in 1999, Pakistan handed over air dominance to India without a fight. Had Pakistan offered combat, as indeed its should have, given the fact that its soldiers were being killed by our air attacks, the pattern of air activity would have been very different. We would have had to fight for air dominance, even if it was to be at the cost of other air operations of war.

There cannot be any hard and fast rules on how to win the air war. Much will depend on the strategies adopted, the type of weapon systems available on both sides and their effectiveness in the types of operations envisaged. The likely duration of war and the possibility of one side or the other being in a position to limit the duration is another important consideration. Such imponderables may alter the nature of the air war but the imperative of winning air domination to whatever extent is possible will always remain. Again, if a particular plan does not work, the flexibility of air power will permit ready and quick alteration to the plan.

Both adversaries will vie to achieve air domination. As a rule, the extent of air domination will be a function of military power. Resources will always be important but possibly more important is the planning and utilisation of resources. A sound doctrinal approach will produce better results. As one side begins to gain advantage in the air domination stakes, it will attempt to capitalise on the gains and seek even greater dominance. However, at no stage can anyone let their guard down. Continuous effort is necessary to maintain the air dominance or improve on it. Good intelligence information is also needed to ensure that we are not surprised by the introduction of more effective equipment, and the enemy can always learn from experience and alter tactics to their advantage. Nothing should or can be taken for granted in war.

Air power is an offensive weapon and must be used offensively. The first requirement is to try and attenuate enemy offensive capability. The object is to force the enemy onto the defensive. One way to achieve this is by attacks all over his country whereby he is forced to not only thin down his defences, but also lower his capability for offensive action. Offensive and defensive counter-air operations will have to be launched and it must be our attempt to challenge enemy air power at every possible opportunity. It is also a corollary in air operations that the optimum use of air power is towards targets where the likely gains are maximised consistent with a low attrition rate.

The winning of air dominance requires knowledge, capabilities and suitable equipment. Such information and capabilities are required for both air combat and air-to-surface attacks. The effectiveness of air power will be governed by the degree of air dominance that can be achieved. The greater the air dominance that one is able to create, the more effective will be the support to surface forces. Undoubtedly, with air dominance, our ability to mount ISR missions and attacks on surface targets will be with greater surety, confidence and effectiveness.

The reverse is equally true with the added disadvantage that the enemy air will be permitted greater freedom of action against our surface forces. These factors should be well understood and be duly considered in the joint planning for different contingencies.

Air power can be a potent weapon if used well, and could be ineffective if the essentials of air operations are ignored. In our case, in both the Kargil conflict and in Operation Parakaram, our potential for air domination was not applied and, hence, wasted.

Much has changed in air capabilities in the last few decades but the concept of air domination is a classic one—never changing. What has markedly altered is the ability to exercise air domination and, by extension, the increasing need to do so.

Applicability of Air Dominance

The applicability of air dominance extends throughout the entire spectrum of conflict that encompasses sub-conventional war, conventional war of different intensities and nuclear war as well. The concept is also applicable immaterial of the type of terrain. However, the means to achieve air dominance to whatever degree is possible or desirable will vary.

It would be incorrect to try and launch any operation with whatever objectives, or howsoever small, without air power. Otherwise, the full potential of military power will not be brought to bear on the enemy. Undoubtedly, a single Service operation is a valid operation of war but that should be reserved for special occasions and specific situations only. A good joint planning mechanism that operates regularly and continuously will ensure the optimum use of military power under all circumstances. One factor that must be shunned is the belief that if we do not use air power, somehow, the adversary will also desist from using his air power. Air power will be used if it is advantageous to use it, and the side that uses air power first will always be at an advantage.

It is generally accepted that air power has a decided impact in conventional war and provides an important leg of the triad in the nuclear deterrence stakes. The role of air power in sub-conventional or 4th Generation War, merits some explanation. There are three major characteristics of air power that impact war. The first is the ability to see from a vantage position. The 'see' includes the ability to eavesdrop on communications, intercept data transmissions and the entire ambit of assessing the enemy electronic order of battle. With better sensors mounted on satellites and UAVs as well, persistence can be ensured to a considerable degree and intelligence information corroborated with inputs from more than one sensor mounted on different platforms. Persistent surveillance can also support the guiding of our troops to make contact with the enemy and to keep our forces abreast of the changing situation. Secondly, air power permits the rapid, fast and safe movement of men and material to wherever required. Resupply and greater concentration can also be effected. Thirdly, air power can hit targets in the air and on the surface accurately, efficiently and effectively. These are all important capabilities that can always be brought to bear on the enemy in all types of warfare, including sub-conventional war. The effectiveness of air power will be dependent on the capabilities. Much can be done from the air but we have to have the required wherewithal. Technology will play an increasing role in the conduct of 4th Generation Warfare and well planned technological advances towards a defined purpose can only improve the effectiveness of air power. There can be no denying the impact of air power. Finally, the example of the Liberation Tigers of Tamil Eelam (LTTE) air force could happen elsewhere as well and the most effective counter can only be air power.

Aerospace Domination

Space is but an extension of the air medium. Similarly, the term air domination should be extended to aerospace domination. The rapidly increasing civilian use of space, and the great advantages that the use accrues, make a space war of sorts highly probable. The civilian space industry is worth over $200 billion and conflict often follows commerce. Similarly, use of space assets in military operations is of increasing significance and, once again, competition for unchallenged use of such assets and their denial to the adversary should be expected and planned for.

It is not yet certain as to how conflict regarding the use of space assets will be conducted. The options are numerous but the importance of aerospace domination is easy to comprehend.

Use of space assets can be countered by either hard kills or soft kills. Apart from the unlikely use of lasers or other destructive means to destroy enemy satellites by use of our space assets, hard or soft kills have to be carried out by using ground-based systems or airborne systems. These can be readily targeted by aircraft and missiles. The ground segment of space capability, including control stations, Research and Development (R&D) facilities, launch pads, and the like are very vulnerable to air attacks, especially if air domination has been achieved. Thus, air domination and space domination do actually coalesce. The term aerospace domination is accurate; it should form part of military lexicon.

Cyber warfare impacts both air power and aerospace power. The obvious advantages of controlling the cyber space are again too obvious to enumerate. Much work is ongoing on developing techniques and safeguards to engage in cyber warfare. Domination in this field is also an attractive proposition. As the air, space and cyber space represent closely integrated mediums, their control should be by a single agency. In our country, the Indian Air Force automatically suggests itself.

Conclusion

The significance and essentiality of securing aerospace domination are all too obvious. Aerospace domination that must include cyber space may not be readily achieved if the adversaries are well matched. Under these circumstances, the domination will have to be fought for with the aim of securing the highest degree of domination that is feasible commensurate with the military requirements. The quest for aerospace domination is far too important to merit anything short of a very high priority, if not the highest priority.

There are costs involved. There will also be many limitations but aerospace domination is a laudable objective; the degree to which it can be achieved will be a function of the respective hardware, training and planning. A strategy enunciation is the first step. Any degree of dominance is better than lesser dominance.

There will always be those who will doubt whether the objective of aerospace domination is feasible and categorically state that the high costs are unwarranted. Again, they will argue that we cannot afford the high costs. The more relevant counter argument is that we cannot afford NOT to find the requisite funding for the best aerospace domination we can secure.

2

Limitations in the Existing Legal Framework in Outer Space

Manpreet Sethi

December 13, 2013, marked the fiftieth anniversary of the adoption of the "Declaration of Legal Principles Governing the Activities of States in the Exploration and Uses of Outer Space." It was in 1963 that the United Nations General Assembly had put down certain principles as guidelines for human activity in outer space. It may be recalled that this was the time when the USA and USSR were engaged in a game of one-upmanship as they vigorously set out into the new domain. The essential principle that was then rather presciently articulated, and which was later enshrined in the Outer Space Treaty (OST) concluded in 1967, was to declare outer space as the common heritage of mankind, free for exploration and use by all states on the basis of equality and international law.

The farsightedness of the declaration is evident half a century since. The principle that it consensually adopted then has allowed scores of other countries to utilise this global commons for their socio-economic developmental needs and also prevented the domain from becoming a contentious territory open to national appropriation. Revolving primarily around this dictum, five treaties were negotiated between 1963 and 1979 to regulate human goings-on in outer space. However, since 1979, there has been no appetite for any further treaty-based legal instruments, though the level and nature of activity in space has grown exponentially over the last fifty years.

Indeed, the last major international agreement on outer space that was concluded through multilateral negotiations undertaken in the UN Committee on the Peaceful Use of Outer Space (UNCOPUOS) was the Moon Agreement[1] in 1979. Even this has been ratified by no more than 15 nations and signed (but not ratified) by another four, with the major holdouts being the USA, Russia, China and several other major space-faring nations.[2] In fact, as is evident from the list of countries that have ratified it, none of them has an ambitious space programme, if one at all, that would make them a major stakeholder in outer space. Those that do, have shied away from endorsing the Moon Treaty.

The Conference on Disarmament (CD) which is another multilateral organisation tasked to negotiate the issue of Prevention of Arms Race in Outer Space (PAROS) has been stalemated since the late 1990s. The issue has been on the agenda of the CD since 1982 but the 67 member body has not even so much as managed to build a consensus over three decades on how the challenge should be addressed – through a voluntary non-binding set of guidelines or through the conclusion of a treaty. Meanwhile, since the CD has been unable to agree upon a programme of work for well over a decade owing to the Pakistani intransigence over the Fissile Material Cut-off Treaty, there is no possibility that its subsidiary body could engage in any negotiations on PAROS till some of the other issues are addressed.

As a result, no real legal breakthrough has been made in outer space in three decades. The current legal framework as relevant to this domain actually reflects the political and technological reality of the 1970s. But, the contemporary situation, as well as the developments on the horizon, have leapt far ahead. In fact, the state of affairs in outer space today, in terms of the number of players, the nature of these players, and the technological capabilities, including those facilitating weaponisation of this domain, is drastically different from what it was when the last of the legal instruments was concluded.

This transformation of the situation makes the existing agreements, the five treaties as well as a similar number of United Nations General Assembly (UNGA) resolutions[3], woefully inadequate to handle emerging challenges and those that lie barely beyond the pale. This paper studies the lacunae as they exist in the extant legal framework. The paper is divided into two sections – the first one describes the changes as they have occurred in the space domain; and the second section examines the five instruments to highlight their limitations in relation to the changed space environment.

The Current State of Affairs in Outer Space

More Players with Divergent Interests

Outer space remained a preserve primarily of the two superpowers from 1957 to the end of the Cold War. During this period, 95 per cent of the activities in space were conducted by the USA and USSR. It is only now, over the last couple of decades, that the presence of other players has become much more pronounced and visible. Over fifty countries access space today either with their own indigenously developed launchers or with those of other countries.[4] Many more access and use space services and products. There are over 1,300 satellites presently operational in space. Since 2011, nearly 80 orbital launches have been taking place annually.[5] There is also a significant increase in government spending on space activities, which is indicative of the kind of priority that nations are currently attaching to national space programmes.

The most obvious contemporary reality, therefore, is that outer space is today crowded with all kinds of players – national, private and consortia. Different players have divergent priorities and security concerns. For instance, national progammes that include military objectives make them less open to calls of transparency on numbers or types of spacecraft or even the manoeuvres they carry out. But, the private players who are primarily driven by commercial/profit considerations are more amenable to accepting rules on transparency but less so on undertaking steps on debris mitigation, such as moving defunct satellites into higher parking orbits or de-orbiting them to burn up in the atmosphere, since these measures entail a financial cost. Therefore, the disparate nature of the actors and their interests in outer space carries the potential for a conflict of interest.

Entry of Private Commerce

A trend that started tentatively in the 1990s, but which has since boomed is the entry of private players into space as providers of a range of services. State run programmes no longer hold a monopoly over space flights. Rather, rapid commercialisation of space services is evident in the fields of telecommunications, navigation, Earth observation and meteorology. These are being used by states as also individual users. Private companies are also offering launch services. An even more recent phenomenon, in fact, is the idea of private space ventures for human space flight. This first captured public attention in the mid-1990s when a small group of entrepreneurs and flight enthusiasts formed the X Prize foundation to raise funds for the purpose. This effort resulted in the successful launch of SpaceShipOne in September 2004.[6] In 2005, Virgin Galactic became the first private company to offer commercial human flights into space. In fact, the owner of Virgin Galactic, Richard Branson has also invested, along with some other billionaires, in the enterprise Golden Spike to undertake a lunar mission in 2020.[7] Bigelow Aerospace is engaged in private construction of prototype orbital space stations. According to an estimate by a marketing company, "over 15,000 passengers could be flying annually by 2021, representing revenue in excess of US $700 million".[8] These figures may seem hard to believe today, but may well turn out to be true given the pace at which people friendly technologies are being developed to provide the experience of outer space to the common men and women.

More recently, there has been the entry of private players for cargo transportation as demonstrated by the launch of the vehicle DragonX by Space Exploration Technologies

(SpaceX) to provision the International Space Station (ISS). The National Aeronautics and Space Administration (NASA) has entered into a contract worth $1.6 billion to SpaceX to run 12 cargo missions. In its maiden flight in June 2012, the unmanned capsule carried 500 kg of supplies and equipment for the ISS and returned with 650 kg of retired material and scientific samples.[9] On September 29, 2013, another private firm, Orbital Sciences also joined the competition in this market to supply the ISS when its Cygnus capsule docked with the space station.[10]

Interestingly, in 2009, the global commercial space industry's total revenue (including satellite manufacturing, launch industry, satellite services and ground equipment manufacturing) was estimated at $262 billion, a figure that overtook global military space expenditure for the year.[11] By 2013, this figure had risen to US $ 304 billion.

In yet another development that will have a widespread impact, a new company, Planetary Resources Inc. announced in 2012 that it had plans to mine asteroids as they zip close to the Earth.[12] This is another idea that may seem far-fetched today, but it has the potential to capture the human imagination and it could become a reality in the future. As the technological and commercial viability of undertaking such resource extraction increases, so would the challenges to issues of ownership of resources in an area which until now has been designated as the common heritage of mankind.

Increased Dependence for Civilian and Military Uses

Outer space is an integral part of life on Earth today. Global information availability, weather forecasting, education, financial services, transportation, navigation, communication, agriculture, natural resource mapping and management, disaster management and emergency response and relief are only a few of the activities that are dependent on assets deployed in space. The reliance of the military too on space enabled services such as intelligence, surveillance, reconnaissance, navigation, early warning and even arms control verification is immense and rapidly growing. It is self-evident, therefore, that any disturbance to these assets would have significant consequences for users on Earth.

The possibility of disruption of space enabled services could arise from two situations: one, as a result of a deliberate act of malintent by a state or non-state actor to interfere with the functioning of satellites; two, as an inadvertent occurrence caused by a collision of a satellite with other objects or debris in space. An eventuality of either type would not only affect services and cause inconvenience to users, but also have the potential to exacerbate inter-state tensions on Earth as allegations and counter-allegations attributing responsibility are made. Sharing of benefits of the peaceful uses of outer space has also led to shared vulnerabilities.

Proliferating Debris and Difficulties in Managing Space Traffic

As privately developed and operated vehicles jostle for space along with the increased number of national satellites being sent up for civilian and military uses, a situation of congestion in outer space is already evident. This increasing traffic, in turn, poses twin challenges – of increasing space debris and space traffic management. Every space mission creates a certain amount of debris as rocket booster stages are expended or unused fuel explodes. Hardware fragments from such occurrences drift in space as debris. According to a well known space security analyst, Ram Jakhu, "Historically, creation of rate of debris has outpaced the removal rate, leading to a net growth in debris population in LEO at an average rate of approximately 5% a year."[13]

But this rate is artificially accelerated when large scale fragmentations are caused by explosions of the kind that China undertook in 2007. That one willful act of conducting an anti-satellite test added 3,000 new pieces of large sized (over 10 cm in diameter) fragments and several thousands of smaller ones, increasing the debris by 14 percent. According to the Space Security Index 2013, the US Department of Defence is using the Space Surveillance Network to catalogue about 16,000 objects of 10 cm or more in diameter, while there are more than 300,000 objects with a diameter larger than one cm and millions of pieces of smaller sizes.[14] That even the smallest piece of debris, travelling at high speeds, can destroy or disable a spacecraft is a sobering thought, even more so for nations that have planned manned missions.

Among the pieces of debris being tracked by the USA are also about 200 satellites that have been abandoned in Geosynchronous Earth Orbit (GEO) and which are occupying or drifting through orbital positions and posing a collision hazard for other spacecraft. The lifetime of debris is very long. Objects in 1,000 km orbits can exist for hundreds of years, those at 1,500 km orbits can have a lifetime of thousands of years and objects in GEO can exist for a million years.[15] Currently, one way of removing defunct spacecraft is to trigger their orbital decay by ensuring that on completion of their operational life, they are made to enter the atmosphere where they can burn up at reentry. But this happens only in Low Earth Orbit (LEO). Those in higher orbits can be pushed further up into graveyard orbits where they may continue to 'live' for thousands of years, but would not be occupying precious slots (a resource that is becoming scarce) nor posing the danger of inadvertent collisions.

The fact that accidental collision of satellites in congested orbits is a clear and present danger was starkly brought to light when an operational American satellite collided with a defunct Russian satellite in 2009. This incident drew attention to the problem of traffic management in outer space. Unless nations know about the presence of other satellites and their orbits, especially when unexpected manoeuvres are undertaken, the crowding of space could cause more such inadvertent accidents. These would not only create more debris but also have repercussions on terrestrial inter-state relations, especially if the satellites involved happen to be of countries that do not share high trust levels and have reason to believe that the collision could have been engineered on purpose.

Shrinking Radio Frequencies and Orbital Slots

While outer space is normally conceived as a limitless global commons, it does have its limitations, especially in terms of radio frequencies and orbital positions. It was in deference to the need of the telecommunications industry that sought a body to regulate and manage the radio spectrum and orbits in a sustainable way that the International Telecommunication Union (ITU) came into being. Its constitution acknowledges that frequency bands used for radio services, including the geostationary orbit, "are limited natural resources and they must be used rationally, efficiently and economically…"[16] The ITU, based in Geneva, today has a membership of 193 states and some 700 private entities.

Over time, and especially with the increase in transmissions to and from satellites as well as with other uses of the radio frequency spectrum, global coordination of the spectrum management has been enabled by the ITU. It ensures avoidance of interference among the many Earth and space stations. It also provides licences for satellites and operational standards to be applied by the member states through their national administrations. But with the increase in the numbers of users of space and space enabled applications, the demand for radio frequencies and orbital slots has risen manifold. Interference in frequencies is already a matter of concern in crowded slots such as LEO. The ITU, however, has no enforcement authority or powers. Member states voluntarily abide by its rules and regulations since it is essentially a coordinating agency for international use of the frequency spectrum.

Imminence of Weaponisation of Outer Space

The use of satellites for military operations is today a routine activity. In fact, the very first utilisation of outer space was for military purposes and a range of other applications such as imagery, navigation, telecommunications and meteorology grew out of military programmes. Operation Desert Storm demonstrated the effective use of space-based assets in active support of ground combat operations, thereby making them an entrenched and integral component of military planning and execution even for countries that did not yet have sufficiently able space programmes.

Growing dependence on space assets for military operations requires countries to protect them from interference by other players who might envisage destruction of satellites as one way of denting the strength of the adversary. For the present, none of the space powers is known to have undertaken overt steps to weaponise outer space in terms of placing weapons in orbit, but research and development on technologies that could change the situation very easily continue. Therefore, the major space-farers are known to be addressing the issue in three ways: firstly, by enhancing physical protection of satellites through their hardening; secondly, by fortifying redundancies by dispersing abilities over a range of satellites; and thirdly, by building capabilities that can enable quick replacement of the destroyed spacecraft.

The reason for these hedging strategies is the sense that weaponisation of space is imminent. One example of this is evident through the fast evolving link between Ballistic Missile Defence (BMD) and weaponisation of space. In August 2012, the US strengthened this belief when a BMD test involved its Space Tracking and Surveillance System to detect and track mid-course reentry vehicles and pass the information to the fire control elements of Aegis BMD to launch interceptors.[17] With this, the BMD moved up into the space layer for sensors. US efforts at building a Space-Based Infrared System (SBIRS) to undertake boost phase interception comprise technological capabilities that are pushing the envelope of military use of space. Interceptors in space could be next. Hedging against such technologies, Russia and China are engaged in own Research and Development (R&D) on their repertoire of space weapons too. For instance, in May 2012, Russia announced that it was developing a sea-based space defence system that will be able to engage targets in LEO. China demonstrated the capability to blind/jam satellites through lasers in 2006 and then the Anti-Satellite (ASAT) in 2007. At the moment, the idea of deploying weapons in space is not popular, but that is certainly not stopping any of the major players from keeping themselves ready for any eventuality. A strict definition of weaponisation of space which has traditionally been seen to mean placement of weapons in space no longer seems to matter since technological trends appear to point towards a range of actions/tools that could be used to disrupt space enabled services. These might range from soft kill actions from Earth such as jamming or blinding of satellites by Directed Energy Weapons (DEWs) or high powered lasers, or hard kill through ASATs. They may also include manoeuvres of existing spacecraft in such a way as to collide with another or even the launch of micro satellites to act as space mines.[18]

In sum then, the current situation in outer space points to a newness in the manner of its utilisation, the nature and numbers of the players involved, and also the scope of that use. And, at the moment, it largely seems to be a case of free for all, except for the limited stipulations placed by the five treaties enacted in the 1960s and 1970s when the state of affairs in outer space was quite different from what it is today. It is in the context of these developments that dot the current situation in outer space that the second half of this article examines the lacunae in the relevant legal instruments that currently regulate outer space.

Examining the Existing Legal Instruments

The UN Committee on the Peaceful Uses of Outer Space (COPUOS) is the main inter-governmental body of 74 member states tasked with the development of international legal principles governing space activities. Established in 1959 by the UN General Assembly (UNGA), it is mandated to review the scope of international cooperation in peaceful uses in outer space, encourage research and dissemination of information on outer space matters, and to consider legal issues relating to space and its exploration. It has two sub-committees (legal, and scientific and technical) that meet annually to consider issues/reports submitted to them by the UNGA or member states. Based on a considered analysis of these, the sub-committees submit recommendations to the UNGA for adoption of resolutions. Like the Conference on Disarmament, COPUOS and its sub-committees work on the basis of consensus.

In the first 25 years of its existence, COPUOS was instrumental in negotiating and concluding the five treaties on outer space that are currently in force. But since then, it has managed to get no more than UNGA endorsements on principles on some relevant specific issues. For example, in 1992, a set of principles relevant to use of nuclear power sources in outer space was endorsed by the UNGA. A working group of the scientific and technical sub-committee provided a safety framework for nuclear power source applications in outer space, focussing on the safety for the relevant launch, operation and end of service phases, which was adopted by the UNGA on May 19, 2009.[19] Similarly, the same sub-committee was successful in approving a revised draft of the Inter-Agency Space Debris Coordination Committee in December 2007 which encourages nations to limit the amount of debris released during normal operations, minimises the potential for break-ups during the operational and post-mission stages, and limits the possibility of accidental collision in orbit. However, none of these has the status of a treaty and they remain by way of guidelines that nations voluntarily accept and implement. Overall then, only five treaties regulate human activity in outer space and these are briefly discussed below.

Outer Space Treaty, 1967

The Treaty on Principles Governing the Activities of States in the Exploration and Use of Outer Space, including the Moon and Other Celestial Bodies was concluded on January 27, 1967, and was the first attempt at regulating human (mostly American and

Soviet) activity in space. Today, it has 102 ratifications.[20] Amongst its main provisions, the treaty provides for freedom for use of outer space for the benefit of all countries, "on a basis of equality and without any discrimination" (Article 1), prohibits national appropriation (Article 2), extends international law and the UN Charter to outer space (Article 3), prohibits placement of a nuclear device in orbit or space (Article 4), endorses the treatment of astronauts as envoys of mankind (Article 5), calls upon nations to bear international responsibility for national activities (Article 6), including liability for damage (Article 7), seeks retention of the jurisdiction by the states over their space objects (Article 8), and, calls upon states to follow international cooperation in space exploration (Article 9).

While the treaty does cover a fair amount of ground on ensuring that outer space remains the common heritage of mankind and in pinning responsibility for damage caused by national activity, it does not cater for many aspects of this activity that could become contentious given the contemporary and possible future developments in outer space. Some of these limitations are identified in the following sub-sections.

Lack of Adequate Supervision: The OST vests responsibility in a state for its national activities in space. This is well understood in cases where the state has original responsibility for its own acts or for those that it authorises. In such cases, through launch and registration, the state assumes and retains responsibility. But the issue becomes more complicated when commercial activity is undertaken from a nation's territory by private service providers or a satellite is launched on behalf of another state. For example, if a satellite is launched using the facilities of a state but its operations are in private hands or under the control of another state, then who exercises the right of supervision? Situations of this kind might multiply if countries/private parties begin to offer commercially competitive launch services for satellites, thereby creating the possibility of the emergence of "registrations of convenience".[21] Clarity on the issue of supervision, therefore, is of utmost importance as traffic in space grows, along with the attendant risks of traffic management.

Fortunately, some of this ambiguity was resolved in 2005 through the UNGA Resolution on the application of the concept of 'launching state' which redefined national activities to include government and non-government actors in space. Therefore, it called upon the states to "consider enacting and implementing national laws authorizing and providing for *continuing supervision* of the activities in outer space of non-governmental entities under their jurisdiction"[22]. The purpose of this was to provide assurance to other parties that all activities would be conducted in accordance with the OST obligations. In order to fulfill this function, the state satisfies itself of the commercial activity being undertaken by a non-governmental entity by making it go through an *a priroi* licensing procedure and by continually monitoring its activities. But the OST does not lay down any minimum standards or procedures to determine compliance. It depends on the discretion of the state, and therefore, it can vary greatly. In any case, the OST is not implemented through any international organisation and; consequently; there are no commonly accepted rules that must be followed in this regard. So, the supervision obligation is to be performed without any binding standards. Of course, there are some recommendatory guidelines on debris mitigation, regulation of radio transmissions to and from space stations, etc. that may be followed as good space etiquette.

Lack of Enforcement on Ensuring Transparency: Article XI of the OST asks for states to "inform the UN Secretary General, the public, and the international scientific community of the nature, conduct, location, and results of outer space activities as soon as the country in question considers such information to be practicable and feasible." This squarely places the onus and initiative of rendering information on the state. But, it also leaves it to the state's discretion to decide when it may wish to provide this information. In fact, by stating that the act may be undertaken whenever it is deemed "practicable and feasible", it has given a very long rope to the states. As experience shows, several countries, especially where activity of a military nature is involved, have never found it practicable and feasible to furnish this information. Since the OST has no authority to enforce any penalties for non-compliance, transparency has suffered. This will have implications for space situational awareness, especially as the number of spacecraft and quantity of debris increase and pose risks of inadvertent collisions.

Lack of Formal Dispute Settlement Authority: While the treaty exhorts states to "conduct all their activities in outer space with due regard to the corresponding interests of all other states", and to "undertake international consultations before proceeding with any activity that would cause potentially harmful interference with the peaceful exploration and use of outer space", none of the national actions is contestable. In fact, the OST has no authority to attribute responsibility in case of a conflict. In any case, given the large number of objects that are already in space, especially in the form of debris, it is well nigh impossible to establish the responsibility of a state in the case of damage to, or destruction of, a satellite of a particular state or private entity. If per chance culpability can established, the Liability Convention could take care of the matter. But in case of an allegation that is not accepted or cannot be substantiated, the OST offers no solution for dispute settlement.

Lack of Controls on Weaponisation of Outer Space: The OST prohibits states from placing in orbit around the Earth, or on other celestial bodies, or in outer space in any other manner, any objects carrying nuclear weapons or other Weapons of Mass Destruction (WMD). Nations are also barred from building military bases and fortifications on celestial bodies or conducting tests of weapons or military manoeuvres. However, the treaty is silent on transit of WMD through outer space, or on keeping weapons in constant orbit (instead of placing them) and neither does it specifically prohibit conventional weapons to be deployed or non-nuclear ASAT tests to be conducted. Indeed, China was not in violation of any law when it conducted the ASAT test in 2007. That it breached a norm is another matter. The treaty also does not expressly prohibit development, testing and deployment of conventional weapons in outer space, nor the development, testing and deployment of ground-based systems that can reach targets in space using conventional, nuclear or directed energy weapons.

Lack of Universally Accepted Safety Standards: Potential risks from space missions may be posed to the safety of the general public (in the air, on the ground and at sea), launch range personnel and/or human beings in orbital and sub-orbital flights. These may also involve risks to the safety of ground facilities, other space systems in orbit and to the space and terrestrial environment. States are expected to take adequate safeguards to minimise risks to the safety of all. But there are no universally accepted safety standards that impose this requirement. The best practices and recommendations are all that states have to go by.

The International Standards Orgnaisation (ISO), the world's largest developer of standards, is presently the only international body that has developed a set of space safety standards for global use.[23] However, these respond only to the industrial and technical needs and are largely "unstructured, sparse, generic, and not endorsed by the majority of national regulatory bodies that deal with space activities."[24] Moreover, since these are for voluntary acceptance and implementation, they do not provide for an equal amount of risk mitigation worldwide, and nor can they prevent unfair competition if a state or private entity opts to use sub-standard safety practices to cut costs.

The need for national legislation on space safety, and its extension into an international harmonisation of standards is imperative to ensure long-term space security and safety. This is going to be even more important if commercial human space flights are to become a viable international business. Harmonisation of national flight safety certification standards, licensing regimes and liability coverage will be necessary. Some lessons for these may be drawn from the nuclear domain where the industry has evolved certain standard operating procedures in order to promote operational safety and efficiency. Accidents like the Three Mile Island in the USA, Chernobyl in Ukraine, and Fukushima in Japan have been the triggers to fortify independent regulatory mechanisms at the national level. Meanwhile, the nuclear industry has found an effective peer reviewing mechanism in the World Association of Nuclear Operators (WANO) which serves to boost confidence in each other's reactors and nuclear operations. A similar approach to safety regulation in space may also be considered. Independent regulatory organisations in each country could be supplemented with international benchmarks that are voluntarily and proudly accepted by all space-farers.

Rescue Agreement, 1968

Basically meant to supplement the OST, the Agreement on the Rescue of Astronauts, the Return of Astronauts and the Return of Objects Launched into Outer Space sought to address the issue of recovery of humans or space objects that might inadvertently land in territories other than those of the launching state. In order to safeguard the astronauts, the agreement confers ambassadorial status on them and requests states parties to assist them for safe return, as also help in the recovery of space objects.

Two aspects of this agreement have shown up legal limitations in the developing reality of outer space. The first pertains to the definition of an astronaut.[25] The agreement defined any individual who had been to space as an astronaut, but this was at a time when the people visiting space were essentially space scientists, technologists or engineers. And, their numbers were fewer. As tourists begin to travel to space, would all space passengers be deemed as astronauts? Secondly, at the time when the agreement provided for the provision of assistance to states to help in a rescue mission and to offer ambassadorial status to the astronauts, the number of nations engaged in any form of space activity was small. With the possible boom in space tourism, expecting states to carry out rescue missions, when necessary, would open up questions of who would pay for the rescue endeavour, as well as the treatment of the rescued. Commercial human space flights will demand greater clarity on these issues.

Liability Convention, 1972

The Convention on International Liability for Damage Caused by Space Objects holds the launching state or states (defined as a state that launches or procures the launching of a space object or a state from whose territory or facility a space object is launched) liable to pay compensation for any damage (of the nature of collision, debris creation or radio frequency interference) caused by its space object to the Earth, aircraft in flight, or damage to other space objects if they act negligently. It was invoked in 1978 when the Soviet spacecraft Cosmos 954 crashed, scattering radioactive debris over Canada. The USSR paid $3 million to Canada under the Liability Convention.

Over time, as the nature of population in space changes, establishing culpability in order to claim liability will not be easy as the convention was concluded at a time when there were few players in outer space and even these were only representing the government. But, with increasing actors, including of the commercial variety, and increase in orbital debris, pinning blame to claim damage is going to be very difficult. Meanwhile, the advent of commercial human space flights will bring related complications of liability in the event of accidents, insurance requirements and also the legal status of documents that claim to convey the informed consent of passengers. In any case, the Liability Convention relates to third party liability and not contractual liability as relevant to passengers or loss or damage of cargo.[26] Neither does it specify a method or formula to determine due compensation for the third party claimant, but has left it open to interpretation by just stating that the compensation must be determined according to international law and the principles of justice and equity. However, if the matter cannot be settled between the two parties involved, the convention does provide for third party arbitration through the setting up of a Claims Commission. This would consist of a representative from the launching state and one from the claimant state, and a chairperson jointly chosen by the two. The determination of the commission would be binding.

While the need for a Claims Commission has not occurred until now, the possibility of the situation remaining unchanged is becoming dimmer by the day owing to the complex nature of outer space today. An inadvertent collision of an operational satellite with a piece of debris could throw open severe challenges since proof of negligence and culpability will not be easy to establish. It may even be conjectured that the nature of the relations on the Earth of countries suspected to be involved will most likely play out in how the issue is handled.

Registration Convention, 1975

Given the international nature of space activities, the ability to undertake correct attribution of responsibility demands an open, transparent and accessible registry of all spacecraft launches. It is with this in view that the Convention on Registration of Objects Launched into Outer Space was concluded in 1974 to fulfill the need for providing some identification of the objects in space in order to attribute responsibility in case of damage.

For this purpose, the UN began to maintain a public registry in 1962 though the convention actually came into force later. It mandates that each state should maintain a registry of the objects it launches into space, and where more than one state is involved in the launch, then they decide which one would reflect the object in its registry. The state is required to provide information on five subjects: the name of the launching state or states; registration number of the space object; date and territory or location of launch; basic orbital parameters, such as inclination, apogee and perigee of the spacecraft; and the general function of the spacecraft. This information is to be provided "as soon as practicable" to the UN Office on Outer Space Affairs (OOSA). This phrase was used in order to enable the state to ascertain the relevant parameters after the satellite had reached its position. But, many nations, including China, have never found it practicable to furnish this information to OOSA. Moreover, where information has been provided by nations, its relevance and veracity has often been overtaken by later manoeuvres in orbit or due to the influence of natural forces on a satellite. In any case, it is not mandatory for states to maintain stated orbital parameters after the registration.

As the objects in space increase and space situational awareness becomes a necessity not just from the defence point of view but in order to minimise risk of collision with debris or defunct objects, the need for maintaining the registry from the point of view of attribution becomes less than adequate, even as it grows more than necessary. The convention does not require the state to update the orbital parameters. Countries such as the USA that have the wherewithal to maintain their own space situational awareness have paid scant attention to the limitations of the convention and maintain their own data base to cater for the requirements of their space objects. However, the benefit of this is not available to all space-faring nations.

Moon Agreement, 1979

The Agreement Governing the Activities of States on the Moon and Other Celestial Bodies ordains that the Moon and other celestial bodies are the common heritage of mankind and that activities on such bodies would be governed by an international regime that will provide for the exclusively peaceful uses of the Moon, non-disruption of its environment and sharing of natural resources with developing nations in some way, which is not yet defined. Therefore, while it firmly establishes the principle of non-appropriation by nations or private entities, it does, however, allow extraction of resources from these planetary bodies whenever it becomes technologically and commercially feasible as long as the "technology and means to obtain those resources can be shared with [those] who could not otherwise obtain it on their own."[27] In fact, the Moon Treaty does accept the need to elaborate on the concepts of common heritage of mankind and sharing parameters as technology comes of age. But, its attempt in the late 1970s was to place the celestial body beyond the purview of human activity that was *commercially exploitative* of its resources in any way. By establishing the principle that any activity that sought to use its natural resources would have to share the benefits, the agreement de-incentivised national or commercial private activity that could have led to a race for getting to the potential resources on the Moon.

However, this is no permanent solution to the issue since, as technology makes it feasible to prospect and exploit resources on the Moon or other celestial bodies, the Moon Agreement may not be able to provide any legal hindrance, particularly since none of the major space-farers, and particularly those who already have, or are planning to send, manned missions to the Moon, have accepted the treaty. The USA, Russia and China have not signed the treaty and India has not ratified it. Therefore, the Moon Agreement remains a toothless tool that may quickly lose its significance as technology and politics overtake the current scenario. And this may happen sooner than expected. According to recent reports, mining in space, especially of asteroids, may soon be a possibility. Deep Space Industries (DSI) and Planetary Resources are two American companies that plan to send up small exploration satellites, that the DSI calls FireFlies, and which will be like flying cameras to send images of asteroids by 2016. Once scientists have studied these images and established the composition of minerals that may be available there, the plans are to extract and use space minerals as "interplanetary gas stations or to build, fuel and support colonies on Mars".[28]

Conclusion

It is evident that outer space is not yet a well regulated international commons. At times, owing to the lack of consensus on definitions and, at others, due to political compulsions, nations have been unable to go beyond the basic framework that was established in the 1970s. As aptly stated by Dr GS Sachdeva, a space law exponent, "The few treaties in operation have evolved out of circumstantial necessity and have conceded several compromises to achieve conclusion of negotiations, possibly to ensure immediate objectives in mind."[29] The extant treaties also do no more than define the overall limits applicable to a nation's space activities.

The USA is the most vocal opponent to the creation of new legal instruments to govern outer space. Not only does it seek to protect its own freedom of action in space by refusing to accept any constraints on its future capabilities, it also appears to be deterred by the thought of having to engage in a treaty making exercise in an environment in which the stakeholders have multiplied. International, regional and national concerns and interests will have to all be reconciled at the same time, a prospect that is less than welcoming for a country that was once a superpower that could dictate its terms or which at the most had to negotiate with only one other challenger.

Besides the USA, none of the other major space-faring nations has shown any great appetite either for accepting legally enforceable agreements that restrict its right to conduct research and development, testing or operation of activities in outer space. Rather, the general mood has been to develop "soft" laws on these issues. These are by way of non-binding instruments in the form of resolutions or declarations or principles or codes of conduct. While helpful generally, these suffer from the disadvantage of creating a false sense of security since all nations may or may not accrue the same amount of legitimacy and rigour of implementation to them. These may be "declarations of collective wisdom of contributing space stakeholders"[30], but not all stakeholders in space may accept these, leading to political problems.

However, the challenge is that despite the lack of political initiative to craft anything substantive, absence of cooperation in outer space is certainly not a desirable option. It may no longer even be a viable option because if states and private enterprises are to continue to use space, respect for each other's rights and acceptance of own responsibility will have to be a *sine qua non* of the behaviour of each space-faring nation.

In fact, it is not just to reap the commercial potential of space that cooperative effort is required, but the militaries too have a common interest in the sustainability of the domain and its protection against common risks of traffic management and debris mitigation so as to prevent any military incident from being inadvertently triggered. Common sense demands that countries come together to constructively address the limitations in the existing legal framework in outer space by building on the blocks that already exist. Bringing them up to date should be taken as a collective endeavour endowed with the necessary political will and wisdom.

Notes

1. Agreement Governing the Activities of State on the Moon and Other Celestial Bodies, December 18, 1979.
2. The treaty has been ratified by Australia, Austria, Belgium, Chile, Kazakhstan, Lebanon, Mexico, Morocco, Netherlands, Pakistan, Peru, Philippines, Saudi Arabia, Tunisia and Uruguay. France, Guatemala, India and Romania have signed but not ratified the Moon Treaty. For more see, "Status of International Agreements Relating to Activities in Outer Space as at 01 Jan 2013", COPUOS Legal Subcommittee Document A/AC.105/C.2/2013/CRP.5.
3. These resolutions include the 1963 declaration of legal principles governing the activities of states in outer space; the 1982 principles governing direct broadcasting satellites; the 1986 principles governing remote sensing; the 1992 principles on the use of nuclear power sources in outer space; and the 1996 declaration on international cooperation in outer space for the benefit of Third World countries. These principles, in contrast to the treaties, are not legally binding though they do carry the moral force of the UNGA.
4. RS Jakhu, T S Gobba and PS Dempsy, eds., *The Need for an Integrated Regulatory Regime for Aviation and Space: ICAO for Space?* (Germany: Springer – Verlag/Wien, 2011), p. 5.

5. For a comparative analyses on country-wise launches over the years, see "Orbital Launches of 2013", Gunter's Space Page at http://space.skyrocket.de/doc_chr/lau2012.htm, accessed on January 15, 2014.
6. SpaceShipOne's aerospace vehicle won the Ansari X Prize in 2004 by launching two sub-orbital flights up to an altitude of 100 km. These carried weight equivalent to that of three humans and returned to Earth two weeks apart. Jakhu et al, n. 4, p. xxi.
7. "Branson Keen on Moonwalk in 2020", *The Times of India*, December 4, 2012.
8. Jakhu et al, n.4, p. 11.
9. Saswato R Das, "A New Era Blasts Off", *The Times of India*, June 27, 2012.
10. For more on this, see "Swans and Falcons", *The Economist*, October 2013.
11. Jakhu et al, n. 4.
12. Kenneth Chang, "In Pursuit of Riches in the Asteroid Belt", *Indian Express*, April 29, 2012.
13. Jakhu et al, n.4, p. 83.
14. Cesar Jaramillo, ed., *Space Security Index 2013: Executive Summary*, as available at http://www.spacesecurity.org, accessed on December 22, 2013.
15. Jakhu et al, n.4, p. 83.
16. Ronald J. Spencer Jr, "International Space Law: A Basis for National Regulation", in Ram S Jakhu,ed., *National Regulation of Space Activities* (Springer Science, 2010)
17. "Northrop Grumman Built STSS Demonstration Satellites Participate in Test of Next Generation Aegis BMD Weapon System", http://www.nasdaq.com, accessed on September 4, 2012.
18. For more on this concept, see GS Sachdeva, *Outer Space: Security and Legal Challenges* (New Delhi: Knowledge World, 2010), pp. 197-202.
19. UN Document, A/AC.105/934, 19 May 2009.
20. The OST is now being accepted as Customary International Law and, hence, binding on all states irrespective of signature or ratification. It is, thus, binding on non-treaty states as well as new states subsequent to the treaty. Refer GS Sachdeva, Chapter 1—Jus Cogens of Space Law in *Outer Space: Law, Policy and Governance* (New Delhi: Knowledge World, 2013).
21. As cited by Spencer Jr, n. 16, p. 13.
22. UNGA Resolution No. 59/115. "Application of the Concept of the Launching State", January 25, 2005. Emphasis added.
23. The International Standard Organisation (ISO) came into being on February 27, 1947, to facilitate international exchange of goods and services through coordination and unification of industrial standards. 163 national standards organsiations are members of ISO.
24. Jakhu et al, n. 4, p. xxii.
25. Sachdeva, n. 18, pp 89-96.
26. For more on this subject, see an excellent exposition in Ibid., pp 144-148.
27. Michael J Listner, "International Space Law: An Overview of Law and Issues", *New Hampshire Bar Journal*, vol. 52, no.1, Spring 2011, p. 64.
28. Susan Thomas, "Rock Science: Asteroids as Space Mines", Reuters report, as reproduced in *The Times of India*, December 8, 2013.
29. Sachdeva, n.18, p. 59.
30. Ibid., p. 5.

3

Organising Air and Space Power for Enhancing Comprehensive National Power

KK Nair

Power is defined and interpreted variously. While power by the strictest definitions of physics is a product of force and velocity, in more generic terms, it is a complex product of a variety of factors; the most important being knowledge, wealth and violence. Within the narrow confines of the subject under discussion, the common assumption of power implying a capacity to control or force a desired outcome would suffice. The capacity to control outcomes is a direct result of harmonious and efficient exercise of the trinity of mind (knowledge), money (wealth) and muscle (violence). These are the primary components of power. They are interrelated, and enable a variety of consequences. In terms of the nation-state, they translate into the ability to use intellectual power, economic power and military power in pursuit of national interest.

With regards to the interrelation of these three Instruments of Power (IoPs), a sound economy sustains a sound military (and vice-versa) and both, in turn, are sustained and utilised by a sound intellect. A range of employment avenues and strategies accompanies each of the above instruments of national power. For example, military power can be used for a variety of purposes ranging from disaster relief to counter-insurgency operations to actual fielded combat. Similarly, a sound national economy enables a variety of options ranging from imposition of sanctions to inducements by preferential trade agreements, financial assistance, etc. Finally, knowledge, by itself could be applied variously to ensure optimal pursuit of national interests. National power, hence, would need to be viewed as a comprehensive matrix of a variety of factors, the most prominent amongst them being a nation's economic, military and intellectual power.

Each of the above instruments of power, in turn, is a combination of a variety of 'sub-instruments', all of which, again are interrelated and critical for the pursuit of national goals. For example, the variety of 'sub-instruments' in a military context would include national armies, navies, air forces and their sub-components like an army's infantry, artillery, armour, etc. and likewise for the navy and air force. These components serve the purpose of combat as also shaping of international relations. They demonstrate national resolve and political intent. Gunboat diplomacy, stationing of fighter aircraft on operational readiness, massing of troops on the border, etc. are classical examples.

The impact and criticality of the sub-instruments in shaping national and international affairs, however, are perennially changing and require persistent watch and adaptation. The extent and mix of actions employing one or more of the instruments or sub-instruments of power would also not be constant. Based on the prevailing and evolving situations as well as requirements, the extent and mix of actions would change necessitating inclusion and promotion of more potent options to beef up the overall national index of power or '*Comprehensive National Power'*.

India and Comprehensive National Power

The term Comprehensive National Power (CNP) is Chinese in origin and as the term suggests, refers to the comprehensive power of a nation-state. It represents an adaptation of Western methodologies for monitoring and assessing national power fused with traditional Chinese concepts of statecraft and strategy, which place a heavy emphasis on calculations and estimates of relative power among nations. It applies quantitative and qualitative evaluations of national military power, economic power, science and technology, and foreign affairs to determine the relative CNP of nations. In brief, the concept revolves around the ability of a nation-state to harness knowledge, compete economically, and wage high-technology warfare as critical components of national power[1].

Overall, the above concept is not a recent discovery and has been in vogue since ages. As a matter of fact, the ancient Indian conceptions of the intellect (*Brahman*), the military (*Kshatriya*) and the economy (*Vaishya*) broadly mirror the above concept. The conceptual parameters of the power structure and its gainful exercise were also apparently well understood considering the fact that the ancient dynasties of the Guptas, Nandas as well as the Mughals secured and sustained their massive kingdoms on these.

Nevertheless, inability to monitor change and adapt the power structure and its attendant instruments (as well as sub-instruments) of power to evolving concepts and requirements led to serious degradation in CNP, with disastrous consequences for the nation-state. For example, towards the end of the Mughal period, dynamic debate and intellectual reason were replaced by mindless dogma, travel overseas was prohibited and import of goods as well as ideas reduced to a trickle. An insular power structure, thus, missed out on the gains of the industrial revolution sweeping the West, with serious implications for the economy as well as the military. National economy as well as military institutions were degraded as never before. Traditional industries were rendered obsolete, and archaic, slow moving Indian military structures could not withstand the onslaught of far-reaching, highly mobile British firepower, etc. The above instance is not just one of a kind—many more such examples resonate across India's history.

As India moves ahead into the new millennium, the above stated conceptual paradigms are not about to change. What would be significantly different would be the consequences of sluggish adaptation of the national Instruments of Power (IOPs) to the opportunities and challenges of the information revolution of the present times and the foreseen future. The changes would be unprecedently quick and become increasingly critical with every passing year. India is a globally acknowledged knowledge power and its economy is stable. Both the above instruments have adapted fairly well to the gains and challenges of the information revolution. A knowledge commission is in place, as also are commercial endeavours aimed at optimally exploiting the gains of the information revolution. Nevertheless, the same cannot be said about the military. The military is yet to adapt to the information age and gross imbalances or inadequacies in the IOPs are fraught with disastrous consequences. Hence, there exists an emergent need to harness new opportunities and organise their gainful exploitation and integration in tune with prevailing and future requirements and capabilities.

Examining National Objectives and Military Instruments of Power (IOPs)

Our prevailing military IOPs are primarily derivatives of the dynastic armies of the past. Dynastic military IOPs had dynastic objectives; a piece of territory here, a fair maiden there, a royal retribution, etc. The means of developing and employing military IOPs were also simple and largely involved pitting mass against mass as exemplified by the massive Rajput and later Mughal styles of warfare. Objectives during the colonial era expanded, yet the primary objective was to extract economic resources by acquisition and exploitation of territorial gains. Nevertheless, the colonial rifles and artillery of the industrial age complicated warfare with their increased ranges and accuracy. They also added the options for gainful employment of military power as never before. Towards independence in 1947, the options and complications in organising and exercising military IOPs only increased further with the arrival of air power in India. The development of nuclear weapons and ballistic missiles in the later decades enhanced it even more. The variety and complexity of objectives attainable by military IOPs, particularly those organised around exploitation of air and space, has now increased as never before.

At the same time, the requirement of pitting mass against mass to seize territory, deliver punishment or to forcibly extract resources from other territories has reduced significantly. As a matter of fact, with regards to territory, the present Constitution of India contains no provision for forcible acquisition of territory. Neither is it found in the general provisions across the Constitution nor in the specific parts dealing with 'territory' in Part-1, Articles 1-4 of the Constitution of India[2]. Consequently, it would be safe to surmise that the focus of India's modern military IOPs is no longer on the traditional objective of territorial acquisition and more on achievement of sustained, uninterrupted national growth and development. The national objectives consequently are more varied and complex. They include the standard political and security objectives as also the multifaceted objectives of socio-economic growth. It is in the above context that the qualitative lethality of the military IOPs using air, space and information systems to obtain national objectives gains significance. Not only has the quantum of velocity and force in delivering decisive power onto the objective in physical terms multiplied manifold, the possibilities of accurately delivering national power across various objectives in various ways has increased as never before. The aforementioned military IOPs could deliver firepower across vast swathes of territory with astonishing rapidity and also deliver succour to stranded persons with equally astonishing rapidity. The effect is demonstrably dramatic in both cases and serves a variety of national objectives.

With regards to firepower, the ability to use air, space and information systems to perform military tasks more efficiently is the crux of modern war-fighting: the much sought after Revolution in Military Affairs (RMA). The operational validity of the same has been evidenced in every post Cold War conflict involving the USA. US military IOPs, in particular its air force, transcend geography and fight across continents from standoff ranges using the realm of air and space to obtain national objectives. Its demonstrated bias in organising military IOPs around air and space is its unique source of strength. The above has not gone unnoticed and most nations across the globe attempt to emulate the US model of organising air and space for efficacious exercise of national power.

By contrast, in our unique context, the lessons of recent conflicts are yet to sink in. Dynastic and colonial hangovers persist in the organisation and employment of our military IOPs. This is despite the fact that national objectives and situations have undergone an enormous change. For example, the organisational bias of progressively increasing the mass of troops stems primarily from the need to occupy and secure territory ('add boots, keep ground occupied'). The need to secure territory would always prevail and persist. However, extra-territorial ambition (if at all any) was totally renounced post independence and yet India has been progressively organising its military IOPs by adding more troops. Logically, over a period of time, with military modernisation and increased efficiency, the number of troops should have increased marginally or actually reduced. The situation is the other way round. Across the world, the trend is to shed mass for mobility and speed: India apparently is amongst the few non-conformists. Going by the figures given by the International Institute of Strategic Studies, over a period of time, India and Pakistan have been consistently bucking the trend by adding more personnel to their armed forces. Table 3.1 below serves to validate the inference;

Table 3.1: Addition/Reduction In Regular Armed Forces Personnel

Country	Period							
	1978-79	1983-84	1989-90	1994-95	1998-99	2004-05	2011	2012
US	2,068,800	2,136,400	2,124,900	1,650,500	1,401,600	1,473,960	1,563,996	1,569,417
FSU/RUS	3,683,000	5,050,000	4,258,000	1,714,000	1,159,000	1,037,000	1,046,000	956,000
CHN	4,325,000	4,100,000	3,030,000	2,930,000	2,820,000	2,255,000	2,285,000	2,285,000
IND	1,096,000	1,120,000	1,260,000	1,265,000	1,175,000	1,325,000	1,325,000	1,325,000
PAK	429,000	478,600	520,000	587,000	587,000	619,000	617,000	642,000

The above figures are apart from the equally large paramilitary forces personnel. The above trend of continuously adding personnel is despite the fact that in terms of employment of military IOPs, the lethality and potency of modern air power in obtaining solutions were amply evident post World War II.[3] Tremendous confusion and misgivings on the employability of air power prevail (and persist) in the Indian context, leading to sub-optimal utilisation and exploitation of these potent military IOPs.[4] Space capabilities and information systems have multiplied the efficiency of air power manifold. In our unique context, both space and information systems are formidable national strengths, and yet, both are yet to be harmonised. The point is, the components, as also sub-components of the national IOPs are individually strong and yet not integrated into collectively strong and cohesive IOPs.

Reviewing Organisation and Employment of Military IOPs

Thus, in terms of both organisation and employment, there exists an emergent need for the military to adapt, evolve and change. The above is more so because, in the present times, military efficiency is no longer a measure of the numerical head count of troops or weapons available. It is instead the measure of the ability of a nation to employ its air, space and information systems to obtain dominant information and link all its military IOPs for efficacious delivery of power.

The emphasis on information is paramount. The above is especially evidenced in the evolution of modern fighter planes. The worth of modern fighter planes is no longer a measure of its system of propulsion or weapons. It rests on its information-processing capabilities. They are more of information systems and less of 'dumb' platforms. Apart from platforms, even munitions are getting 'smart' with every passing day. Paradoxically, while the quality of machines has been rising exponentially, the same is not true in the case of military manpower[5]. The present emphasis across the globe is on knowledge systems rather than the numerical head-count of troops and the trend would only intensify in the future.

However, so deep is the national obsession with numbers that the Indian Air Force's (IAF's) demand in year 2005 for an Aerospace Command was rejected to "*cap the number of commands per service at seven*"[6]. The above is notwithstanding the fact that the numerical force levels of the IAF have been progressively falling; from the accepted levels of 64 squadrons in 1961, 40 squadrons by the Nineties and 34 squadrons at present[7]. Apparently, deeply entrenched conceptual biases of the past drive the development, deployment and employment of military force structures in our unique context. The above is not to suggest that present military IOPs are ineffective. The military is a very potent national IOP, it ranks amongst the largest and best in the world, and its personnel are amongst the most numerous, highly skilled, motivated and equipped to fulfill military commitments. The only problem is that the above is largely true in the context of an era that has passed. As we move further into the future, as information-intensive systems and platforms evolve as well as proliferate further, the problem would only magnify. The military IOPs of Prithviraj Chauhan or the later Mughals were not inherently ineffective; rather they rendered themselves ineffective by not changing and adapting to the times.

Adapting Military IOPs to the Information Age

The obvious alternative would be to accept change and adapt by harnessing the immense potential of air, space and information systems. To arrive back at numerical force levels of the initially envisaged 60 squadrons within a span of even two decades would be highly improbable, if not impossible. A balance would have to be sought, and the tradeoff would be in terms of replacing numerical mass with information intensive platforms. The investments would need to be in terms of information intensive, multi-role platforms like modern air-borne and space-borne systems. We can ignore the trends and lessons of the Soviet Military Technical Revolution (MTR)[8], American Revolution in Military Affairs (RMA) or Chinese "*informationalization*", etc, sweeping the world at our own peril. The very essence of these concepts is contingent on the exploitation of the characteristics of air and space and, hence, militaries worldwide are evolving and largely organising around it. In the present and future, nations with greater air and space power capabilities would have greater information, military and economic edge.

Advocating for a larger measure of air, space and information systems by itself doesn't imply doing away with the mass. The above does not render the proverbial "*boots on the ground*" obsolete. Air and space power cannot hold ground, and boots would be essential for the same. Nevertheless, in our unique context, while boots on the ground are already aplenty, boots on aircraft rudders are dwindling and brains on information systems are scarce. The above is in serious need of redress, if military IOPs are to prevail and live up to the challenges of the modern information age.

Imperatives of Organising Air and Space for CNP

It would, hence, be imperative to adapt and organise for the changed present and future. India is at the threshold of a revolution, it has demonstratively powerful and growing capabilities impacting all the three constituents of comprehensive national power. Across the world, it is not only recognised but also acknowledged that India is the information capital of the world and its economy is on the upswing. Both these components are in a process of intense change and adaptation. Military IOPs are yet to match the extent of change and adaptation. Organising the military IOPs for adapting to the information revolution involves much more than changes in technology and also involves alterations in the traditional concepts, inter-Service relations as well as force structures. It would also involve a greater interaction between military and civilian institutions. The above is particularly true since the main catalysts of the prevailing change are air, space and information systems. All three impact the civilian realm in equal, if not greater measure. The revolutionary impact of information on the nation is well known, what is less well known is the impact of air and space in revolutionising CNP. The above is of particular relevance since national air power is by definition, the total aviation capability of a nation, "*military and civilian, existing and potential*". As a matter of fact, the inherent flexibility of air power allows it to promote all the three primary constituents of national power. It is inherently knowledge sensitive; it impacts and promotes economic, political and military power.

Harnessing the Indian Air and Space Revolution: Apart from national air forces which enable military power projection, it also needs to be borne in mind that national civil aviation as well as the industry and infrastructure supporting aviation is one of the most powerful drivers of national economies. Growth in national aviation is a catalyst to economic growth and vice-versa. The above is particularly relevant in view of the fact that our national economy grew at a rate of 9.1 percent during the first half of 2006-07, Gross Domestic Products (GDP) growth rate spiked to 9.7 and in 2008, spiked again to 9.4 in 2011. The GDP rates have fallen since, but the fall is not expected to last[9] in view of the fact that India has been the 9th fastest growing economy since 1980 and it is expected to sustain the growth till at least 2020. The sustained growth is expected to lead to an unprecedented rise on the demands on civil aviation. Aircraft orders to meet the growing demand are expected to continue rising till 2020. Secondly, India's burgeoning middle class, which drives the booming economy, is increasingly choosing air over rail travel. The above has led to an increased demand for civil aviation. For example, during the Paris air show in 2005, India's order for 400 aircraft was the largest in the world. The boom in demand may not rise consistently, but it certainly would increase in the future. To put matters in perspective, passenger traffic is expected to rise by more than 50 percent. India's forecast growth of passenger traffic at 7.7 percent is well above the global average of 4.8 percent and even above China's 7.2 percent[10]. India is currently the 9th largest aviation market handling 121 million domestic and 41 million international passengers.[11] Overall, air transport (including air freight) in India has attracted Foreign Direct Investment (FDI) worth US$ 456.84 million from April 2000 to July 2013, as per the data released by the Department of Industrial Policy and Promotion (DIPP)[12]. All of the above is considering that the domestic regional aviation market is yet to open up. The potential, at present is only unfolding and as time progresses and the economy stabilises, the demands on civil aviation can only be expected to increase.

It is, hence, not surprising that while most of the globe post September11 experienced a drawdown in civil aviation, India registered a reverse trend. At the same time, the present global recession complicates future projections. The future is always fraught with uncertainty. The Indian economy would not be immune to the global meltdown and the impact would certainly be felt. However, since the aviation market and industry are characteristically capital-intensive and cyclical, with long lags between investment decisions and project completions, the impact of short-term recession would be cushioned.

With regards to the military component of national air power, India's military aviation sector is also amongst the fastest growing in the world. Around 500 aircraft and acquisitions worth billions are expected within the next few years[13]. The IAF, as part of its modernisation drive, is expected to procure air assets worth over $ 38 billion by 2020.[14]

With regards to space, its impact on revolutionising national development and commerce is apparent to the entire nation. India ranks among the top six space-faring nations of the world in terms of budget and technological capabilities. In 2009, the Indian Space Research Organisation's (ISRO's) budgetary allocation was ₹ 41.67 billion (US$ 0.91 billion), in 2010-11 it rose to 57.78 billion (US$ 1.26 billion) accounting for about 0.14 percent of the GDP, and it continues rising[15]. The commercial-aerospace industry plays a progressively larger role in the space missions and taps the outsourcing work offered by ISRO. As evidenced from the successful launch of the GSLV D-5 in January 2013, it is demonstrably evident that India's cryogenic technologies have matured. This augurs well for all the three prime components of national power. It serves the needs of knowledge and information, the economy as also the military. Apart from launch, India's national space programme is focussed primarily on space-based telecommunications and observation which form the backbone of modern information systems. The Indian Navy has obtained its dedicated military satellite for communications[16]. With the successful launch of the GSLV D-5, the other Services would soon receive their much sought communication capabilities. A complement of observation satellites serves a certain amount of military and civil purpose, navigation satellites are on the anvil and overall the major components enabling air and space-based "*informationalization*" are in place. Purposeful and efficient utilisation would demand integration of these components.

Quite evidently, the forecast growth of our national air and space capabilities lends credence to the fact that our nation's comprehensive power is also poised for dramatic change and growth. It also demonstrates the fact that the growth is largely unsynchronised. The individual components are apparently not in concert. All revolutions carry with them the attendant perils of chaos and self-interest. Our case may be expected to be no different. The opportunities would be enormous; the attendant chaos would also be so. Left disorganised, significant national gains may be frittered away.

Impact on the IAF: Apart from the fact that growing aviation demands drive national economies, it also needs to be borne in mind that growing economies have always needed military prowess to sustain and grow. For example, in the ancient and medieval ages, the political and economic interests of Rome were promoted and secured by land-based power projection. Later the British promoted and secured their interests with sea power and in more recent times, the US promotes and secures its global interests by synergistic application of air and space power. The lessons of history are amply clear that as and when economic strength grows, conflicts of interest arise, and military force would be essential to ensure continual growth and development. With rising regional and global influence come regional and global responsibilities. Political and economic influence, foreign investments, etc would need to be supported in their endeavours by instruments of power which are highly mobile, have enormous reach, are rapidly responsive and extremely flexible. The above qualities are endemic to air power and in particular, air forces.

The point is that while land forces would continue to be largely engaged in tackling the mischievous proclivities of contiguous nations like China, Pakistan and perhaps Bangladesh, the navy and particularly the air force would have an extremely extended sphere of influence. With increasing global interaction and influence come global responsibilities, and the role of air power in managing contingencies and crises would only increase. It would be called upon, time and again, to deliver well beyond national borders and shores and even into remote, inaccessible landlocked areas. It would have to fulfil its obligations rapidly, delivery of power and influence would not only be in terms of delivery of conventional or nuclear munitions or firepower, delivery of airborne military power (like airborne troops, special forces, etc) but also humanitarian assistance best exemplified by the largest evacuation ever conducted in human history. It needs to be borne in mind that the evacuation of 117,000 Indians during the Gulf War was the largest ever such operation carried out. Similarly, the rice dropping over Jaffna was a pertinent example of political signalling as was the devastating bombing of the governor's house, Dacca, in 1971, which snapped the spine of the enemy. Numerous examples abound: the intent is not to recount air power history, but to drive home the point that the enormous strategic reach, the enormous potential to deliver military, political and economic power and prevail would be put to test more often and the nation would expect the air force to live up to the challenges. The above would be more so because of the simple fact that up to 90 percent of our national air power assets (in terms of machines, manpower and allied infrastructure) are with the IAF.

With the largest reservoir of national air power assets, the IAF would wittingly or unwittingly get pushed into the forefront of the revolution in air power because, apart from the military assets, the mantle of civil aviation in terms of human resources might also gradually pass onto the IAF[17]. It is in the above context that we need to look at options which would enable more efficacious fulfilment of the role of air power and in particular air forces in furthering national objectives. Hence, it would be essential to explore unconventional and perhaps asymmetric means to obtain the best out of air power and indeed the entire vertical dimension above the surface of the Earth.

Examining Air Power Options in Air, Space and the Vertical Dimension

It is universally acknowledged that air power is a product of 20th century warfare, and as we progress into the new millennium, air power is on the threshold of becoming the power of air and space: aerospace power. Before space became a consideration, air power characterised by aircraft and allied equipment was, and continues to be, the primary constituent of air power. However, ever since the vertical dimension beyond the atmosphere opened up in October 1957, the options and opportunities have multiplied and expanded exponentially. The options include a vast array of equipment like aircraft, drones, Unmanned Aerial Vehicles (UAVs), balloons, satellites, missiles, etc, and their allied equipment which can be applied to fulfill a variety of missions and roles. An expansion in the variety of flying machines and inclusion of space as a constituent of air power has multiplied the potency of air power manifold. The above has been a persistently decisive factor during the recent conflicts.

The advantages afforded by the vertical dimension along with the unique capabilities of air and space power produce a wide variety of options and opportunities for accomplishing national objectives. The above is not unduly surprising, in view of the fact that both the mediums of air and space enable complementary competencies and, hence, demand a mix of air and space capabilities for executing operations from the vertical dimension in support of national security objectives. As a matter of fact, since the dawn of the space age, the mediums of air and space have experienced a natural progression of synergy to the extent that it has actually enabled migration of certain aerial capabilities like weather observation, reconnaissance, navigation, etc further up into space. More significantly, it has also integrated air and space capabilities into terrestrial war-fighting to the extent that acquisition of aerospace capabilities has become the most sought after global norm rather than the exception. In correspondence with these environmental changes, a tremendous growth in air power capabilities (in terms of both air and space) in military, civil as well as commercial activities has occurred in the new millennium and is likely to continue growing rapidly with the potential to not only enhance but also dramatically change a nation's comprehensive power. It is in the above context that we need to accept the fact that national expectations on the role of air power and, in particular, the role of the IAF in the changing environment, would only tend to exponentially increase. The IAF would need to adapt and balance its capabilities with the requisite force structuring, doctrine, capability acquisition, etc to complement the pace of national growth in a knowledge and technology intensive dynamic environment.

Air Power: Earth-bound, Far-Earth, Near Space and Space: The driving maxim of air power is "*concentration of force*" and the same in modern times has extended vertically to include space systems like satellites and missiles as well as everything in between like near space balloons, far Earth UAVs, common aerospace vehicles, etc. Hence, it would be essential to organise the synergistic development and exploitation of air and space power as a single operational entity. To fulfil national obligations, as well as the challenges of modern warfare, it would be essential to exploit the entire vertical dimension above the surface of the Earth more completely and efficiently and this would demand synergistic utilisation, integration and application of both air and space power. It would be essential to foray beyond the atmosphere and harness the hitherto untapped potential of both air and space capabilities. This would allow for more efficient use and exploitation of the inherent attributes of air power, and by extension, of the entire vertical dimension above the Earth. The obvious option would be to consolidate existing air and space capabilities, plan for the future, and also evolve capabilities further and farther, beyond the realm of the atmosphere onto the realm of space. It would be all the more imperative to exercise the above option in view of the simple fact that extant civilian space capabilities do exist, a spillover of capabilities has already taken place and the recent test case of the Gulf War and almost every conflict since then has continuously validated the concept. The operational logic of synergistic application of air and space power is proven and valid in the present as well as the foreseeable future.

While attempting to duplicate the entire range of aerospace capabilities available to nations like the US or Former Soviet Union (FSU) would be too ambitious and perhaps self-defeating, enormous national gain would be forthcoming by effectively harnessing extant national space capabilities for optimal air power exploitation. We have a fairly advanced space programme for economic and development purposes which already provides inputs and resources for defence, especially in imagery and communications. Further programmes with dual use applicability are on the anvil. As a matter of fact, India's space programme has revolutionised national civil affairs to a much greater extent than military affairs. National aerospace capabilities, hence, would largely be built around or as an extension of these endeavours.

Putting the Act Together

In view of the foregoing, it is conclusively apparent that there exists an emergent need to treat the entire vertical dimension as a single entity and harness the cumulative potential of air and space systems; civil and military, existing and potential. The individual competencies of all these diverse components of aerospace power would need to be assimilated, employed and wielded as a single composite entity for commercial, military and political gain to the nation. For example, the total acquisition of civil aircraft and military aircraft up to the year 2025 is expected to number over 1,600 and monetarily worth hundreds of billions of dollars. On the other hand, our space assets presently earn the nation revenues of around $ 90 million which is expected to rise. The political, economic and military clout such acquisitions and sales would accrue would be immense. Such clout wielded in concert would have a more gainful impact on the national power indices rather than the prevailing disjointed efforts.

Such mammoth transactions also arrive with a variety of attendant opportunities and chaos. Left directionless, the opportunities in air and space might go untapped, significant gains may be frittered away piece-meal, and large scale chaos and rivalry would prevail. It might even breed self-destructive mutual antagonism as evidenced in the prevalent "*pilot poaching*" trends debilitating both military and civil aviation. The above is in sharp contrast with global trends wherein overall national air power efforts are getting increasingly integrated. Integration of military and civil production of aircraft and allied systems is on the rise. In the case of space, military and civil programmes are deeply intertwined, and at times, almost indistinguishable, as in the case of China. The integration extends beyond the platforms and allied systems onto the support infrastructure also. In our unique case, such integration is largely absent at present. The anticipated expansion in capabilities would need to be sustained by an equally efficacious support infrastructure. For example, maintenance support would be essential for sustaining the expansion, yet the same is in a state of serious neglect. National Maintenance, Repair and Overhaul (MRO) opportunities are aplenty, but this vital sector is presently characterised by neglect and chaos. Most heavy maintenance of civil aircraft is carried out abroad, whereas the military does the same locally and with a much more diverse set of aircraft. The IAF's large reservoir of trained aviation technicians goes untapped, in spite of the fact that hundreds superannuate annually and join the ranks of the jobless. Apart from services, manufacture is characterised by overzealousness to import technology. India's globally renowned innovative acumen and spirit of entrepreneurship goes unnoticed. The immense potential of local industry to contribute and gain goes untapped.

On the other hand, India's civilian Department of Space (DoS) boasts of the largest constellation of remote sensing satellites in the world and provides services and products across the globe. Yet, its military is unable to tap into it and scouts across the world, finally ending up with imagery from commercial international firms like Space Imaging, Israel's Offeq, etc. Evidently, while individual competencies are significant, the cumulative potential of air and space systems is yet to be realised or tapped.

Secondly, with regards to employability, the inherent flexibility of air and space systems enables a wide variety of common options for civil and military applications. Apart from aircraft and satellites which could be put to both military and civil uses, other platforms like UAVs, etc could also be utilised for a variety of applications ranging from policing jobs to disaster mitigation, etc. Similarly, surveillance, communication, navigation as well as search and rescue assets, both military and civil, air-borne and space-borne would need to be integrated to afford optimal utilisation of assets and coordinate efforts. A case in point is the envisaged networking of civil and military radars for a composite air picture. The same would need to be integrated and extended vertically further into space by utilising the civilian space assets. The threat to platforms is no longer limited to the atmosphere, it extends into space, and situational awareness of the realm above the atmosphere would, hence, be imperative in the present times as also in the future. The foreseen crowding of the national air space and the challenges of air space management in the near future would also demand greater coordination of air and space assets. It would be even more imperative in view of the anticipated test flight of India's "Multi-Purpose Aerospace Vehicle" which would transcend both the realms of air and space[18].

Air and space assets, nonetheless, would be scarce and costly. Hence, there would be a need for a central body to arrest duplication and coordinate national efforts for common gain as well as coherent direction during times of crises and contingencies. It would be imperative to streamline the acquisition, development, management and employment of these potent elements as a single entity for comprehensive national gain.

An Aerospace Commission to Synergise Air and Space Power: Paradoxically, in an era of magnificent machines, it is man and management modes which would the ultimately decisive. Therefore, it would be essential to have a singular national body constituted with suitable men and management modes tasked with streamlining the foreseen surge in national aerospace capabilities into potent national indices of power. The body could be instituted with the task of consolidating national requirements and guiding the acquisition, management and development of national air and space capabilities and competencies. At the same time, individual competencies and tasks would be left untouched. The guiding principle would be centralised direction, decentralised control and execution. The aim would be to centralise direction while leaving organisational control and execution of committed tasks untouched. The point is not to add an additional layer of bureaucratic control, but to have a single potent body which enables cross-exchange of resources and judicious sharing of potent capabilities in tune with the larger needs of building CNP. Thus, while the prevailing Space Commission would continue guiding the drive for national space competencies, the IAF's operational tasks would be left untouched, the Directorate General Civil Aviation (DGCA) would continue regulating civil aviation, etc. At the same time, means of consolidating competencies for mutual benefit (without affecting individual competencies) could be explored, scarce resources in terms of personnel, equipment and services could be traded internally, mutually damaging rivalries could be resolved, etc. In view of national interest and the greater common good of all, a roadmap and the means to tread on it could be decided and acted upon. In sum and substance, hence, the conceptual framework of the institution dedicated to the development and exercise of national air and space power (and by extension, CNP) would be of a non-intrusive yet effective paternal character. It would herd the diverse components onto the path of nation building, enable the means to tread the path with optimum efficiency, and leave the actual tread to the prescribed organisations In keeping with the immense unpredictable pace of technology, a system to monitor and enable mid-course corrections would also need to be included. The body would need to be inherently dynamic and adaptable for harnessing newer and more potent opportunities and options.

Broadly, the following institutional structure could be envisaged.

Fig 3.1

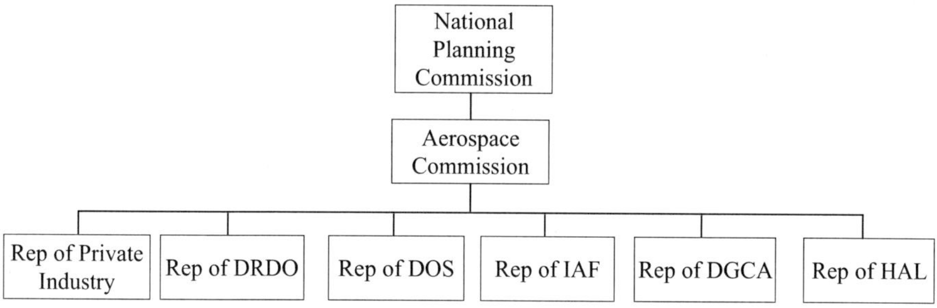

The envisaged commission would:

- Obtain inputs from all the components and adopt a dynamic national aerospace vision as well as roadmap to guide development of national aerospace capabilities and competencies.
- Exercise its authority to enable the means of fulfilling the vision and treading the roadmap.
- Formulate a national aerospace policy for developing, sustaining and employing aerospace power in pursuit of national interest.
- Perodically review measures aimed at efficacious development and exploitation of aerospace power and recommend the options and opportunities laterally and vertically.
- Provide an authoritative inter-phase among the military, civil and commercial bodies as well as international bodies. Overall, it would harness and network the strengths and individual competencies of the aforestated IOPs for common gain within the aegis of national interest.

The above list is by no means exhaustive and is only illustrative of the wide variety of tasks it would be called upon to perform once it is instituted. In sum and substance, the framework of the commission would need to be dynamic and adaptable to withstand the rigours of ever-changing technology and national interests.

Organising Air and Space to Fulfill Military Aspirations: While the Aerospace Commission would further the cause of fulfilling national aspirations, military aspirations would need to be addressed by organising the wide range of the options and opportunities afforded by the realm of air and space. Apart from aspirations, these would be essential for more efficacious exploitation of military IOPs. Air and space-based systems provide vital capabilities to successfully execute national tasks. They also have the potential to be used across the range of military operations at the strategic, operational and tactical levels of war in order to accomplish national security objectives. More pertinently, the lessons of recent conflicts conclusively establish that information derived from air and space platforms would be vital for success in conflicts. Achieving advantages in both the mediums of air and space before and during conflict would be critical to success on the battlefield as well as for effective deterrence and national well-being. The prevailing environment and revolution in information-intensive systems has led to a situation wherein air power as a composite of air and space capabilities has become the prime instrument of military power.

Hence, it would be imperative to obtain a certain level of space capabilities or at least a modicum of '*information-dominance*', if not '*informationalisation*' or any other kind of RMA for military IOPs to prevail in the present age. The requirement for information intensive air-borne platforms is being addressed (to a certain extent) by existing structures like the IAF—what needs serious redress are space-based systems for military uses. Acquisition and development of information systems in stand-alone modes leads to sub-optimal utility. Gainful utilisation of information would demand a judicious mix of air and space-based systems. Hence, apart from information intensive air-borne systems, there exists an emergent need for examining the options afforded by space. Information, nevertheless, is one of the aspects; overall, the following aspects would need to be addressed.

- Securing of our space and terrestrial assets and thereby ensuring uninterrupted national development.
- Coordination of military requirements and development of military space capabilities.
- Integration of air and space-based information systems into the conventional military apparatus.

Addressing the above three aspects would be an onerous task. Firstly, the key issues impacting each of the above aspects would need to be identified. Existing and foreseen priorities, options and opportunities for tackling the issues would need to be worked out and decided upon. Thereafter, actions would need to be coordinated amongst the bodies concerned for addressing the above aspects. At present, no single agency exists to address the above, resulting in sub-optimal exploitation of extant national space capabilities by the military. Hence, there exists an emergent need to constitute a centralised body which would address all the aforementioned aspects.

With regards to identifying a suitable body for organising air and space capabilities, force structures of military IOPs are, by and large, governed by the operational environment. Military power of specific Services builds upon the operational characteristics afforded by the environment in which they are designed to operate. Suitable organisational structures use their expertise to build upon these characteristic capabilities and convert them into strengths. These capabilities undergo refinements in technology, doctrine, tactics, experience and practice, etc to translate them into strengths unique to a particular service Thus, the army builds its military strength upon the operational characteristics of land, the navy on water and the air force on the entire vertical expanse above the Earth. No known upper limit of operation or defence has been laid down for the air force, since the same is not possible. The characteristics of air and space in the vertical dimension enable distinct capabilities. While the air force has translated the capabilities of air power into formidable military strength, the vast capabilities of space are yet to be tapped. Hence, force structures to harness extant space capabilities as well as undertake integration of air and space would be an essential prerequisite for later conversion of space capabilities into strengths. The above in no way implies that capabilities would remain under the isolated purview of the IAF. Air and space capabilities inherently promote joint application of military power. For example, air power capabilities exist with the other two Services also, but the nation's strength in terms of air power rests with the IAF. Thus, while the proposed structure would make space capabilities available to all the military IOPs, overall aerospace strengths could be nurtured under the IAF and made available to military as well as national IOPs. For a beginning, constitution of an Aerospace Command would be a harbinger of the much sought after RMA. The organisational framework of a structure aimed at integrating air, space and information systems into the nation's military IOPs cannot afford to be rigid. It would be inherently flexible to address and integrate the rigours of evolving technologies military requirements and doctrine. Air and space capabilities inherently promote joint application of military power. In our unique context, military doctrines are increasingly moving towards joint application of military power for national gain. Hence, apprehensions over ownership issues are largely unfounded and finally, too premature at this stage.

Conclusion

It goes without saying that constitution of an Aerospace Commission and an Aerospace Command would not be the end of the entire affair. It would only be the first contributory step in organising national air and space capabilities for comprehensive military and national gain. It would be the first step to enabling employment of national air and space capabilities as a composite potent entity instead of the prevailing disjointed effort. Nevertheless, the globe gets smaller with every passing day and the time-distance relationship shrinks further with evolving capabilities of air, space and information systems. As a consequence, the national imperatives of organising the above stated instruments become increasingly critical with every passing day. Hence, it is imperative that we put the act together; the faster the better for comprehensive national power and gain.

Notes

1. For details, refer Angang Hu, *Economic & Social Transformation in China* (New York: Routledge, 2007) ch. 2, pp 34-41, and Ye Zicheng, *Inside China's Grand Strategy: The Perspective from the People's Republic* (Kentucky: University Press of Kentucky, 2011), ch. 1, pp. 17-26.
2. Refer to Constitution of India at the site of India's Ministry of Law and Justice at lawmin.nic.in/coi/coiason29july08
3. For example, while air power pre-World War II was largely perceived as an essential prerequisite for pursuit (or support) of the air-land battle or naval engagements, post-World War II, the ability of air power to independently pursue military objectives has become increasingly apparent with every major conflict.
4. For example, historically, combat air power, though available was not put to use on a number of occasions, including the Chinese aggression of 1962, due to flawed perceptions on its employability. For a more exhaustive account of historical instances of sub-optimal utilisation of combat air power, see Air Cmde Jasjit Singh, "Some Reflections on The IAF", *Air Power Journal,* vol.1 no.1, (Monsoon 2004), pp. 158-165.
5. By all accounts, the quality of military manpower available since independence has either degraded or maintained status-quo or at best marginally improved.
6. The Group of Ministers on higher defence management, during the National Defence Alliance (NDA) regime, had restricted the number of commands to six in the case of the army and air force. The present United Progressive Alliance (UPA) government accomodated an additional command for the army, taking the total number of commands to seven, equal to the existing air force commands. For details, see "Govt Caps Commands per Service at 7, Rejects Aerospace Plan", *Indian Express,* September 15, 2005.
7. See PTI report, "IAF Needs 39 Squadrons, has Only 34: Defence Committee", *The Economic Times*, April 29, 2013.
8. The Soviet concept of Military Technical Revolution (MTR) evolved in the 1950s and involved utilising information obtained from satellites, high level aircraft and computers for acquisition and targeting of the adversary with nuclear and conventional munitions by long range aircraft and ballistic missiles. Later American concepts of RMA, net-centricity, transformation, etc built up on the same basic premise as also do present Chinese theories of informationalisation.

9. See, "Economy, Market on High Octane", *The Times of India*, January 13, 2007 and World Bank GDP Growth Rate Data at http://data.worldbank.org/indicator/NY.GDP.MKTP.KD.ZG and India GDP Annual Growth Rate at http://www.tradingeconomics.com/india/gdp-growth-annual.
10. As revealed by Airbus's global market forecast in Press Trust of India Report, "India to Face $105 Bn Demand for Aircraft", *The Financial Times*, December 7, 2006.
11. See, Indian Brand Equity Foundation Report dated September 13, 2013, at http://www.ibef.org/industry/indian-aviation.aspx
12. Ibid.
13. Refer Rajat Pandit, "Aviation Majors Eye Indian Defence Market", *The Times of India*, December 21, 2006.
14. Refer FICCI Report, "Indian Aviation: Spreading its Wings" February 2013.
15. Refer Deloitte Report, "Overview of Indian Space Sector-2010," August 2010.
16. Refer PTI News Report, "India's First Defence Satellite GSAT-7 Launched Successfully", *The Times of India* , August 30, 2013 and Madhumati D.S. "Navy's First Satellite GSAt-7 Now in Space", *The Hindu*, August 30, 2013.
17. The above is largely inevitable considering that by 2020, there would be more than 15 airline operators, air traffic of over 100 million, need for more than 4,000 pilots and MRO opportunities of over $ 2 billion. The above needs could only be fulfilled by ex-IAF personnel, since producing such a large number of personnel within a span of 5-6 years would be next to impossible. Data sourced from UKTI report on Indian Aerospace Industry.
18. For details on Multi-Purpose Aerospace Vehicle, see speech of President of India, Dr. APJ Abdul Kalam, "Vision for Aeronautics Missions", JRD Tata Memorial Lecture, Bangalore, August 20, 2005. Available at home site of President of India, http://presidentofindia.nic.in/scripts/sllatest1.jsp?id=579 -->

4

Understanding Pakistan's COIN Strategy

Shalini Chawla

The military has evolved into the most powerful institution within Pakistan, asserting itself into the national policy decision-making processes and the country's governance even when a civilian government has been installed. Other institutions in the state have not been able to develop due to a number of factors. The military today stands as the most dominant institution, deciding the political, strategic, social and even religious discourse in Pakistan.[1]

The dominance of the military has created problems in the state and the state has been driven by the interests of the military. Although this is not the sole reason for the fragmented society and politics which Pakistan has experienced over the decades, it certainly is a major contributor to it. The military usurped political power for the first time under Gen Ayub in 1958 when the first Marshal Law was imposed on October 7, 1958, as a joint decision of President Iskander Mirza and Gen Ayub Khan. One could say that this marked the beginning of the penetration of the military (since Ayub, as the commander-in-chief had already been functioning as the defence minister since 1954) into the bureaucratic structure of the country as Ayub initiated military control over the political and civil systems. The bureaucratic structure was empowered due to the military's involvement and backing. In the late 1950s and 1960s, the military managed to boost its image as the sole defender of the nation, not only of the territorial front but also domestically in the wake of weak political institutions which were unable to stabilise the country. Since then, there has been a gradual increase in the military's involvement in the various facets of the state, making it the most powerful entity. All the military takeovers in Pakistan have been welcomed by the masses because each time, the military takeover came due to a weak, corrupt civilian regime, which left the nation in pitiable economic and political turmoil. This has formed a vicious cycle in Pakistan, where a fragile and fraudulent civilian leadership stresses the nation politically, socially and economically and the masses are eager to see the military leadership take over in order to bring the anarchy of the civilian regime to an end. The military takes charge and the masses are happy for some time, before the political parties again start to assert themselves, and the suppressive policies of the military regime shakes up the masses, who now want the democratic system back in place in order to participate in the decision-making.

At another level, the Pakistan Army has pursued a consistent strategy of covert war and promoting/sponsoring/executing insurgency across its borders. Stephen Cohen, one of the leading American experts on Pakistan and its army, states in his book, regarding the Pakistani officers who were trained in the US: "The American doctrine was primarily concerned about *suppressing* such a war, but Pakistanis also studied it in terms of *launching* a people's war against India, or developing a people's army as a second line of defence".[2]

In an another book published two decades later, he reemphasised this factor:

> A special forces unit was established in 1959 with American assistance, and the professional military journals explored the concept of low intensity conflict in considerable detail. Studies were made of Algeria, Yugoslavia, North Vietnam, and particularly China; several of them concluded that guerella warfare was a "strategic weapon", a "slow but sure and relatively inexpensive" strategy that was "fast overshadowing regular warfare."[3]

On the other hand, Pakistan's history is replete with instances of insurgencies, especially in its non-Punjabi provinces (even if the pervasive violence in Sindh, especially Karachi, is not taken into account). This has mainly been driven by the fact that the ruling elites (military and civil), an overwhelming proportion of whom belong to the army and the civil bureaucracy, sought to deny the legitimate rights, leave alone satisfy the aspirations, of the people of the provinces while drawing upon the economic output from these provinces.

It is, therefore, not surprising that insurgencies in Pakistan are as old as its history and the nation experienced its first insurgency in the 1940s when the Balochis rebelled against the state. Balochistan has been a troubled area from the time of Pakistan's creation—the region was strongly against annexation to Pakistan. It has been flush with guns and known to be ruled by guns. The province has experienced a series of insurgencies which the Pakistani government has tried to suppress by military firepower. The Baloch leadership was never in favour of joining Pakistan and always desired and demanded an independent Baloch federation. In 1948, despite all the efforts by Pakistan and formalisation of the merger between the princely state of Kalat (which *de-facto* represented Balochistan till

1947) and Pakistan, there was immense resistance from Balochistan. It was not simple for Pakistan to incorporate Kalat into Pakistan except through the formal accession of the princely state after the lapse of British Paramountcy on August 15, 1947. As a result, the Pakistani forces were mobilised for operations against the state of Kalat and it was under this threat of force that Kalat ultimately signed the "Instrument of Accession" on March 28, 1948. As a consequence of the state's policies since then, the Pakistani government has faced regular revolts from the Balochis at not very infrequent intervals. Each time, the military has reacted with the use of heavy force involving a significant number of ground troops and air operations, leading to massive civilian casualties, and, inevitably, to further alienation. An example of the army's brutal role was seen during the six-day battle at Chamalang in the Marri area in September 1974. An army ground and air offensive was launched in the winter of 1974 on the Baloch tribes, who had gathered for an annual pilgrimage to the Chamalang plains, inflicting severe human and livestock casualties.[4]

The ongoing Baloch insurgency was seriously aggravated in 2005 and intensified with the killing of 79-year-old Baloch leader Akbar Bugti on August 26, 2006, using an American supplied F-16 combat aircraft. Insurgency has grown tremendously and Balochistan, which was anyway a production house for the Mujahideen training, has turned home for many terrorist organisations, including the mostly deadly terrorist entity – the Tehrik-e-Taliban Pakistan (TTP). The Balochis have been extremely hospitable and welcoming towards the Al Qaeda fighters and Taliban militants as most of the Taliban leaders and soldiers are graduates from *madrassas* in Balochistan which flourished under the patronage of the Inter-Services Intelligence (ISI) and Central Intelligence Agency (CIA) during the 1980s. After the US led North Atlantic Treaty Organisations (NATO) troops targeted the Al Qaeda, their natural instinct was to return home to Balochistan. After 9/11, the insurgency has grown further and the Pakistan military has shown no restraint in handling the rebellion with any means other than heavy military firepower. The inclusion of other terrorist organisations in Balochistan has added an altogether new dimension to the insurgency, which the state seems to be totally incapable of handling even with military assistance from the US and NATO troops.

The insurgency in East Pakistan in 1971 was due to Pakistan's own policies and a manifestation of three decades of frustration and a growing sense of alienation which the people in East Pakistan (which was actually the majority province) experienced. The civilian and military governing authorities in Islamabad paid no attention to the social, political and economic woes of East Pakistan, which remained deprived of political and economic development. The governing authorities at Islamabad displayed a highly insensitive and intolerant attitude towards the Bengalis who were considered inferior. The two sides of the country were totally different in every respect. And, ultimately, even after the victory in the 1970 national elections, Bhutto was against calling the Parliament which would have inevitably resulted in a Bengali majority from East Pakistan. There was total unwillingness to hand over power to the elected majority and the elected party was vigorously opposed by the army, the Punjabis and Bhutto, which resulted in a rebellion and, ultimately the creation of Bangladesh (substantively due to the unwillingness of the Pakistani leadership to negotiate a political solution and attempt accommodation with the deeply alienated Bengalis). Pakistan's military government led by Gen Yahya Khan responded with a counter-insurgency strategy that at best can be described as "enemy-centric." The military's genocide in 1971 was horrifying, leading to the slaughter of a huge number of men, women and children, especially the intellectuals and educated people. It is estimated that three approximately 100,000 Bengalis were killed, if not more (most sources indicate a genocide that resulted in 3 million casualties). The military response was certainly not the solution to the problems of East Pakistan—the issues could have been tackled with a peaceful approach.

More recently, Pakistan got involved in counter-insurgency following the terrorist attacks in 2001 on the US; as a frontline state in the war on terror along with the US and NATO troops, Pakistan conducted increasingly intensive operations in the Federally Administered Tribal Areas (FATA) and Northwest Frontier Province (NWFP) (now Khyber Pakhtunkhwa—KPK). Pakistan's frontier region, a troublesome region at the best of times, is now engaged in a full-blooded insurgency which the Pakistan military and the paramilitary troops are simply unable to control. The nature of insurgency has intensified and the number of insurgents has multiplied beyond proportion.

KPK and FATA became extremely fertile ground for *jihadism* as they have all the essential elements to facilitate a deadly insurgency which has emerged as the biggest challenge for Washington. KPK and FATA have been ultra conservative regions and have suffered a deep sense of alienation from the governing establishment in Islamabad. The area is extremely underdeveloped and the federal authorities have never been too concerned regarding the diversion of developmental funds in this province. Development, literacy, health facilities all remain at the minimum level in FATA. The underlying cause of unrest in these areas is political and economic in nature.

In the 1980s, the frontier province became the staging post for the *jihad* because of its proximity to the eastern and southeastern Afghan provinces of Paktika, Nangarhar, Kunar, Zabul and Kandahar. The lawless tribal areas served as transit posts for both weapons and Islamist zealots pouring in from all over the world to join the anti-Russia *jihad*. Hundreds of *madrassas* blossomed in the region producing the world's deadliest terrorists. The military in Pakistan fully utilised the period to accelerate its covert war in Jammu and Kashmir (J&K).

Increased militancy and the rising number of insurgents in the FATA and KPK, which now present a conglomeration of various insurgents and terrorists groups to the Pakistani military and NATO forces, have been subject to deep focus for the past four years. The underlying causes for insurgency were anyway present and the triggering factor was the Lal Masjid incident in 2007 which increased the intensity of, and speeded up, the terrorist activities in the region. The tribal areas are not only hospitable to the insurgent groups but also provide the maximum number of training schools for their further growth. Shuja Nawaz has very rightly said about FATA:

> The most dangerous spot on the map may well be the source of another 9/11 type of attack on the Western world or its surrogates in the region. Should such an attack occur, it likely will be spawned in the militancy that grips FATA and contiguous areas in Afghanistan and Pakistan today. The principle actors are the Taliban, in both countries; their allies former Soviet-era Mujahideen commanders, including Gulbadin Hekmatyar of the Hezb-e-Islami and the Haqqani groups (headed by Jalaluddin and his son Siraj); Sunni militants from central and southern Punjab; and Al Qaeda, which benefits from links of these insurgents. [5]

Most of the Taliban leadership of Afghanistan and followers of at least two major Mujahideen commanders—Jalaluddin Haqqani (formerly of the Maulvi Khalis group within the Hizb-e-Islami and then member of the Taliban government, and Gulbudin Hikmatyar (of the eponymous group Hizb-e-Islami), of the Afghan War against the Soviets in the 1980s—are believed to have taken refuge in FATA, where they have been welcomed by their fellow tribesmen.[6] These factions of the Taliban continue to prosecute their war against the United States and the new Afghan government. Apart from these, elements of Al Qaeda continue to use FATA as their training and recruitment ground and also there are reports that the Taliban and Al Qaeda have formed an "effective military alliance of convenience".[7] Added to this deadly extremist mix is the TTP factor, whose avowed aim is to revolt against the presence of US and NATO forces within Pakistan, and enforce the establishment of *Sharia* as the rule of law within Pakistan. The TTP has taken up the battle against the Pakistani state and has been very selectively targeting the military. The TTP probably tops the list of deadly terrorist attacks, including the assassination of Benazir Bhutto in 2007, the attack on the Marriott Hotel in Islamabad in 2008, and various other subsequent attacks.

The TTP has also established links with the Afghan Taliban and the Al Qaeda. FATA has increasingly emerged as a principle sanctuary for the TTP terrorists and, thus, the insurgency which now has the full-fledged support of the locals is in full swing. Although, some Pakistani scholars hold the view that the TTP is losing its 'brand value', the fact remains that the attacks by the TTP pose a significant challenge which the Pakistan Army is trying to eliminate militarily but without much success.

Underlying Causes of Insurgency

After studying the various insurgencies in Pakistan, some of the underlying common factors can be pointed out. Firstly, alienation of the people in various parts of the country ethnically different from those in Punjab (which rules Pakistan) stands as a common factor in all three cases, i.e. East Pakistan, Balochistan and FATA/KPK. All the three regions have been alienated from the federal government. In the 1950s, Muhammad Nazimuddin's proposal of providing an equal number of seats in both the Lower and Upper Houses of Parliament to both the wings was rejected by the West Pakistan political leaders. Again, the One Unit Plan which came up after the Constitution was passed in 1956, was not welcomed by the East Pakistanis as they felt it would reduce their strength at the Centre. East Pakistans always felt devoid of power.

Balochistan again has been deprived of rights and facilities by the federal administration. The region always resisted annexation to Pakistan and in the 1970s, Bhutto displayed a completely intolerant attitude by not accepting the participation of the Balochis in the governance. FATA and KPK have been totally alienated, so much so that FATA is termed as "*Ilaaka Ghair*" which means alienated territory in the Urdu language. The province stood governed by the Frontier Crimes Regulations (FCR) based on the 1920 British law. The region is completely isolated from the Centre and has absolutely no role in the national decision-making in any form. FATA has always had very limited participation in the political system of Pakistan. In 1997, universal franchise was extended to FATA, but it could only send representatives to the federal legislature.

Secondly, underdevelopment of each of these regions has been a visible indication of the ethno-centric policies followed by the majority Punjabi rulers of the country. East Pakistan stood in complete contrast to the West as far as development was concerned, not only in terms of the infrastructure but also educational institutions.

Balochistan, although extremely rich in natural resources, has been deprived of its due share in the developmental process in Pakistan. One of the major factors generating tremendous unrest among the people of Balochistan is that they have not received an appropriate share in the gains which the government generates out of the region's natural resources. This is one of the main reasons behind the attacks on the Chinese workers at Gwadar port. The port is operated by a state-run Chinese firm – China Overseas Port Holding Company—but provides little in terms of employment and opportunities to the locals and this is a pressing cause of resistance in the area. The Balochis are deeply dissatisfied with the amount of royalty which has been offered to them for Gwadar. Similarly, the dispute over sharing the revenue from the Sui gas plant, the largest gas plant in Pakistan, has soured the relationship between the Pakistani government and the Balochis.

FATA's underdeveloped state obviously, does not need any elaboration and has been described well by Shuja Nawaz:

> FATA has suffered from lack of proactive and participatory government mechanisms and has been subject to an anachronistic, top-down administrative system that served the colonial British power but is not suitable for a modern society. Because of these conditions and general neglect by successive central governments in developing the economics and polity of the region, it will continue to provide a favourable environment for terrorism and militancy.[8]

Thirdly, insensitivity on the part of the governing leadership towards the locals has aggravated the problems. But this is a natural outflow of alienation, and the federal government has paid scant attention to the repeated requests from the region regarding their problems. It was very clear in East Pakistan, when the West Punjabi psyche was to look down upon the East Pakistanis and also sideline even the humble requests made on pertinent issues by them. For Balochistan and FATA also, the Pakistani leadership has displayed a rather harsh and insensitive attitude towards the demands from the locals.

Fourthly, the military and also the civilian leadership in Islamabad are primarily driven by their larger interests to seek strategic depth in Afghanistan to stand at par with their superior neighbour, India. Islamabad seems to have failed to realise that the real strength of the nation would be to have complete support from the tribal areas – the Pashtun community which has a nationalist fervour and could be diverted towards seeking the national objectives along with the military leadership.

Fifthly, another common feature in all the insurgencies within Pakistan is the treatment/countering of insurgency through military means. Starting with the first outbreak of Baloch insurgency in the 1940s, the Pakistan government has invariably opted for the use of brute military force. One cannot say that the military means can be ruled out to counter insurgency but definitely the military solution alone is never an answer to the problem of insurgency. The conduct of the counter-insurgency strategy has to be a conjunction of military, political, economic, and, for that matter, even physiological actions.

Pakistan Military's Counter-Insurgency Strategy Post 9/11: Has it Been Successful?

The Pakistan military had inherited significant experience of counter-insurgency in the KPK during the British Raj which tended to rely largely on the extensive use of military force. Regrettably, it did not review this as a sovereign state dealing with its ethnically diverse provinces after 1947. But even then, it had acquired substantive experience with counter-insurgency in the past, beginning with the Faqir of Ipi's continuing *jihad* in KPK from the British days, starting in 1936, then against the Pakistan government, finally, ending only when the Faqir died in 1960. One could argue that Pakistan carried forward the "enemy-centric" approach to counter-insurgency from this experience though there should have been deeper and sober introspection after its creation as a sovereign state. It continued to acquire extensive experience in Balochistan and then in East Pakistan. Many Pakistani scholars refrain from calling the outbreak of rebellion in East Pakistan an insurgency, but the fact is that the 1971 rebellion and the creation of Bangladesh certainly had the characteristics of an insurgency. In Balochistan, the military opted to use a heavy hand each time, and but did not manage to eliminate the insurgency from the region, and it kept popping up at frequent intervals.

In the meantime, in the 1980s, Pakistan became the frontline state for the United States in its war against the Soviets and, thus, gained enormous experience in conducting/waging insurgency. Here, it also acquired enormous experience and expertise as well as weapons and equipment, including the knowhow to generate funds through illegal funding from banks created for this purposes with money from the narcotics trade. The United States not only provided ample resources to foment the insurgency but also provided support to the Pakistan Army and the ISI with the essential training and infrastructure to conduct the "holy war" against the Russians. During the 1980s and specifically after the Soviets left Afghanistan in 1988, the Pakistan military conducted the insurgency in Kashmir and other parts of India, including Punjab. So, obviously the military is well-versed in conducting insurgency rather than countering it, which is a total reversal of its role.

Pakistan's approach in dealing with the widespread insurgency in Balochistan and specially FATA in the last 7-8 years has been centred on the use of brute force. This is evident in the statement made by former Director General Military Operations (DGMO), Maj Gen Ahmed Shuja Pasha in 2008, that to counter irregular warfare "all that you need is a well-trained infantry soldier".[9] In the last nine years, the Pakistan Army has not been able to control the insurgency; rather, the military actions have managed to unite the terrorist organisations and have added the support of the international organisations to the regional insurgents who seem to share a common objective which is anti-state, anti-military. The view has now apparently changed under the US nudging and training, and there is some realisation in the armed forces for adoption of a broader approach to counter-insurgency.

Between 2001 and 2012, the Pakistan Army conducted a number of military operations in FATA and the Malakand and Swat regions. The early efforts in South Waziristan were not very successful and involved cordon-and-search operations during which the army lost men through ambushes and also surrender.[10] The United States decided to assist the operations with drone strikes on the selected targets ostensibly against suspected Al Qaeda hideouts. But, eventually, the drone strikes went up in numbers, not only targeting Al Qaeda but the other terrorist outfits also. The military operations involving an increasing number of drone strikes did manage to destroy some of the insurgent infrastructure led by the old *maliks* in FATA but what was more disturbing, the outcome was the emergence of the new young leaders guiding the insurgency in the region, with support from the other militants.

The continued military operations against the insurgents in the tribal areas have shifted from one area to another in the last six years. But a decisive victory against the insurgents is not likely. The insurgents frequently change their positions and establish fresh bases with local support in no time, forming extended terror zones for the military. The counter-insurgency tactics followed by the military have only multiplied the insurgents in numbers and also increased the frustration and anger in the people's mind. Although the Pakistan military has claimed to kill a large number of insurgents/terrorists, the fact is that the Taliban has not only spread its wings fully in the Khyber-Pakhtunkhwa province but also in Punjab, the heartland of Pakistan.

Fig 4.1: Annual Number of Unmanned Drone Strikes in Pakistan, 2004-10

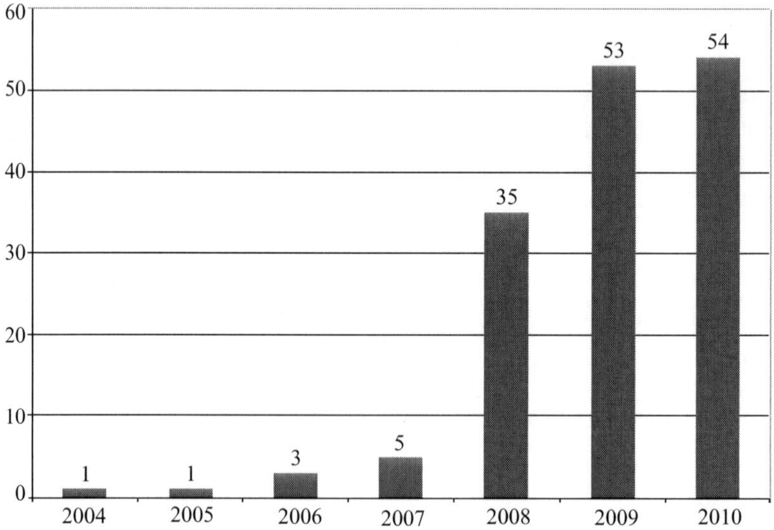

Source: Ian S. Livingston and Michael O'Hanlon, "Pakistan Index: Tracking Variables of Restructure and Security", *Brookings Report,* August 31, 2010, p. 7.

The US-Pakistani air strikes (which have been on an increase—see Fig 4.1) have proved to be completely counter-productive in achieving the military and strategic objectives. On the military front, the air strikes have not proved successful against the Al Qaeda leadership, which was the prime motive of initiating them. The air-based firepower reveals the extreme weakness of the CIA and Pentagon in the tribal areas, and not their strength. To be actually effective in the tribal land, the US and Pakistani forces need many more human resources and smart intelligence actions on the ground. A simplistic and easily executable air strike strategy often proves to be vague and relatively more effective operations have been those on the ground, in close partnership with the Pakistani security forces. [11]

On the non-military side, the air strikes have done insurmountable damage. The strikes have resulted in colossal civilian casualties which has aggravated the anger in the people. FATA and KPK have anyway been isolated and have never shared emotional proximity with the Pakistani governance—they have felt isolated for decades and the air strikes were for them another indication of insensitivity from Islamabad. This anger has been exploited by the insurgents to gain popular sympathy and also new recruits. This seemed to be the motive behind Faisal Shehzad, the Pakistan-born US citizen who confessed to the planning of New York's Times Square bombing in May

2010. He is an educated youth and not a part of Al Qaeda or the Taliban but confessed that he intended taking revenge for the civilian casualties in the drone strikes.

There was immense resentment against the air strikes as they were seen as impinging on Pakistan's sovereignty. At least three Predators are said to be deployed at a secret Pakistani air base and can be launched without specific permission from Islamabad.[12] This has obviously multiplied the anti-American sentiment among the people and resulted in rising mistrust for American actions.

The air strikes have produced, and will continue to produce, more insurgents and supporters for the Taliban and Al Qaeda, as many youngsters, after the civilian casualties and loss of families, are forced to join the insurgency campaign. The tribals very comfortably accept the ideology of the Taliban which is based on an extremist interpretation of the *Sharia,* and a desire for revenge provides an additional incentive. It is not wrong to say that the air strike strategy is a booby trap for Taliban insurgents and also Al Qaeda, which turns out to be the most effective recruitment vehicle for them.[13] The air strikes have facilitated the task of the insurgent groups who had to otherwise work towards generating hatred in the minds of the people and convince them to join them in their fight against the state.

The counter-insurgency strategy by the Pakistan military in KPK and the search for Al Qaeda and the Taliban has not succeeded primarily due to a number of reasons. Two of these reasons stand out: (i) Pakistan's unwillingness to decimate the Taliban; and (ii), Pakistan's continuing "enemy-centric" counter-insurgency strategy. After 9/11, Pakistan was compelled to divorce itself from its long-standing ally, the Taliban, and support the US completely in the war against terror. US Deputy Secretary of State Richard Armitage, told Lt Gen Mahmood Ahmed, Pakistan's ISI chief, immediately after the 9/11 attacks, that Pakistan has to make a choice: "You are either 100 percent with us or 100 percent against us—there is no gray area".[14] Gen Musharraf was left with little choice but to accept the US proposal and join President Bush in the war on terror. Pakistan was asked to curb all domestic expressions of support for terrorism. It received alluring military and economic aid not only from the US but from all across the globe for taking a stand against terrorism and becoming a US ally. The economic aid post 9/11 was much needed by Pakistan and got the nation out of the economic doldrums.

The military has been engaged in the war on terror for more than 10 years now. But the terrorist and insurgent groups have not only expanded, they perpetrate attacks with increasingly deadly methods. The expansion in the number of terror outfits is quite amazing and it is unlikely that Al Qaeda and the Taliban have managed to expand to this extent without the support or consent of the military and ISI. Pakistan had promised to sever its links with the Taliban, which it considered its "strategic assets", and the other extremists. Pakistan has also allowed the US free access to wage a war against its own people. From 2003 onwards, taking advantage of Washington's involvement in Iraq, the Pakistan military reestablished its links with the Taliban and the Haqqani network. The Pentagon was confronted with a better equipped, psychologically stronger and more motivated Taliban. [15]

Pakistan was certainly not going to destroy its own creation, the Taliban, which it views as its most important strategic asset to fulfil its objective of gaining strategic depth in Afghanistan. Pakistan also did not touch the other terrorist organisations which have been serving its interest against India and are tools of the military's covert war strategy which it has followed against India for the last four decades. The top leadership of Al Qaeda also was sheltered as these factions were operating from major cities like Karachi and Peshawar. The military has been very focussed on sheltering groups which serve its larger national strategic objectives.[16] It has continued to distinguish among militant and insurgent groups operating in FATA and KPK and to use the tribal areas for training proxy groups to be used in India and also Afghanistan against Karzai's regime. The military has not only refused to target these select groups but has provided support to them. Support to some proxy organisations and their allies has created a conducive environment for militancy to grow and undermine the government's efforts to establish law and order and handle the security situation.[17] The military discriminates between the 'Good Taliban' and the 'Bad Taliban', and this is less out of ideological sympathy and more out of strategic calculation. Pakistan's "selective" approach has been a major hindrance in its counter-insurgency efforts.[18]

Conclusions

Literature and attention to counter-insurgency was nearly absent in most countries (especially in the West) till 1999, probably because the United States did not wish to remind itself of its major failures in counter-insurgency in Vietnam. It was due to the growth and expansion of trans-national terrorism and support for generating insurgencies in other countries (especially during the Cold War, though followed indigenously by countries like Pakistan from the very beginning of the Cold War) after the first bombing of the World Trade Centre in 1993 that the US elites and government began starting to pay greater attention to trans-national terrorism and then to counter-insurgency.

Current strategic and academic literature identifies the following counter-insurgency strategies:

- **Population-Centric Strategy.** Under this strategy, people's social, economic and political grievances are held foremost even though force may have to be employed to ensure stability for a period long enough for such measures to begin to take effect. India's counter-insurgency is broadly based on this model. Even where used, the employment of force and firepower is to be tightly controlled and minimum force applied. The concept is based on the fundamental principle that population is the centre of gravity for the insurgents as well as the counter-insurgent authorities. Hence, the civil casualty factor is given strong emphasis where the insurgents would try and provoke a strong reaction by the government forces which could lead to a crossfire and, potentially, collateral damage and casualties, thus, increasing the alienation factor among the general population and their tilt towards the insurgents.
- **Leader-Centric Strategy.** This strategy views insurgency and counter-insurgency as a conflict between the elites in which the elite with superiority in certain leadership attributes usually wins. Mark Moyar has been a great supporter of this strategy and, in fact, attributes the outcome of every insurgency since the American Civil War in terms of the qualities and attributes of leaders on either side.[19] He naturally also supports flexibility and delegation of authority to counter-insurgent forces. Moyar argues, "Sound counterinsurgency methods dictated from on high in the form of orders or doctrines, have consistently failed when good leaders were lacking. The installation of good leaders, by contrast, has most often produced success even if those individuals were not told in detail how to do their job."[20] But he concedes that "only threat and use of force can stop hard core insurgent leaders from attacking the counter-insurgents."
- **Network-Centric Strategy.** The "network-centric warfare" concept after the 1991 Gulf War had held that future wars would be won by technology driven networks. While in the early stages of the US-Coalition wars against Iraq and in Afghanistan, this concept tended to get support, the bubble of technological omnipotence was soon burst by the failure of high technology to defeat the Afghan and Iraqi insurgents. This is not to say that technology is not important in counter-insurgency, but that technology has to be relevant to the nature of the war and its utility and success will depend upon force employment and not the mere possession of technology and size of forces arrayed on either side.[21]
- **Enemy-Centric Strategy:** This type of strategy seeks to destroy the will of the insurgents by the sheer power of superior firepower and mobility normally associated with modern military forces. Our present studies clearly show that the Pakistan military has been pursuing an enemy-centric strategy to deal with the insurgency in

its western and eastern provinces which placed little faith in political accommodation and socio-economic steps to alleviate the causes of insurgency while using superior firepower to impose stability and security for the general public.

The Pakistan military has adopted an "enemy-centric" approach in every counter-insurgency operation, where the regular army prides itself in its military professionalism for a conventional war and where the driving psyche is to treat all opposition as "enemy." This has resulted in adoption of various tactics and approaches to deal with the people of the region from where insurgency erupts, as an enemy that threatens their positions. Given the nature of the Pakistani state, and the military's overpowering position, it was the most apparent approach to be followed in dealing with the insurgents, in the past and at present. The current enemy-centric strategy by the Pakistan military is not new and it has followed the same in the past. The difference at present is the involvement of the superpower in the counter-insurgency and also the availability of the most sophisticated military assistance from the West.

The enemy-centric approach aims to destroy the will of the insurgents and also their ability to fight back. Initially, when an insurgency erupts, the insurgents are fewer in number with limited means and support and, hence, the enemy-centric approach of counter-insurgency could potentially bring desirable results and could manage to nip the insurgency in the bud. One can say the approach worked in Balochistan in the early decades. But the other side of the enemy-centric approach is that it can lead to civilian casualties, generate support for the insurgents due to aggravated anti-state/military sentiments and a feeling of revenge erupting because of the civilian casualties. Even if the military is able to manage the insurgency in its nascent stage but does not take care of the aftermath of the military operations, the insurgency could gather support over a period of time, and would erupt again. Hence, the cycle of insurgency, fed by an enemy-centric strategy by the government and the absence of attention to the root causes of the insurgency, continues, as has been observed in Balochistan and KPK.

The Road Ahead

Altering the Strategic Calculus

To be able to control the insurgency and actually get normalcy in the region, the Pakistan military and government need to make serious amends to their ongoing approach not only towards the insurgency but also their overall military strategy which is very India-centric. The military has been very selective and partial in its approach of dealing with the militants and has continued to shelter the terrorist outfits which it considered as important tools for its strategy of covert war through terrorism against India. The military's prime concern and main objective is centred on countering India and to be at par with India due to the perceived security threat. Gen Musharraf acted against the militant outfits immediately post 9/11 under US pressure. Around 200 religious extremists and militants who were arrested by law enforcement measures in November 2001 were released after a few months as the government declared that it did not find sufficient evidence against them.[22] Musharraf banned leading anti-India organisations like the Jaish-e-Mohammad (JeM) and Lashkar-e-Tayyeba (LeT) but almost all of them have been functioning with changed names. Hassan Abbas, in his detailed study about these organisations, says, "True that Lashkar-i-Taiba was among the banned outfits and its chief Hafiz Saeed was under arrest, but this group's parent organisation, Dawat-ul-Irshad was operating without hindrance or restrictions."[23] The LeT has been renamed as the Jamaat-ud-Dawa and is operating in full swing. The organisation, in fact, is quite popular among the masses as it offers significant social service, free of cost, which the Pakistani state is unable to provide.

Even with the Taliban, the military was not in favour of cutting off the ties as it wants the Taliban to serve its larger interest in Afghanistan after the departure of the US. The Pakistan military has adopted the strategy of covert war against India and is convinced about the use of terror as a foreign policy tool. As long as the Pakistan military supports the militants and terrorism as an instrument of state policy, it will not be possible for it to control the insurgency and militancy within the state. There is a clear need for Islamabad to alter its *strategic calculus* and end its support to the militant groups.

The state needs to realise that its real assets are its own people and, thus, the focus has to be much more on addressing the alienation and grievances of the people. This, in normal practice, is best achieved through democratic principles and practices. Through democratic means, the risk and potential of alienation can be reduced substantially which, in turn, would lead to reduction, if not elimination of the possibilities of the rise of insurgency. Although Pakistan has a democratic façade currently, the real decision-making lies with the military. Adoption of true democratic principles, where the state adopts a broad-based decision-making system, would fundamentally change the relationship between the state and society. The Pakistani state has to be more sensitive to the needs of the people rather than the present feudal system managed and run by the army and a militarised culture. This will be an ideal counter-insurgency strategy by dealing with the reasons that give rise of insurgency.

Provincial Autonomy

To be able to control the insurgency and not allow it to grow, Pakistan needs to take effective actions to modify the existing system of governance which is extremely "autocratic" in nature, and in which the entire power is centred in Islamabad. Pakistan needs to provide more political, social and economic autonomy to the provinces and have a regional balance in terms of treatment from the federal government. All the Pakistani provinces need to get equal attention and equal powers in terms of running the governance. Eminent Pakistani scholar Shuja Nawaz, commenting about the genesis of insurgency in Pakistan says:

> When you create a buffer zone, when you call a territory '*Ilaaka Ghair'* you are basically excluding them from the heartland... there are Pakhtuns in NWFP, now Khyber Pakhtunkhwa, they are part of Pakistan, but why on earth, sixty-three years after independence, do we have a territory in Pakistan still referred to as *Ilaaka Ghair*? It is being treated as a foreign territory, then it will behave like a foreign territory, then it will do its own things and that's the root cause."[24]

He further adds:

> The problem is of the relationship between the Centre and the periphery in Pakistan, as a result Pakistan which had a bit of a Constitution, became a highly centralised autocratic system....power shifting to Islamabad.[25]

In 2010, the process of devolution of some powers to the provinces began, but the process is indeed long, and will take time, even if the succeeding regimes continue the process. Pakistan needs to "rebuild the civilian institutions that can run the provinces independently".[26]

Investment in Socio-Economic Development: Build-up of the Human Capital

Pakistan has paid little attention to its socio-economic development. All the socio-economic indicators project that the national spending on the important social sectors like education and health has been much less than that on defence. Pakistan spends a low percentage of its Gross Domestic Production (GDP) on the education sector which is actually a pillar of the nation's stability. The existing educational institutions are insufficient in the country whereas the numbers of *madrassas* are alarmingly high and the numbers of students enrolled in the *madrassas* are also very high (Fig 4.2). An inefficient education system is bound to produce restricted job opportunities for the youth who would then be easily inclined towards *jihad.* The story of Kasab, one of the terrorists involved in the Mumbai blast on November 26, 2008, is a prime example of diversion of youth towards terror outfits due to lack of job opportunities. The militants and insurgent groups are constantly in search of youth who may be easily motivated for the purpose of insurgency. The deteriorating education system and the rising rate of unemployment provide the insurgent groups ample raw material which can be shaped according to their requirements. Fig 4.2 shows an increase in the number of students enrolled in *madrassas* in the last two decades. If the state focusses on developing a sound educational policy, with affordable good schools, the enrolment in *madrassas* can be controlled. Pakistan's population is growing at 3 percent and the educational institutions need to grow at the same pace. The areas infected by insurgency have literally no education system in place (Fig 4.3).

Fig 4.2: Estimated Growth Rate of Different Types of Schools in Pakistan

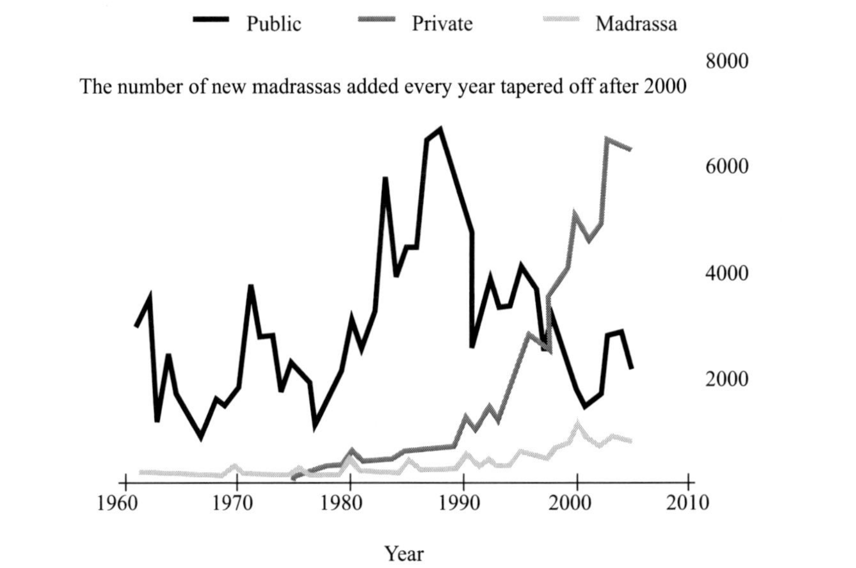

Note: As of January 2010, there were on estimated 1,500,000 student offending Madrassas in Pakistan.

Source: Ian S. Livingston and Michael O'Hanlon, "Pakistan Index: Tracking Variables of Restructure and Security", *Brookings Report,* August 31, 2010, p. 29.

Fig 4.3: Enrolment in Government Schools in Pakistan, in NWFP (KPK) and FATA

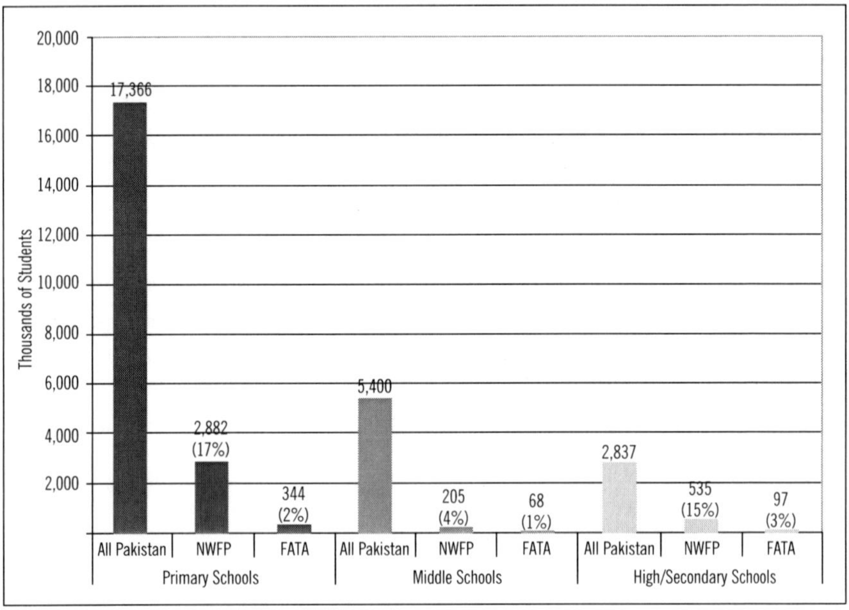

Source: Ian S. Livingston and Michael O'Hanlon, "Pakistan Index: Tracking Variables of Restructure and Security", *Brookings Report,* August 31, 2010, p. 29.

Pakistan has focussed on building up its military capability from the time of its creation. A major portion of the national budget has been invested in defence and the development sector has stood neglected for a long time, which is now actually resulting in various social and economic calamities for Pakistan. Important social sectors like education and health receive around 2.5 percent and 0.5 percent of the GDP share, as compared to defence on which the state spends more than 3.5 percent of the GDP.[27] Pakistan has up till now received close to $ 22 billion in aid from the United States but around 85 percent has been spent on defence and military modernisation and only 15 percent has been used for the socio-economic development of the country. Pakistan needs to allocate a larger share of aid and also national income towards building its human capital, specially in Balochistan, KPK and FATA.

Population-Centric Strategy

While the use of conventional military power cannot be ruled out in the counter-insurgency strategy, any such strategy has to be conducted in conjunction with the military, paramilitary, economic, political or, for that matter, even psychological actions.

Pakistan needs to adopt a population-centric strategy and not an enemy-centric one, which it has been following. The strategy has to be based on the basic code that the population is the centre of gravity and, hence, the civil casualty factor has to be given strong impetus. Military actions would automatically work towards increasing alienation among the masses if the human factor is not given due consideration. The civilian casualties, displacement of the people, and destruction during the operations need to be carefully dealt with.

Fig 4.4: Key Actors in Insurgency

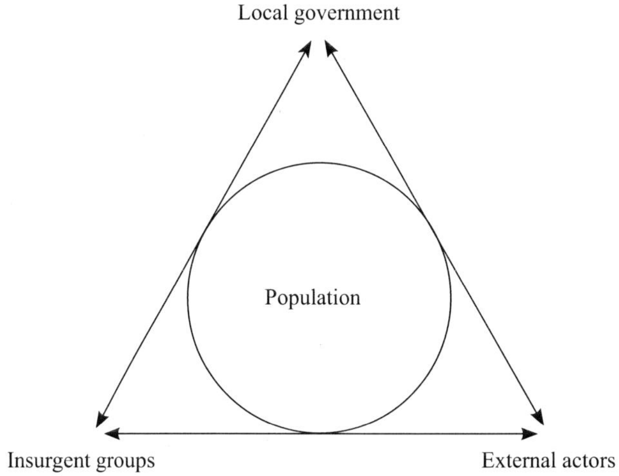

Source: Seth G. Jones, C. Christine Fair, "Counterinsurgency in Pakistan", *RAND* National Security Research Division, 2010, p 89.

The local population becomes extremely important in counter-insurgency and also, for that matter, in waging insurgency. The main actors in an insurgency are the local government, the insurgent groups, the external actors and the local population. As we can see in Fig 4.4, the local population is extremely critical for all the other three actors. The insurgents aim to gather more and more support from the people to continue and win the insurgent movement and, thus, any counter-insurgency strategy would have to also work towards gaining support from the people in the region.

The strategy needs to involve the socio-economic development of the areas which is badly needed.[28] To win support from the people, Pakistan has to invest in the development of FATA and Balochistan. Population support would build up if the developmental process begins in some form or the other. There has been realisation on this front and Obama's Af-Pak strategy lays emphasis on investment in development, but ultimately, it will be the political and military will to do so that would create a difference in Pakistan.

Also, Pakistan needs to encourage and facilitate the participation of the people in the counter-insurgency strategy. The civilians need to participate in the deliberations and this could potentially build more trust between the governing bodies and the population. The political will to do so is completely lacking in Pakistan.[29] Sharing of information with regards to the overall strategy with the people, and also having inputs from the people could produce a positive outcome.

Notes

1. Discussion with Ayesha Siddiqua Agha, February 25, 2011, at Jamia Millia University, New Delhi.
2. Stephen P. Cohen, *The Pakistan Army* (Oxford: Oxford University Press, 1998), p. 65.
3. Stephen P. Cohen, *The Idea of Pakistan* (Oxford: Oxford University Press, 2004), p. 104
4. "Balochistan In History: Baloch Insurgencies 1948-1977" at <www. http: balochistanhistory. blogspot.com>
5. Shuja Nawaz, "FATA -A Most Dangerous Place", *CSIS,* January 2009, Washington D.C., p.V
6. Ibid., p. 7.
7. Ibid.
8. Ibid., p. 8.
9. Shuja Nawaz, "Learning by Doing: The Pakistan Army's Experience with Counterinsurgency", *Atlantic Council,* February 2011, p. 3.
10. Ibid., p. 8.
11. Dr Hubertus Hoffman, "Tribal Areas (FATA): US Air Strikes Counterproductive - Smart Power is Better than Hard Power", *World Security Network: Networking a Safer World,* April 8, 2008.
12. K Alan Kronstadt, "Pakistan-US Relations", *Congressional Research Services (CRS) Report,* February 6, 2009, p. 22.
13. Hoffman, n. 11.
14. Owen Bennett Jones, *Pakistan: Eye of the Storm* (New Delhi: Penguin Books, 2002) p. 2.
15. Siddharth Vardharajan, "Six Lessons from a Flawed 'AFPAK" Strategy", in *Counter Terrorism in South Asia,* an ORF-Heritage Foundation Dialogue (New Delhi: KW Publishers, 2011). pp. 172-173.
16. Interview with Prof Sumit Ganguly, professor of political science, Tagore Chair in Indian Culture and Civilisation, Indiana University, Bloomington, on September 28, 2010, at the Institute for Defence Studies and Analyses, New Delhi.
17. Seth G. Jones and C. Christine Fair, "Counterinsurgency in Pakistan", *RAND* National Security Research Division, 2010, pp. 83-84.
18. Discussion with Dr Michael Krepon, co-founder Stimson Centre, on March 8, 2011, at the Centre for Air Power Studies, New Delhi.
19. Mark Moyar, *A Question of Command: Counterinsurgency from Civil War to Iraq* (New Haven: Yale University Press, 2009).
20. Ibid., p. 4.
21. Stephen Biddle, *Military Power* (Princeton: Princeton University Press, 2004)
22. Hassan Abbas, *Pakistan's Drift into Extremism: Allah, the Army and America's War on Terror,* (Armonk: M.E. Sharpe, 2005) p. 224.

23. Ibid., p. 225.
24. Discussion with Shuja Nawaz on March 15, 2011, at the Centre for Land Warfare Studies, New Delhi.
25. Ibid.
26. Ibid.
27. The actual defence spending in Pakistan is much more than the allocated defence budget. The actual figures can be concluding by adding the US aid and equipment which is not a part of the official budget. See, Shalini Chawla, "Trends in Pakistan's Defence Spending", *CLAWS,* Manekshaw Paper, No. 5, 2008.
28. For details on the acute requirement of development in FATA, see Naveed Ahmad Shirwari, "Understanding FATA: Attitude Towards Governance, Religion & Society in Pakistan's Federally Administered Tribal Areas", *Community Appraisal and Motivation Programme (CAMP),* Vol IV, at http://www.understandingfata.org/reports.php#
29. n. 24.

5

Airlift Operations: The Path Ahead

Ashok K Chordia

The Times had written an editorial in October 1903, criticising earlier efforts to build heavier-than-air flying machines because according to it, the technology was theoretically impossible. Two months later, the Wright Brothers launched their plane at Kitty Hawk.[1] Much less than a century later, the C-5 Galaxy that took to the sky had a wingspan larger than the first powered flight of the Wright Brothers. The impact of the computer's potential, likewise, was largely missed in 1945 when a prominent member of a National Research Council study committee stated boldly that the United States would never need more than five or six electronic computers – he missed the American computer market of a half-century later by a factor of tens of millions.[2] The tremendous pace of progress in all walks of modern life, including the field of aviation, makes predictability of the path ahead ever so difficult. It becomes even more complex because often the driving forces that seem obvious to some are hidden to others. A picture of the future cannot possibly be a *mean* of all the different perceptions put together.

With the improvement in the aircraft design, airlift naturally became a sought after choice for transportation of men and material for both civilian and military purposes and all along, technology had a marked effect on the mechanics of airlift. The last hundred years, the years after World War II in particular, have seen phenomenal improvement in speed, range, reach, endurance, payload, avionics, etc. Cargo can now be delivered almost anywhere on earth, speedily and efficiently. The hypersonic jet Waverider was tested in August 2012; its successful flight would have resulted in the distance between New York and London being covered in an hour.[3]

The aerofoil shape that is the basis of all flying machines, has been almost perfected, and further improvement is likely to be at a relatively slow pace. But today's aircraft is not merely an assembly of an airframe and an aero-engine; it is a complex system of systems; each system has components and each component is made up of many materials. The discovery of a new material, lighter and stronger; a path breaking development in the design of a component; invention of a computer chip that can process data at the speed of thought (exaggeration intended) or even ground equipment that improves efficiency – each of these developments, individually and collectively – can turn a glacial pace of development into a torrential one. For example, a rather simple looking improvement in the aircraft design – the *aft-end* opening of the cargo compartment in flight has had a profound effect on paradrops: it has enabled faster exit of sticks of paratroopers which, in turn, has reduced the spread on the ground, resulting in concentrated drops and speedier rendezvous of the airborne forces after landing. Thus, in a length of drop zone in which a Dakota aircraft with only one side door for exit for paratrooping could drop just about 20 paratroopers, an IL-76 with a four-point exit (two side doors and two exit points at the aft end) can drop over a 100 paratroopers – an astounding increase of 400 percent in the capacity to paradrop. Today, a formation of IL-76 and AN-32 aircraft can paradrop a battalion group in a drop zone smaller than 5 sq km sq. Contrast this with the Allied paradrop over Sicily (Operation Husky, 1943) wherein paratroopers were scattered 60 miles across the island of Sicily.[4]

Developments in aircraft design apart, parallel improvements in the delivery systems have revolutionised aerial delivery. The invention of the ram air parachute has made standoff paradrops possible. With the use of these aerofoil shaped parachutes in High Altitude High Opening (HAHO) mode, a special forces team can exit an aircraft miles away from the objective unseen by the naked eye. They can steer their canopies and land accurately on targets as small as a tabloid – an entire team can manoeuvre into a drop zone the size of a school's sports ground.

Nanotechnology is one of the most useful and promising areas for Research and Development (R&D) today, which is influencing all walks of life in a big way; airlift too shall feel its impact. Miniaturisation of components *ceteris paribus* generates space, which can be used for mission supporting equipment on board the aircraft or for additional payload. With time, the dependence on airlift is not likely to reduce; rather it is likely to increase. The threats to airlifters are also likely to multiply – machines operating far beyond direct human control will become increasingly inevitable. Robotic airlift promises to keep human lives out of harm's way while supplying the needy.

Summing of the Classical Debate

Need is a powerful driver. Airlift of supplies to the high altitude areas in the Himalayas demands extraordinary power in the airlift aircraft. The C-119 Packet, the Indian Air Force's (IAF's) workhorse of the 1960s did not have sufficient power to operate in those altitudes. *Jet packs* were fitted on the aircraft to provide the additional power.[5] It was an effective modification that enabled the IAF to overcome the hurdles. In another instance of airlift in critical times, the need to land a fixed-wing aircraft in an extremely restricted area to rescue hostages in the second attempt of the Iran hostage rescue led the Americans to experiment with a Hercules aircraft (rockets fitted all around) and to achieve a Super VTOL (Vertical Takeoff and Landing) capability (Operation Credible Sport, 1980).[6] Though one of the two prototypes crashed during the trials, the experimental test flight was successful; the second aircraft was not used, as Iran returned the hostages. That operational necessities drive technologies and tactics is a given. Moving large volumes; delivery at lightning speeds; clandestine delivery with focus on stealth; delivery in a peculiar terrain demanding special capability and delivery through extreme weather – these, and many more, are the operational needs that steer airlift technology; new needs accelerate the change.

Another school of thought maintains that it is technology that drives tactics and operations. There are examples wherein inventions have shaped and metamorphosed military concepts. To begin with, aircraft and parachutes were not invented with purely military applications in mind, but eventually they were adopted to enhance mobility – existing technologies were harnessed to support war. Radars and computers were designed and developed for use on the ground. In due course of time, they found use on airborne platforms.

While scientists and technologists come up with desirable (read *demanded*) solutions to problems, scientific research and emerging technology also throw up ideas that remould the existing tactics rendering the old war-fighting methods redundant – the invention of the tank is a classic case: it wrote the epitaph on trench warfare. It is time now to lay the classic debate on *'whether technology drives operations or operations drive technology'* to rest – the two have a symbiotic relationship and there are drivers and determinants that drive both.

Key Drivers and Determinants

Of the numerous factors that can possibly affect future airlifts, some are the key drivers, which are most likely to steer the course; alongside, are the critical uncertainties that weaken any objective assessment:

	Key Drivers	Some of the Critical Uncertainties
1.	Wars	Nature? One/ two Front? Which Front? ...
2.	Disasters	Nature? Location? Intensity? ...
3.	Geopolitics	Air Evacuation: Time? Place? Manner? ...
4.	Infrastructure Development	Location? Type? Cargo?...
5.	Increased Flying Activity	Accidents? Search and Rescue (SAR)? Combat Search and Rescue (CSAR)? Where? When? ...

Wars

Many crystal ball gazers and military thinkers prophesy short wars; they visualise a brief and localised nature of future wars. The emphasis is on sub-conventional/ unconventional wars, insurgency and guerrilla wars sponsored by non-state actors. But, if one were to go by the live examples of the recent times, wars have been of all types – short and long; between countries; between a country and non-state actors; and within a country, between ideologies. That the US would be involved in prolonged major wars as in Iraq and Afghanistan was unthinkable after the disintegration of the Soviet Union in 1991. India has been facing insurgency and border terrorism, which started as a brief military engagement but has turned into a prolonged war of sorts. The nature of future wars cannot be taken for granted.

Coming to the art of fighting wars – it keeps evolving. There are some successful repetitions of the application of the principles of war. Yet wars cannot be generalised as that would limit response and diminish the possibilities of favourable outcomes. From sub-conventional armed conflict to a full-scale war – hostile interactions among warring sides continue to differ occasionally and sometimes, drastically. But one requisite of war-fighting that has not changed for ages, and is not likely to change ever, is the need for superior logistics support and mobility. The characteristic speed and flexibility of airlift makes it a preferred choice for transportation during war and peace alike; cost considerations do influence decisions. Besides, the element of surprise is a spinoff of the inherent properties of airlift and since each type of war poses different challenges, the airlift requirements are occasionally dissimilar – airlift also evolves with each war.

Humanitarian Assistance and Disaster Relief (HADR)

Environmentalists warn that due to the existing high rate of deterioration of the environment, natural disasters would strike planet Earth more often than in the past. The recent disasters are not an aberration, but the beginning of a future in which mega-disasters would be a matter of routine. According to an International Development Ministry (UK) report, "The scale, frequency and severity of humanitarian disasters will continue to grow, and at an accelerated pace." The report predicts that by 2015, climate-related disasters will affect roughly 375 million people every year.[7] The disasters will necessitate major relief operations the success of which would depend on the ability to move large numbers of men and tonnes of material expeditiously to affected locations, and simultaneously, on the ability to evacuate the distressed to havens. The trend was evident in the cloudbursts accompanied with flash floods and landslides in Uttarkashi (June 2013) wherein the *IAF's biggest ever helicopter-based rescue operation* saved many lives.[8] The process of reconstruction and rehabilitation following disasters also needs mountains to be moved under conditions of poor or no surface transportation. Rescue and relief operations following accidents like the Bhopal gas tragedy (1984) and the nuclear disaster triggered by a tsunami at Fukushima (2011) can be managed better with airlifts. In turn, operations of this nature influence the way airlifts are managed. For example, the bellies of the four helicopters used for dowsing the fire in Fukushima had to be coated with lead to shield the aircrew from nuclear radiation.[9]

Geopolitics

The requirement of a military response to an SOS call from a friendly foreign country as in the case of Operation Cactus (the Maldives, 1988) is a persistent possibility. War and war-like situations apart, the geopolitical environment the world over is in a state of uneasy equilibrium. The ideological and human rights movements in Algeria, Tunisia, Yemen, Libya, Egypt, and now Syria, have spread like wildfire. Such people's movements result in exoduses, forcing people of a different country/ ethnicity to flee the country in turmoil. The fleeing population faces death, destruction, looting and arson while crossing the borders by surface means. Millions died during the exodus following the partition of India in 1947; a very few lucky ones were airlifted. Asians crossing over to Kenya by road/ rail were looted when they tried to escape the wrath of the India-phobic dictator, Idi Amin of Uganda (1972)[10]; those evacuated by air, escaped the harassment. Indians were evacuated from Kuwait, Iraq, Yemen and Libya under similar circumstances. Geopolitical conditions around the world, Asia and Africa in particular, have turned exoduses into a commonplace phenomenon necessitating evacuation of people. Airlift continues to provide immediate succour. Such situations too, shape airlift in some ways.

Infrastructure Development and National Progress

Roads, bridges, dams, oil refineries, power plants, a versatile communication system and armament factories, etc. are the result of sustained development. Creation, operation, repair and maintenance of mega infrastructure depends on the ability to position material and people in large numbers where required. Though roadways, railways and waterways are cheaper means of moving goods and connecting people, sometimes the terrain restricts movement of cargo by these means and delays projects, particularly when a consignment is over dimensional. It is imprudent to build long stretches of roads in difficult terrain for a one-time use – say, transporting large radars/ telescopes to mountaintops because such roads are of no use practically once the specialist equipment has been transported. Airlift removes hurdles of this nature. Besides, some strategic stores, regardless of their dimension and weight, are necessarily airlifted. Recurring requirements of this nature have prompted the use of air cranes, which are powerful rotory-wing aircraft with the capacity to airlift heavy underslung loads.

Search and Rescue

For many reasons, the quantum of flying in both military and civilian sectors keeps rising. A simple probabilistic derivation, therefore, suggests an increase in flying related incidents/ accidents. A proportionate increase in the need for search and rescue of people in distress is, therefore, a foregone conclusion. Airlift plays a key role in the search of crashed aircraft and rescue of the survivors. Growing intolerance towards the loss of lives demands eternal readiness with airlift. *Golden Hour*[11] rescue also demands a high level of preparedness. Combat Search and Rescue (CSAR) during hostilities is a given too. The exemplary attempt to rescue the survivors of the two American UH-60 Black Hawk helicopters (Black Hawk Down, 1993) has set a benchmark for such operations.

Derived Wisdom from the Past

Need to Consolidate Airlift Resources

A sure conclusion is that airlift will continue to be vital for both military operations and for civilian or humanitarian purposes – except when the demands increase manifold, often exceeding the capacity. As always, budgetary constraints shall limit affordability of large fleets of airlift platforms and delivery systems. The three Services, paramilitary forces and civil administrations will vie for a share of the resource. Prioritisation of requirements within a Service or an organisation will be relatively easy but with each organisation justifying its needs, prioritisation across the big list of end-users might be contentious. Therefore, the clamour to *own* the airlift resources shall be at an ever-increasing pitch. The lessons of history and accumulated wisdom, however, proclaim prudence in maintaining airlift resources under one umbrella rather than distributing them and diminishing their effectiveness.

Indigenous Capability

Capability building is an arduous, long path, an unending exercise. A formidable airlift capability is the result of long years of perseverance. The success in R&D may come by instantly or elude the scientists for long periods. It is natural that the countries that develop new technologies do not easily share them with others, not even with their strongest allies. Towards the end of World War II, the Americans had gone to the extent of putting the Indian and the Royal Air Force (RAF) air crew under house arrest at an air base near Purulia to prevent them from getting a glimpse of (then) America's latest secret – the B-29 Super Fortress bomber.[12] The superior performance of the US Air Force and ground forces in the Gulf War also demonstrated that dollars allotted in the 1980s for training, readiness, and spare parts were well spent.[13] Countries that create and develop airlift capability with an eye on the strategic goals are able to meet challenges and tide over crises with much ease.

Judicious use of Capacity

All airfields do not have sufficient cargo for visiting airlift aircraft. A heavy lift aircraft like the C-17 in particular may not find a payload of 70 tonnes at each base. Therefore, some airlift capacity always goes unused. Movement of an empty airlifter is the lost capacity that cannot be recovered. Management of such *incidentally surplus* airlift capacity merits thought.

Management of Turnaround/ Maintenance Time

According to a *Discovery Channel* documentary, a C-5 Galaxy aircraft requires 16 hours of maintenance for every hour of flying. The C-5 is not an exception; all modern transport aircraft, including the C-17 and C-130J, require detailed maintenance each time they take to the air. Considerable time is spent in routine maintenance and turnaround of an airlift aircraft between missions/ sorties. Further, it is not always possible to use an aircraft modified for one purpose, for another – special role equipment is required which takes time to be installed or removed. An aircraft readied with seats to carry troops cannot carry containers or stretchers. Retention of modifications for special roles restricts loading of an aircraft to its *full* capacity e.g. the weight of the anchor cables used for paradrops or the rollers used for supply drops, when fitted in an aircraft but not used, and other specialist equipment, like cranes and gantries installed in an aircraft are a compromise with the overall capacity of an aircraft. Considering the constraint of numbers, management of roles, maintenance schedules and turnaround times comprise the key to deriving optimum returns from the airlift resources.

Infrastructure

Availability of infrastructure is an important element that affects exploitation of the the full potential of the platforms. Ideal conditions are not possible across the length and breadth of the country. Therefore, there is stress on the management of the existing infrastructure and sometimes situations demand construction of new infrastructure speedily to meet immediate requirement. Construction activities close to the border in peace-time breed distrust with the neighbours and can have serious implications; some unpleasant outcomes were evident from the standoff between India and China in May 2013. Such incidents pose hurdles and prevent development of military infrastructure. This dilemma can be overcome by building infrastructure at lightning speeds when there is a clarion call. Airlift became a necessity to maintain troops and support 40,000 refugees in the Poonch sector when the road link to Jammu came under threat of being cut off (Indo-Pak War, 1947-48). Six thousand refugees working round the clock constructed an airstrip within one week.[14] Runways were similarly constructed at a fast pace during the Berlin airlift.[15] Ability to create infrastructure speedily is a force multiplier.

Pooling Civil-Military Airlift Resources

Military airlift resources are not adequate to meet all contingencies; capacity needs augmentation during major crises. The civil air fleet in India has worked in tandem with the Indian Air Force (IAF) on numerous occasions in the past. In response to a radio broadcast made by Sardar Patel, the civilian aircraft operators came forward to extend their support in Jammu and Kashmir (Indo-Pak War, 1947-48).[16] Years later, the Kalinga Airways were called upon to support the military airlift in the days leading to the India-China War (1962) and all through the war itself[17] – their contribution was praiseworthy. Yet at one point during those operations, it was decided to do away with their support, apparently due to the fear that they might not be able to face the pressures of actual conflict; their reliability was doubted. The decision was ignored at the behest of the then chief of the Air Staff.[18] The fears expressed in 1962 came true during the Kuwait airlift on the onset of the Gulf War (1990-91) – in the midst of the crisis in the Gulf region, Air India pilots and staff threatened to ground the flights meant for evacuation of the Indian expatriates, unless a some of their crew, stuck in Kuwait, were recovered. They did fly subsequently to evacuate people but avoided the zones threatened by war.[19] Augmentation of military airlift capacity by civilian resources demands serious thought.

Notwithstanding the enormousness of their airlift capacity, the US armed forces too face situations when they need to augment it. They have a formalised system for co-opting the civilian airlift capacity when a situation demands. The Civil Reserve Air Fleet (CRAF) ensures dedicated and formally quantified augmentation of the military airlift capability by the civilian airlines in times of national emergencies.[20]

Airlift Platforms: Means to an End

Airlift aircraft are but means to an end, and much depends on how they are employed to get maximum advantage – airlanding/ paradrop of supplies and Low Altitude Parachute Extraction System (LAPES) are some of the options. Apart from transport aircraft gliders, hovercraft, airships and even bombers have been utilised to undertake airlifts in the past. The Halifax bombers that rained havoc over Germany at the peak of World War II, airlifted salt during the siege of Berlin.[21] Similar attempts by the IAF to airdrop rations and ammunition using the Tempest fighters to support troops at the besieged fort at Skardu (Indo-Pak War, 1947-48) were not so successful; the limited range and load carrying capacity of the aircraft coupled with the hurdles posed by weather and terrain prevented a favourable outcome – Skardu fell to the infiltrators.[22] Though high speed of the airlift platform is a desired performance characteristic, an airborne platform that can fly at varying speeds (very low to very high) serves greater purpose. STOL (Short Takeoff and Landing), ESTOL (Extremely Short Takeoff and Landing) and VTOL (Vertical Takeoff and Landing) capabilities often become necessities. Development of the tilt-rotor aircraft[23] (like the V-22 Osprey) and the quadrotor aircraft is a step in this direction. Availability of versatile airborne platforms coupled with their innovative use can overcome many an airlift challenge.

Unmanned Airlift Platforms

The density and lethality of the air defence environment and extreme weather conditions increase the vulnerability of the airborne platforms and deter airlifts for the fear of loss of aircraft and accrual of casualties. Growing intolerance of the civilian population, the government and the media towards loss of lives creates pressure. The planning and execution of airlifts, therefore, aim at ensuring minimal loss of lives and cargo. Unmanned aerial vehicles/ systems lower casualties. Airmules,[24] Robocopters, Snowgoose and now, a 16-seater Jetstream aircraft test flown in the UK in May 2013[25] are likely to soar in the skies in the future. The Americans have designed the pilotless cargo drone to deliver vital supplies to territories plagued by roadside bombs.[26]

Trends Likely to Influence Future of Airlifts

Aircraft development has followed a near set pattern – improvement in speed, payload, STOL/ VTOL and stealth characteristics, range, endurance, avionics, etc. Progress in these fields is inevitable and would continue at varying paces. Discussed here are some of the inventions and landmark events that are different from the *routine* advancement and are likely to influence the future airlifts significantly.

Robotic Airlift

Airlift platforms are vulnerable to enemy missiles, air defence fighters and artillery. The Germans suffered heavy losses in terms of aircraft and aircrew while trying to supply their troops encircled by the Russians at Stalingrad during World War II. The French suffered similar heavy losses during the siege of Dien Bien Phu (Indo-China, May 1954). A large number of American helicopters were lost in the Vietnam War while airlifting troops and supplies. Such losses led to renewed efforts to address the vulnerability of airlift platforms: stealth, to avoid detection, and greater stress on creation of favourable air situation and protection of the airborne force using fighter escorts. The idea of development of unmanned aerial vehicles for airlift is the outcome of the need to avoid loss of lives during airlift through a hostile or hazardous environment. The K-MAX helicopter, a joint Lockheed Martin and Kaman Aerospace venture[27], is a step in this direction. By the end of January 2012, the K-MAX helicopters had airlifted over 100,000 lb. of cargo on more than 50 unmanned resupply missions in Afghanistan.[28] Unmanned airlift could be meaningful in peace-time too. It could be of tremendous utility in evacuating people from a hazardous environment as in Bhopal (Union Carbide, December 1984) or from the nuclear disaster site as in Fukushima (2011).

Despite its advantages, the path to robotic airlift needs to be trodden with extreme care and caution. On a challenge, Texas college researchers managed to take control of a drone of the US Homeland Security in the presence of the operators.[29] That hijacking, even if for fun, has ominous implications: if amateurs can do it, professionals can do it as well, may be, with élan. An unmanned airlifter laden with supplies or casualties landing in the adversary's hands is an unwelcome proposition. Development of tactics to counter an adversary's tactics is an endless endeavour – there must be a dogged determination to stay ahead. *Optionally manned* aircraft could be a part solution to the problem.

Quadrotor Aircraft

Quadrotors are very stable flying machines with great potential as airlifters, though presently the development is focussed on surveillance and reconnaissance. Making use of the stable configuration of the quadrotor, Domino's Pizza has experimented with the delivery of pizzas to its customers.[30] Larger versions, as and when developed, would be capable of airlifting sizeable cargo. Even at this point in time, with a little ingenuity, unmanned quadrotors, in their present forms, could well be used to deliver critically required medicines, hand-held Global Positioning System (GPS), mobile phones, torches and matches, etc. to people in distress. Similarly, quadrotors could make invaluable deliveries in the midst of special operations like the ones undertaken during the Mumbai (Taj Hotel, 2008) and Nairobi (Westgate Mall, 2013) terror strikes.

Airship: A Revival

Today, an airship sharing the air space with other aircraft, would appear anachronistic; even a suggestion to consider an airship as a viable and effective mode of transportation, could be seen as putting the clock back. The fact is: airships have sailed far ahead of the ghastly *Hindenburg* disaster (Lakehurst, New Jersey, May 6, 1937) in which 35 people were killed – a disaster that tolled the knell for airships.

According to a study (2011) under the United States Congressional Budget Office, concern had arisen during the 1990s that rapid deployments like those to the large air bases in Saudi Arabia during the first Iraq War, would not be possible in the future if such air bases were not available. It was argued that transport airships capable of landing in any suitably large open area could reduce dependence on overseas bases.[31] The report suggested that over the previous two years, the Department of Defence (DoD) had funded more than $500 million for projects on *lighter-than-air* platforms. The Pelican and the Sky Tug are hybrid airship projects for airlift of 20 to 60 tonnes over 1,000 to 3,000 nautical miles.[32] These payloads and ranges compare well with some of today's leading airlifters: the C-130J, the C-17 and the C-5.

Presently, airships are being used mainly to carry overdimensional cargo like the long blades of windmills, which cannot be carried by trailers to locations on hilltops due to the difficulty in manoeuvring through winding roads and hairpin bends. It is believed that China has also used (tugged) aerostats in Mongolia for movement of cargo. Skylifter, an Australian firm, is developing an airship that will carry up to 150 tonnes over 1000 km. According to the firm, once developed, the airship will carry rural hospitals and disaster relief centres to remote areas.[33] Large airships with payloads of 500 to 1,000 tonnes would yield greater throughput capacity than many of today's airlift aircraft.[34] Besides, the use of airships would prolong the calendar life of the other airlift platforms.

Skydive at Mach 1.2

On October 14, 2012, an Austrian, Felix Baumgartner skydived successfully from 1,28,000 ft Above Mean Sea Level (AMSL) over New Mexico. The landmark jump provided a plethora of scientific and medical information for aerospace researchers – over 100 million physiologic points from the mission of October 14 alone. The invaluable data would be used for the development of high performance, high-altitude parachute systems. According to the research team studying the record jump, the lessons learned will generate new ideas for emergency evacuation from vehicles, such as spacecraft, passing through the stratosphere.[35] That declaration from the scientists seems to the proverbial *tip of the iceberg*. The possibility of a man *flying* at a speed in excess of Mach1 is a great technological leap. This development, along with some others, can revolutionise aerial delivery of special forces (discussed later).

Flying Soldiers

Yves Rossy, a former Swiss Air Force pilot has developed a system comprising a backpack with semi-rigid aeroplane-type carbon-fibre wings, powered by jet engines.[36] With the contraption, he has flown long distances over different terrains at speeds ranging between 200 to 300 kmph (kilometres per hour). Rossy's invention has promise for future single man flight. What started as an aero-sport adventure experimentation, has generated ideas for military application.

Similarly, a futuristic engineless parachute system with electronic guidance and head-up display navigation has been tried successfully. The equipment is cleverly tucked away, enabling "stealth" flights. As per the manufacturers, this high-tech human gliding device allows jumpers to leap from planes and glide in any chosen direction at about 60 mph. Presently, a parachute is used for landing. Development of a version that could be landed without a parachute is under way. The system is designed for High-Altitude, High-Opening (HAHO) jumps. It is highly manoeuvrable and has a glide ratio of 5:1. Over 50 test flights were undertaken in 2006. The next step is to mount small engines, which would present more aerial delivery options.[37]

Imaginative Leap into the Future

He who predicts the future lies even if he tells the truth.

— An old Arab proverb.

It is, but natural that today's infant technologies will impact airlift of the morrow. Therefore, drawing from what is possible today, one is less likely to go grossly wrong – except in case a revolutionary technology alters the landscape entirely; just as the invention of the aircraft gave a new dimension to warfare itself and later, the invention of the helicopter (VTOL technology) transformed war-fighting still further. Discussed here are some of the airlift scenarios based on empirical data and plausible technological/ tactical realities.

Airlifters Flying Under Voice Commands

Unmanned Aerial Vehicles (UAVs) are *flown* by pilots sitting in control centres miles away from the scene of action. They use miniature joysticks and other instruments, which are physically manipulated electro-mechanical devices meant to control the UAVs. This physical handling of the *controls* suffers from the obvious lag between a decision and movement of fingers to operate the *control*. Making machines respond to voice commands is a rather old technology but capable of getting a more prompt response. Getting UAVs to respond to voice commands might just be a possibility. An airlifter *piloted* by *voice commands* might be a reality in the future. Experiments with brain impulses to control devices are already in progress and have potential for unmanned airlifters too. Unmanned airlifters with artificial intelligence might be yet another possibility.

Inflight Transfer of Cargo

Aerial refuelling is the mechanical transfer of fluids between two aircraft in flight. Among the many skills, it entails superior formation flying while the fuel is transferred. Taking the technology and this skill to a different level, it might be possible in future to transfer stores and still later, even personnel from an aircraft to another. Such a capability would eliminate the need of multiple landings by an aircraft to muster special forces teams and special equipment on its way to execute a special operation. Every landing, thus, avoided would save precious time, so critical to special operations and disaster relief operations alike. Stunt skydivers with powered wings have been docking with parachutists in flight. There are others who have achieved the feat of bailing out of an aircraft and entering another one, also in flight.[38] It is only a matter of time that such possibilities find military applications.

Airships in Disaster Relief

Helicopters were used to douse fires in Japan's Fukushima Daiichi nuclear power station that followed the huge earthquake and tsunami (Japan, March 2011). Those helicopters were handicapped – they could carry just about 2.5 tonnes of water, with little effect on the blaze; their bellies had to be coated with lead to lessen the effect of nuclear radiation – a compromise with the payload. Pilots who flew those sorties did so at the risk of their lives. A pilotless airship (a possibility in the near future) even with a capacity of 60 to 70 tonnes would achieve spectacular results, with no risk to lives, and much larger quantity of water being delivered in every lift.

Airships as Airborne Aircraft Carriers

Airships were daringly used as "*flying aircraft carriers*" in the 1930s – the USS *Macon* and the USS *Akron* were used for launching Curtiss Sparrowhawk biplane fighters.[39] With some ingenuity, it might be possible to develop and use airships effectively for search, rescue and relief operations. Small, manned or robotic aircraft, like the airmules, could ply casualties; carry relief teams, medicines and food for the victims in and out of an airborne hospital. An airship could possibly have carried hundreds of residents upwind and saved them from the poisonous gases emanating from the Union Carbide pesticide plant (Bhopal, 1984). With an airborne aircraft carrier, it would also be possible to keep vigil over an area for long hours (with surveillance UAVs operating from the airship) and delivering troops instantly at the desired locations. Their use in anti-Naxal operations could be a possibility.

Man-Bird at Mach 1

The possibility of an individual falling at a speed higher than Mach 1 has been tried successfully (Felix Baumgartner, October 2012)[40]. An individual *flying* with powered (jet) wings is also a possibility (Yves Rossy's experiments).[41] An individual flying at speeds in the region of Mach 1 using powered *wings* might just be a corollary. Thus, it might be possible in the future, for a special forces team to be able to bail out of a transport aircraft; *fly* at a speed close to Mach 1 to an objective several miles into enemy territory; destroy an installation and *fly back* to another airborne platform holding position elsewhere.

And May be ...

Albert Einstein's theory, which describes the relationship between mass and energy, has led to discussion and experiments on *teleportation* – a process (many believe) by which matter could be converted into energy; that energy could travel at the speed of light and, at another place (call it "*consignee end*"), get converted into matter. While not much is known about the status of the experiments, the subject has become very popular with fiction writers. But then, *The First Men in the Moon* (1901) was also scientific fiction which remained H. G. Wells' imagination till Neil Armstrong landed on the moon in 1969. Time will tell, but science and technology have a way of surprising mankind. Whatever else would happen is left to the reader's imagination.

Future of Airlift: The Indian Scene

For tomorrow belongs to the people who prepare for it today

— African Proverb

Wars, routine air maintenance and Humanitarian Assistance and Disaster Relief (HADR) operations are the main drivers of airlift operations. Analysts usually narrow down to two conclusions when discussing India's future wars: firstly, state sponsored insurgency, and secondly, a one or two front war with a nuclear overhang. With airlift operations in mind, two more scenarios could be thought of: firstly, a major natural (or a *man-made*) disaster striking the country in the midst of a two-front war; this possibility cannot be dismissed summarily seeing the regularity with which disasters have struck the Indian subcontinent over the last few years. And, secondly, one or more of the remaining neighbours colluding with the adversaries and opening up a third front of sorts;[42] this is an extremely remote possibility, which could come true if India were to ignore their concerns blatantly, leading to their alignment with the adversaries. Any such new scenarios would magnify the need for logistical support and, hence, the demand for more and varied airlifts.

Adequacy of airlift capacity is a function of availability of resources, which is a constant at any given time; and the commitments, which are variable. It is difficult to assess the adequacy in absolute terms because of the critical uncertainties of time, place and manner in which an airlift might be required. It is possible that the airlift capacity of the country even with augmentation of the IAF's capacity by the civil air fleet might be inadequate to satiate a specific need. In the war with China (1962), the IAF's airlift capacity had fallen short despite augmentation by the civil air fleet – the contribution of Kalinga Airways in that war is well known.[43] To augment it further, the US had provided a squadron of C-130 Hercules aircraft to fly sorties between Delhi and Leh for about six weeks.[44] A repeat of support of this nature is doubtful because India has not reciprocated such gestures.[45] Historical records suggest that despite augmentation by both Kalinga Airways and the US Air Force (USAF), the overall capacity was inadequate to meet the demands – the IAF air-dropped supplies at a scale nearly four times its total capacity to bridge the gap.[46]

Considering the notional shortfall, the aim should be to meet all the arising commitments within the available means. Maintaining a large fleet of transport aircraft within the constraints of the defence budget and augmenting the capacity by pooling in all airlift resources of the country is a run of the mill approach to addressing the need. It is possible to increase capacity and enhance capability by managing and utilising the existing resources more efficiently. Here are some points to ponder over:

- A high level of understanding among the stakeholders is essential. Awareness of each other's strengths, limitations and weaknesses, and genuine demand and provisioning of airlift rather than airlift resources, serves a more fruitful purpose.
- It is worthwhile to consider devoting the incidentally surplus airlift (discussed earlier) to meet the airlift requirements of other government/ semi-government

and even private organisations. Such utilisation of airlift would be a net national gain.

- India has added 1.25 lakh km of roads per year for 8 years (2004-12)[47]. This is sure to relieve the IAF of some of the trivial airlifts. While continuing to create a network of roads in the future, long stretches of straight wide roads could be made for air landing relief material during crises. A C-130J capable of landing on unprepared surfaces (like the makeshift airstrip at Daulat Beg Oldie) could be able to land on such *prepared* surfaces during national emergencies.
- Capability available elsewhere in the world cannot be India's starting point: mere possession of the C-130J aircraft is not a licence to undertake an Entebbe-like raid nor the acquisition of Chinook helicopter, the certification to enact an Operation Neptune Spear. India needs to write its own script; realistic joint training and preparedness to address contingencies, is the way ahead.
- An agency that can create infrastructure rapidly is a force multiplier. Creation of a Seabees-like team to raise infrastructure would be a big step towards achieving high levels of preparedness.[48]
- Airlift capacity needs augmentation during crises. An analysis of the operational needs of the country against current realities can help create an organic national capability by integrating the civil and military airlift capabilities. It is very important to have a formalised system, which assures *reliable* build-up in emergencies. Creation of a Civil Rescue Air Fleet (CRAF)-like organisation would guarantee better support.[49]
- Use of appropriate Material Handling Equipment (MHE) and reduction in the turnaround time across the board can bring about marked improvement in efficiency. A work-study devoted exclusively to these aspects can cause a major transformation.
- A focussed approach to keep pace with the world leaders in technology is important. It may be difficult to take big leaps but it should be possible to conjoin the available technologies, innovate and keep moving.
- The human element is primal in effective airlifts. Improvement in the quality of their training, education, dedication and morale is bound to pay rich dividends. People need to reinvent themselves with some radical (human) engineering to meet future challenges. A transformation of minds and work ethics can attain high levels of proficiency, which, in turn, can bring about perceptible asymmetry despite limited resources and constraints. Transformation also implies changes in doctrine, strategy, tactics, technology, force levels and force employment.

Embarking on the Path Ahead

The extensive use of airlift foretells its importance as a tool for force projection and force application in spite of the improved surface transportation and despite the increased vulnerability of the airlift platforms. The need for improved mobility in the future will demand airlift of ammunition, fuel, food and at times, even water directly to the frontline. Therefore, the air force needs to be ever prepared to not only airlift a mechanised force into a hostile country, but also sustain it once it is there. Prompt and speedy airlifts will serve as force enhancers. Conceptually, the aim must be to be able to create a dilemma for the enemy that cannot be overcome. In time, space and volume, the delivery should be overwhelming. A formidable military airlift capability is necessary to achieve this end. A build-up of such a capability addresses the peace-time requirements of HADR too.

Preparing for the '*unforeseen*' or the '*unpredictable*' is oxymoronic – the path ahead should ideally mean, "Being prepared with the ultimate in capability within available resources at any given time." Whether it is rescuing President Gayoom or President Jayewardene, whether it is the Maldives or Sri Lanka, it is basically the capability to rescue a hostage on an island. It is a capability, which could be rehearsed in the Andamans. Ability to meet contingent requirements must follow obviously.

Like the other elements of air power, airlift operates at much higher levels of technologies than the rest of the technologies put together. The tremendous pace of development in this sphere introduces uncertainty in calculations. It is advantageous to possess the most advanced means to achieve ends – there must be a conscientious and relentless pursuit to acquire the latest and the best that technology can offer. But the zeal for the *state-of-the-art* systems must not overshadow the ability to innovate and achieve the difficult and the impossible within the available means. Adaptation to change ensures speedier all round progress and averts decline, which follows long periods of routine mundane operations. It must be understood that technological perfection is an endless pursuit – a mirage.

It is difficult to evaluate the impact of a new technology on airlift because sometimes the pace at which a technology matures is so fast that it gets outdated even before it is dovetailed with tactics and strategy. Quite often, the rate of change scores over the quantum of change. The fast pace makes the coming together of doctrine and mature technology impossible. In fact, *mature technology* is a misnomer because technology is ever evolving. Therefore, a good policy would be to *use the technology of the day to maximum advantage* by reforging tactics on the basis of realities. In war-fighting, tactics supported by superior technology can more than make up the asymmetry of numbers.

At any given time, whatever works is the best.

Apendix "A"

(Refers to Footnote 48)

SEABEES

The Seabees are the US Navy's Construction Battalions (CBs), adept at creating infrastructure speedily. They were formed following the attack on Pearl Harbour when the task of turning imminent defeat into victory seemed almost insurmountable. These battalions were created in an answer to a crucial demand for builders who could fight. They are renowned for building bases, bulldozing and paving thousands of miles of roadway and airstrips, and accomplishing numerous other construction projects in different war zones since World War II. They constructed six 8,500+ ft runways at the rate of one runway per 53 days; over 18 km of taxiways; hard-standing to accommodate over 400 bombers, and accommodation for 50,000 personnel and office complexes, on the islands of Tinian and Saipan in a record time of less than a year during World War II.[50] About 2,600 Seabees were deployed in about 20 different countries around the globe supporting a variety of humanitarian missions and contingency operations in 2012. Seabees were among the first forces in Afghanistan after the 9/11 attacks to upgrade and repair airfields.[51]

Appendix "B"

(Refers to Footnote 49)

CIVIL RESERVE AIR FLEET (CRAF)[52]

The Civil Reserve Air Fleet (CRAF) of the US supports the airlift requirements of the Department of Defence (DoD) in emergencies when the need for airlift exceeds the capability of the military aircraft fleet. All CRAF participants are US carriers fully certified by the Federal Aviation Administration, and meet the stringent standards of Federal Aviation Regulations pertaining to commercial airlines.

The CRAF has three main segments: international, national, and aeromedical evacuation. The international segment is further divided into the long-range and short-range sections and the national segment into the domestic and Alaskan sections. Assignment of aircraft to a segment depends on the nature of the requirement and the performance characteristics needed.

The commercial airlines contractually pledge aircraft to the various segments of CRAF, ready for activation when needed. To provide incentives for civil carriers to commit aircraft to the CRAF programme and to assure the United States of adequate airlift reserves, the government makes peace-time airlift business available to civilian airlines that obligate aircraft to the CRAF. DoD offers business through the International Airlift Services.

CRAF presents benefits and opportunities for both the DoD and US airlines. By all accounts it appears to be a symbiotic relationship. Yet, as circumstances change, pressures and diverging interests may emerge that could bring changes to CRAF. A number of factors may be considered when examining the future size, character and role of CRAF. These factors include cost, other potential government / commercial arrangements, potential change in DoD requirement for CRAF, and an industrial base for, or financial assistance to, US air carriers.

Notes

1. Peter Schwartz, *The Art of Long View: Planning for the Future in an Uncertain World* (Chichester: John Wiley & Sons, Reprinted 2007), p. 13.
2. As cited by Richard P Hallion in John Andreas Olsen, ed., *A History of Air Power* (New Delhi: Vij Books, 2010), p. 371.
3. BBC News – "Hypersonic Jet Waverider Fails Mach 6 Test," available at http:// www .bbc .com/ news/ technology - 19277620, accessed on June 6, 2013.
4. Lt. Gen. Edward M Flanagan Jr. (Retd), *AIRBORNE: A Combat History of American Airborne Forces* (New York: Ballantine Books, 2002), p. 81.
5. Dr. PB Sinha, Col AA Athale & SN Prasad, *History of Conflict with China, 1962* (New Delhi:

History Division, MoD, GoI, 1992), p. 346.
6. "Crash Landing", *Popular Science*, vol. 251, July 1997 (Canada: Bonnier Corporation:, 1997), p. 32.
7. Natural Disasters Will Increase: British report - Technology & Science - CBC News available at http:// www .cbc .ca/ news/ technology/ story/ 2011/ 03/ 28/ disasters –paddy –ashdown –britain .html, accessed on March 17, 2013.
8. "Operation Rahat", *The Times of India*, Monday, June 24, 2013.
9. "Habitat" available at http://inhabitat.com/japans-nuclear-crisis-escalates-helicopters-dump-water-on-crippled-fukushima-plant/daiichi02-2/, accessed on September 28, 2013.
10. Niranjan Desai, "Revisiting the 1972 Expulsion of Asians from Uganda", in *ORAL HISTORY, Foreign Affairs Journal*, vol 7, no. 4, October–December 2012, pp. 446-458.
11. Golden Hour is the crucial period of time that rescue teams need to act in order to give the survivors of a crash or a disaster the best chance at survival.
12. Air Chief Mshl PC Lal, *My Years with the IAF* (New Delhi: Lancer International, 1986), pp.36-38.
13. Richard H. Shultz, Jr. and Robert L Pfaltzgraff, Jr., *The Future of Air Power in the Aftermath of the Gulf War* (Alabama: Air University Press, 1992), p. 92.
14. Air Mshl Bharat Kumar (Retd), *An Incredible War: IAF in Kashmir War 1947-1948* (New Delhi: Knowledge World, 2007), p. 179.
15. Lt Gen William H. Tunner USAF, *Over the Hump* (Washington D.C.: Office of Air Force History, US AF, 1985), p. 211-212.
16. Kumar, n. 14, p. 44.
17. Sinha, et. al, , n. 5, p. 347.
18. Air Mshl Bharat Kumar (Retd), *Unknown and Unsung: Indian Air Force in Sino-Indian War of 1962* (New Delhi: Knowledge World, 2013), p. 59.
19. K. P. Fabian, "Biggest Ever Air Evacuation in History," ORAL HISTORY, *Indian Foreign Affairs Journal*, vol. 7, no. 1, January-March, 2011, p. 97.
20. Read more about CRAF in Appendix "B".
21. Tunner, n. 15, p.205.
22. Kumar, n.14, pp. 88-89.
23. Tilt rotor aircraft have been in use for some time. Issues of noise and rubble (raised at the time of landing/ takeoff) still need to be addressed.
24. "The AirMule" is a compact, unmanned, single-engine, VTOL aircraft. Still under development, it can evacuate two casualties. It could be used for other payloads and other missions. It is suited to special robotic operation, for example, via Tele-Presence," accessed on December 18, 2012.
25. "Pilotless Flight Trialled in UK Shared Airspace", *BBC News* - 13/05/13 9:14 PM, available at http://www.bbc.co.uk/news/technology-22511395, accessed on May 13, 2013.
26. "Cargo Drone to Rescue of Areas Strewn with Bombs", *The Times of India*, January 9, 2012, p. 13.
27. *Jane's Unmanned Aerial Vehicles and Targets*, issue 33, November 2009, p. 322.
28. Paul McLeary, "K-MAX Chugging Along in Afghanistan", posted at 3:58 PM on February, 03, 2012 in *Aviation Week* (Online), available at http://www.aviationweek.com, accessed on June 19, 2013.
29. "Students Hijack a Drone for $ 1,000 Bet", *The Times of India*, Sunday, June 30, 2012, p.18.
30. "Sorry, The Future Will be Filled with Drones", *The Resident,* available at http://www.youtube.com/watch?v=qIzIJK8CRTI, accessed on July 4, 2013.
31. Author's discussion with Mr. Pankaj Som Chaturvedi of TRA Aerospace Pvt. Ltd. and report of a study titled, "Recent Development Efforts for Military Airships November 2011," available at

site http://www.cbo.gov/sites/default/ files/cbofiles/attachments/11-01-Airships.pdf, accessed on August 19, 2012.
32. Ibid.
33. "Giant Airship That Can Carry Entire Buildings 2000 km," *The Times of India*, Wednesday, October 6, 2010, p. 21.
34. Despite low throughput, fixed-wing aircraft and helicopters have a distinct advantage over airships. They can *commence* delivery much sooner than airships. It is important that due credence is given to urgency while planning airlift.
35. Jonathan Amos, "Skydiver Felix Baumgartner Breaks Sound Barrier", *BBC News,* available at http://www.bbc.co.uk/news/science-environment-19943590, accessed on June 13, 2013.
36. "Jet-Man Performances," available at http:// www. jetman. com/ performance. html, accessed June 13, 2013.
37. Jeff Salton, "Gryphon Winged Suit Drops in for Some Serious Air Time," dated December 8, 2009 available at http://www.gizmag.com/wingsuits-gryphon/13512/, accessed on June 13, 2013.
38. "Plane-to-Plane Skydive on Discovery Channel," available at http://iloveskydiving .org/view/ videos/ plane – to - plane-skydive-on-discovery-channel/, accessed on September 30, 2013.
39. *USS Macon and Sparrowhawk,* available at http://www .youtube .com/ watch? v= IWoE QR l8d Cs & feature =related, accessed on September 5, 2012.
40. Amos, n. 35.
41. n. 36.
42. Shishir Gupta has alluded to this scenario in "Trouble on the Horizon", *Hindustan Times*, (New Delhi), October 6, 2013, p. 13.
43. Sinha, et. al.,n. 5, p. 346.
44. Mshl P.C. Lal, n. 12,, p. 115.
45. The allusion is to India's reluctance to refuel the US aircraft during the Gulf War.
46. n. 18, p. xviii.
47. Deepak Kumar Dash, "India Added 1.25 Lakh Km of Roads Per Year in Last 8 years", *The Times of India*, July 25, 2012, p. 11.
48. The Seabees are the US Navy's Construction Battalions (CBs). They are adept at creating infrastructure at breakneck speed. Read more about the Seabees in Appendix "A".
49. The Civil Reserve Air Fleet (CRAF) of the US is a well organised system of augmenting airlift capacity. Read more about the CRAF in Appendix "B".
50. "The Use of Tinian Island During World War II", available at http://web.mst.edu/~rogersda/ umrcourses/ge342/Tinian%20Island.pdf, accessed July 23, 2011.
51. Additional Seabee Battalions Deploying to Afghanistan Story Number: NNS091222-01; Release Date: 12/22/2009 7:58:00 AM on Navy.mil the official website of the US Navy available at http://www.navy.mil/search/display.asp?story_id=50316, accessed on August 4, 2011.
52. Christopher Bolkcom, "Civil Reserve Air Fleet (CRAF)", CRS Report for Congress, Congressional Research Service, Library of Congress, available at http:// www .fas .org/ sgp/ crs/ weapons/ RL33692 .pdf, accessed on June 13, 2013.

6

Cruise Missiles in South Asia: Strategic Implications

Sitakanta Mishra

The threat of ballistic missiles and nuclear weapons does indeed remain a great concern in South Asia, but is not the only form of contingency that this region is currently experiencing. One perceived strategic implication of the (nuclear) cruise missiles, especially with Pakistan, is that it has "lowered the index of stability in the region".[1] The upswing in cruise missile inventory in South Asia necessitates revisiting the contours of deterrence stability, and military Confidence-Building Measures (CBMs) in vogue in South Asia. Here an attempt is made to evaluate how the expanding cruise missile inventory of India and Pakistan stresses the regional nuclear stability and the overall security architecture. Will cruise missiles contribute to regional deterrence stability or upset it? How will they impact the effectiveness of missile defence? Will a conventional cruise missile attack on missile defences result in crisis escalation?

A cursory look at the number of missile tests conducted by India and Pakistan over the last one decade would reveal that strengthening of the cruise and short-range missiles inventory is one of the top priorities of both countries' defence strategies. In addition, Pakistan is in the process of expanding its nuclear weapons inventory by adding Tactical Nuclear Weapons (TNWs) and miniaturisation of nuclear warheads. With both countries in the process of consolidation of their nuclear triad, the regulation and management of their arsenal and the variety of delivery mechanisms need serious attention. A CBM between India and Pakistan on pre-notification of the flight-testing of ballistic missiles with the objective of "enhancing mutual confidence and engendering predictability and transparency of intent" has been in operation since 2005. However, a combination of ballistic and cruise missile threat could severely complicate and stress the regional deterrence stability. Though India has achieved substantial headway in Ballistic Missile Defence (BMD), it cannot hope for a credible defence unless its missile defence strategy addresses both ballistic and cruise missile threats.

Why Cruise Missiles?

There is no single reason why South Asian countries have opted for cruise missiles. Technological sophistication, cost-effectiveness, the domino effect of their possession and use by the major powers in different contingencies, and regional security imperatives – all seem to have their role concurrently.

Though the importance of ballistic missiles has not declined, global interest in cruise missiles has increased phenomenally since the 1970s. Technological innovations in the arena of guidance and navigation, propulsion or engine technology, stealth, warhead and the design of the airframe have reached a level of development which allowed an altogether new generation of these weapons and made them more *intelligent*.[2] Since the 1980s, the Global Positioning System (GPS) has been an integral part of missiles. Incorporation of low-observable (stealth) technologies and use of composite materials has provided reduced weight while increasing the thrust. Micro-miniaturisation of electronics has increased computational densities and data storing capacities of the onboard computer. The evolving cruise missile technology seems to be moving from *aid to autonomy*. These and many other innovations have gradually infused some sort of decision-making power in the machines, therefore, they have become more lethal and accurate.

However, technological innovations in the domain of cruise missiles are not taking place in a vacuum. The shape of the battlefield itself has undergone surprising alterations and, thereby, the choices for weapons. Today's war-fighting necessitates targeting of an individual, a bunker or a building; thereby, the selection of weapons for a single-shot kill has been pronounced. Also, their technological novelty, cost-effectiveness, high military payoff, ease of concealment and transportability, make them attractive to countries. The developing countries now consider them as the *poor man's air force*. According to a study, "$50 million could buy one or two advanced tactical fighters or 15 ballistic missiles with three launchers, or 100 off-the-shelf, ready to fire cruise missiles".[3] As per the US Financial Year (FY) 99 Air and Missile Defence Master Plan, given equal funding, any nation could buy 40 off-the-shelf cruise missiles within the cost price of one or two fixed-wing fighters.[4]

On the other hand, starting from World War II till Operation Iraqi Freedom, the use of cruise missiles by the major powers has exceeded that of ballistic missiles by over 3 to 1: the number of cruise missiles used was around 19,465 while the number of ballistic missiles used during the same period was around 5,875.[5] Today, around 130 types of cruise missiles are available with 75 countries of the world. More importantly, defence against cruise missiles is virtually impossible. During the 2003 Iraq War, the Patriot missiles successfully intercepted all nine ballistic missiles fired by the Iraqi forces: but they failed to detect any of the five primitive cruise missiles Iraq employed.[6] The Patriot system was also involved in three friendly-fire incidents, downing two Allied warplanes and killing one American and two British pilots. It was realised as a result that intercepting lower-altitude, slower-flying cruise missiles remains a pressing challenge even for the United States.

Lastly, the utility of modern cruise missiles seems to have attracted the South Asian nations and their choice for specific weapon systems. India and Pakistan are contiguous neighbours and many cities in each side are only a few hundred kilometres away. The Missile Technology Control Regime (MTCR), mainly restricts ballistic missile technology transfers, but allows transfer of cruise missiles of 300 km range and 500 kg payload. South Asian countries find enormous advantages in cruise missiles. They are inexpensive, easy to acquire, hide and use. More importantly, according to David Nicholas, these systems provide "an alternative to maintenance of air superiority through traditional means"; with a handful of cruise missiles, a state could mount a strategic bombing campaign, and, thus, avoid the need to achieve real air superiority.[7]

South Asian Cruise Missile Inventory

Though the missile policies of India and Pakistan mainly constitute the South Asian missile discourse, China's missile strategy has impinged sufficiently upon the strategic affairs of the subcontinent. In addition, Bangladesh is reportedly taking an interest in missiles and has commenced some interaction with China in this regard. However, this study only analyses the contours of the India-Pakistan cruise missile discourse, keeping in mind China's missile strategy vis-a-vis India and the Sino-Pak missile cooperation.

Pakistan's Cruise Missile Strategy: The fear in Islamabad is that India may seek to neutralise Pakistan's existing ballistic missile-based nuclear deterrent by deploying BMD.[8] As a result, Pakistan's strategy now seems concentrated on strengthening of its cruise missile inventory. Though Pakistan's cruise missiles are currently subsonic, as a logical step, it would soon acquire their supersonic versions.

Pakistan's cruise missile inventory mainly constitutes the Babur and Raad missiles. It is speculated that the Babur (Hatf-7) is based on the BGM-109 Tomahawk.[9] Among the many US Tomahawks that were launched against Al Qaeda training camps in Afghanistan in August 1998, six landed in Pakistan, which it reverse engineered. Reportedly, it has also received Chinese assistance in reverse engineering the unexploded Tomahawk[10] which has been test-launched seven times till February 2011.[11] According to *Jane's Strategic Weapon Systems 2011*, initial production of the Babur may have begun in 2006 and the system entered initial operational service in 2010.[12] Pakistan is believed to be working on the Babur II project and it is speculated to be a submarine launched supersonic variant.

Pakistan has developed the turbojet-powered Ra'ad (Hatf-8) cruise missile. First tested in August 2007, it is of 350 km range with a capability to carry a variety of different warheads, including a nuclear warhead. Its tail configuration is believed to have a South African connection.[13] According to Pakistan's Inter-Services Public Relations (ISPR), the Babur and Ra'ad both have "stealth capabilities" and "pinpoint accuracy"; each of them is described as "low-altitude, terrain-hugging", "with high manoeuvrability".[14] The Ra'ad "can deliver nuclear and conventional warheads" and is believed to have "enabled Pakistan to achieve a greater strategic stand-off capability on land and at sea".[15] By April 29, 2011, Pakistan had test-launched the Ra'ad for the third time. Currently, Pakistan is speculated to be working on an upgraded version of the Ra'ad.

In addition, the Sino-Pakistan missile and nuclear nexus and Pakistan's proliferation activities to countries like Iran, Libya and North Korea need to be viewed with further caution. US intelligence reports reveal that China has transferred 34 complete M-11 missiles, missile technology and manufacturing assistance to Pakistan.[16] Even China's supply trail runs to Iran and then into Lebanon, either by sea or over land via Syria, as well as North Korea. Of concern are the missiles exported to Iran, such as the long-range C-802 and the shorter-range C-801 Anti-Ship Cruise Missiles (ASCMs).

Bangladesh's Missile Programme: Bangladesh also has taken interest in missiles and has commenced some interaction with China in this regard. On May 11, 2008, the Bangladesh Navy successfully test-fired the C-802 missile in the Bay of Bengal, following an upgrade to the missile system with the assistance of a Chinese technical team. Bangladesh is also acquiring the European Otomat MK-II SAMs (Surface-to-Air-Missiles) that are defensive in nature and function. But their range of less than 200 km makes them a defence only against India. Strategists view the missile programme that Bangladesh has begun with Chinese help as part of Beijing's considered strategy to encircle India.[17] In which way this nascent programme will move is a matter of speculation.

India's Cruise Missiles Strategy: On the other hand, to bring greater choice to its missile inventory, besides ballistic missiles, India relies heavily on the BrahMos venture which is a multi-role missile, capable of performing either anti-ship or land-attack missions. The air-launched and submarine-launched versions are in progress. It is believed that the joint venture can produce roughly 100 missiles a year, and of the

1,000 missiles produced over the next ten years, half have been earmarked for export. The BrahMos seems to have acquired a robust export market amongst a growing list of interested countries, including Malaysia, South Africa, Kuwait, Chile, and Indonesia. Commemorating the induction of the BrahMos in the Indian Army on June 21, 2007, the then Indian President A.P.J. Abdul Kalam said, "Today, we have an order book worth US$ 2 billion and serious business interest exists for an order of an equal amount". President Kalam went on to express the hope that with such a capability, the missile can be "aggressively" marketed worldwide. Though both the foreign and domestic orders of the BrahMos are undisclosed, the Malaysian Deputy Defence Minister formally announced on July 4, 2007, that Malaysia has plans to procure a number of long-range cruise missiles while taking account of the "sensitivities of neighbouring countries".[18] If things move right, the BrahMos would spread to many more countries and the production of its new sophisticated variants, in the form of hypersonic, multi-role versions, would be smooth.

In late 2004, the Indian Navy first inducted the BrahMos on its surface ships. The Navy's Rajput-class destroyers have eight BrahMos missiles onboard, capable of either maritime strike or land attack. Its Project 15A destroyers will carry 16 BrahMos missiles fired from a Vertical Launch System (VLS) and the Talwar-class frigates will have 8 VLS.[19] The air force version of the BrahMos is known to have commenced in 2005 and initial work has begun with the Sukhoi design bureau, HAL, and the Indian Air Force for interface requirements and installation on the SU-30 MKI. According to the BrahMos Aerospace official website, the test launch trial commenced in 2010 and their induction was earmarked for 2012. Installation on other aircraft will depend on user requirements.[20] According to reports, minor adaptation has been undertaken to reduce the weight of the missile to around 2,500 kg with a smaller rocket booster and additional control fins for launch stability. The air force version will carry a 300 kg warhead, 100 kg heavier than the navy's. For precise attacks against land targets, BrahMos Aerospace turned to an unspecified multi-mode seeker to improve terminal accuracy against lower-contrast land targets.[21]

Originally, the army planned to induct the first BrahMos regiment, comprising three batteries, each having four mobile autonomous launchers. Each launcher has three missiles, making a total of 36 per regiment. According to Dennis Gormley, "After Pakistan's surprise launch of its Babur LACM in August 2005, Indian officials apparently found the army's deployment schedule too dilatory and decided instead to muster a special BrahMos missile regiment. Reportedly, the Indian Army will eventually deploy three full regiments of the BrahMos LACM even though it only planned one at the start."[22] As one regiment has four Mobile Autonomous Launchers (MALs), each with three missiles, the Indian Army would be able to fire a total of 12 missiles at 12 different targets within 30 seconds from each regiment.[23] So far, the second BrahMos unit of the Indian Army has been operationalised in the western sector along the Pakistan border. The third regiment which is to be deployed along the China border in the northeastern sector by the Indian Army has also been given the go-ahead by the Defence Ministry.[s]

Latest reports on the BrahMos suggest that the missile is heading to be known as a "sub-strategic super weapon" capable of being launched from land, sea, sub-sea and air platforms, and, more importantly, capable of carrying a nuclear warhead.[25] The integration of the X-555 and BrahMos navigation systems has produced it as a super rocket with a sub-strategic capability above its tactical range. The proposed Mark II BrahMos missile aims to acquire a range of more than 1,000 km and the reported agreement with France (that, reportedly, hit a snag) for the transfer of technology for the production of French cruise missiles in India is one of the Indian attempts to address the country's security deficit.[26] The BrahMos II, lab tested with a speed of 5.26 Mach, making it the fastest cruise missile in the world, is expected to be ready by 2013-14.[27] Another three such attempts include (1) the indigenous Land Attack Cruise Missile (LACM) strategic system called Sagarika which aims to develop a 1,000-km-range cruise missile to be launched from aircraft and submarines; (2) a new LACM development programme called Nirbhay with 1,000 km range believed to be in the same class as the US Tomahawk; and (3) collaboration with Israel to convert India's Lakshya pilotless vehicle into an LACM with a range up to 600 km carrying a 350-kg payload.

It is a matter of speculation as to which programme will emerge from India's multiple and ambiguous LACM developments but it is evident that "New Delhi is determined not to allow Islamabad to exceed its missile ambitions."[28] With India planning a massive build-up of conventional capability with the BrahMos versions (later on, its nuclear version), it may tilt the conventional balance in South Asia. That is probably why Pakistan wishes to extend the Babur's range up to 1,000 km, which has prompted defence analysts in India to argue for extending the ranges of Indian missiles.[29]

Strategic Implications

Since the cruise missile programmes of South Asian states are in an evolutionary mode and shrouded in mystery, to fathom their precise implications is difficult. However, the future strategic balance in South Asia would largely depend on the pace, numbers and quality of cruise missiles acquired by both countries. It is viewed that the South Asian countries find cruise missiles useful for basic nuclear deterrence requirements.[30] Deployment of

LACMs on survivable submarines or mobile platforms, obviously, provides an assured means of surviving counter-force attacks, assuming that such missiles can penetrate the anti-missile defence. Therefore, cruise missiles as part of the South Asian nuclear discourse must be studied in the context of the strategic stability-instability paradigm.

Undoubtedly, the strategic repercussion of Pakistan's cruise missiles has been strongly felt in India. In an interview, former Indian Navy Chief, Adm Arun Prakash characterised Pakistan's surprising cruise missile acquisition as a destabilising event in the regional strategic environment. According to Vishal Thapar, "The worry is that the next arms race between India and Pakistan will be ... cruise missiles. With Islamabad already declaring its intention to nuclear-tip the Babur, the prospects are ominous. Unlike ballistic missiles, the terrain-hugging cruise missiles are difficult to detect and are also deadly accurate. This is bad news for nuclear deterrence in the subcontinent."[31]

Scholars have different opinions on the issue. Shane A Mason, a graduate research assistant in the Monterey Institute of International Studies, is of the view that Pakistan's nuclear-capable cruise missiles have the potential to complicate India's missile defence strategy.[32] Further, he says, Pakistan's arsenal can obscure the distinction between tactical and strategic weapons, thereby complicating nuclear signalling by creating a degree of uncertainty in the minds of Indian decision-makers. Since the Babur and Ra'ad can be used in a conventional or nuclear role, Indian decision-makers may mistakenly view conventional preparations as strategic ones, or vice versa. This confusion would likely lead India's armed forces to avoid taking any unnecessary risks, like penetrating deep into Pakistani territory, crossing the Line of Control (LoC), and using air power. The Babur and Ra'ad, therefore, are viewed to have brought in a fundamental dilemma in Indian defence planning vis-à-vis Pakistan.

On the other hand, Kalyan Kemburi, a research officer for the China Programme of the Rajaratnam School of International Studies, National Technological University, Singapore, is of the view that the cruise missile in Pakistan could contribute to deterrence stability as it helps fill deterrence gaps by providing a credible retaliatory strike option; it will affect missile defence thinking in the way that it will increase the cost of the adversary's defences as the cruise missile is affordable and virtually undefeatable; and it may fail to augment strategic deterrence, rather it could be destabilising for the region as limited missile defence by India will not create a security dilemma for Pakistan.[33] It would allow Pakistan to maintain its nuclear deterrent against India to some extent. In that case, Pakistan will mobilise all resources at its disposal to build up an assertive cruise missile inventory for both 'first-use' and second-strike missions. This, in fact, argues Kemburi, will give Pakistan a dual advantage: (1) the stealthy cruise missiles will enable it to undertake a nuclear mission under its open 'first-use' policy; and (2) it can also can be used as an offensive counter to the missile defence system deployed by India.[34]

Therefore, the intricate question is: what strategic advantage has New Delhi accrued by opting for cruise missiles when Pakistan has followed suit? One may question whether cruise missiles in Pakistan represent a more significant threat to India than the ballistic missiles. It is known that Pakistan has opted for cruise missiles in response to India's BMD programme. If the goal of India's missile defence programme is to bait Pakistan into an economically ruinous arms race, then it appears to be succeeding. If India goes for a cruise missile defence or an Iron Dome like system in the future, one can only wonder what Pakistan's next move would be. However, by going down the path of maintaining strategic parity with India, Pakistan can only become a weaker, poorer, less stable state, which is certainly not in India's interests.

The destabilising effect of cruise missiles lies first in the fact that they could be used in a preemptive war, or an accidental release. Given the domestic politico-security situation in and around Pakistan, the increasing number and variety of cruise missiles, including the nuclear capable ones, in its inventory, could result in operational hazards and misuse.

Secondly, the concern is about how they will impact the effectiveness of missile defence. "Defending against land-attack cruise missiles (LACMs) will stress air defense systems:" low-flying, low-altitude missiles remain below enemy radar and, in some cases, hide behind terrain features, making effective defence against them difficult.[35] The newer missiles, incorporating stealth features, are even less visible to radars and infrared detectors. Using modern technology and programmes, a target can be attacked simultaneously from different directions, overwhelming air defences at their weakest points. Land-attack missiles can fly circuitous routes to get to the target, thereby avoiding radar and air defence installations. Given the extremely short flight time between India and Pakistan, such missiles will not leave sufficient time for any effective counter-measures to be employed.

Difficult Counter-Strategy

There are available only extremely difficult counter-strategy options against the cruise missile threat today: (1) strategy of preemption; (2) strategy of passive defence; and (3) strategy of active defence. A preemptive strategy of launching air and ground strikes against an enemy's missile launchers, assembly and storage facilities, military bases, roads and railways is based on the logic that "the best defence is good offence", and to that extent, self-defence is always a "just war" worth initiating.[36] However, in political terms, such counter-force strikes, especially if preemptive, are problematic. Among numerous such attempts, three preemptive attacks draw attention. First, the surprise attack that the imperial Japanese Navy undertook on December 7, 1941, on Pearl Harbour. Japan's intention was to create a strategic situation so intimidating to the United States that a negotiated settlement to Japan's advantage would result. Second, the preemptive attack spearheaded by the Israeli Air Force (IAF) on June 5, 1967, that destroyed the Egyptian Air Force. Third, the anticipation that Saddam was developing an "Arab Bomb" and his intense anti-Israeli rhetoric was hostile intent enough for Israel's leaders to initiate a preventive attack on the Osirak reactor. On June 7, 1981, eight IAF F-16s, flown by elite pilots, streaked across the Baghdad sky to attack the heart of Iraq's nuclear weapon effort. Undoubtedly, all these attempts were risky and uncertain, with wide ramifications.

Moreover, there is no guarantee that such attacks will locate and destroy all the missile launchers and entire inventory. As cruise missiles can be launched from various platforms such as an aircraft, a fighter, a surface ship, a submerged submarine and a ground-based Transporter Erector Launcher (TEL), there exist "capability gaps" in different areas to prepare an effective defence structure against them. Each delivery technique presents its own challenges to a defender.[37] Owing to the variety of launching platforms and disguise capability, identifying all of them would be a daunting task. Historically, say Kueter and Kleinberg, neither the British hunt for the German V weapon nor the Scud ballistic missile hunts of Operation Desert Storm in 1991 were anywhere near 100 per cent effective.[38]

A passive defence strategy involves individual and collective measures to reduce the vulnerability to, and minimise the effects of, a theatre missile attack. Two broad procedures are normally practised: (1) passive air defence measures; and (2) attack avoidance measures.[39] Both include the use of cover, concealment, and camouflage, protective cover, and deception. Passive air defence measures, if routinely followed, will reduce the probability of attack and will limit damage in case of an attack. Attack avoidance strategies like bunkering, deep burial, dispersal, concealment or keeping valuable assets far behind front lines are normally practised. However, a passive defence strategy alone cannot ensure absolute defence against precision strikes.

Lastly, when interdiction of incoming cruise missiles fails, the default strategy could be to engage and destroy these before they reach their target, which requires an *active* defence system. Using anti-air missiles of various ranges, it may be possible to intercept anti-ship cruise missiles (although intercepting land-attack missiles remains a Herculean task). Reportedly France, for instance, was able to intercept supersonic anti-ship missiles flying at very low altitude in April 2012 using its principal anti-air missile system.[40]

But the US Department of Defence (in the study named "Integrated Air and Missile Defence) has identified at least nine capability gaps in the US cruise missile defence programme. Most prominent among them is the inability to detect small, low-speed, low-altitude targets. These gaps were not expected to be bridged until 2015.[41] Therefore, the Directorate of Operational Capability Requirements of the US Air Force (USAF) has undertaken a Joint Capabilities Integration and Development System study to determine the best approaches.[42] After nine years of consistent effort, with the Patriot Advanced Capability-3 missile test on April 25, 2012, the US military seems to have moved a step forward in bridging the gap in its capability to defend against a cruise missile attack.[43]

Therefore, the greatest challenge is the detection and tracking of the low-flying stealthy cruise missiles early enough to engage them before they reach the target. For it to replicate the USA type model, India would need an effective Command, Control, Communication, Intelligence, Surveillance and Reconnaissance (C4ISR) system. Such a system is extremely difficult to develop; it would consist of a mechanism to intercept and track incoming threats and also be able to physically destroy them. In such a scheme, the model must be multi-layered. First, the launch platforms must be detected, tracked and engaged. And if this fails, the incoming cruise missiles must be detected, tracked and engaged. Once the threat is identified, a decision on how to engage it must be made. Missiles and gunfire are the only two current options as weapons; Directed Energy Weapons (DEW) are also being studied.[44]

The most critical element is detection and tracking of the missile early enough. Generally, the sensor detection system should be pushed out far from the areas defended to allow optimum elbow room. Traditionally, detection was undertaken by ground-based radars. But the cruise missiles' flight path or trajectory make their detection a daunting task. When advanced nations like the United States have not been able to develop such a system yet, can India afford to, and can it overcome the technical hurdles in achieving such a technology-intensive system to counter the emerging cruise missile threat effectively?

Cruise Missiles and Crisis Escalation

The more intriguing question is whether a conventional cruise missile attack on missile defences will result in crisis escalation. Cruise missiles are considered an "offensive counter to missile defence".[45] Precision capable cruise missiles are effective for conventional strikes against targets of strategic importance. Furthermore, a mix of advanced conventional forces, cruise missiles, C4ISR systems, missile defence, and nuclear weapons bestows on a nation the confidence for preemption. Pakistan has acquired all these capabilities except defence against ballistic missiles. Taking into account the cost involved in building a BMD system, Pakistan seems not motivated and may not be capable of acquiring it. However, the precision strike cruise missiles, especially the Babur and Ra'ad, bestow on Pakistan the option and capability of preemption strikes. As Pakistan claims its nuclear first-strike option is an option of "last resort",[46] it would first use all conventional options in its disposal. Therefore, the cruise missiles in Pakistan's possession would be its best choice for employment mainly to evade or destroy India's BMD-backed strategy, which may lead to escalation of the crisis.

Therefore, cruise missiles should be treated the way ballistic missiles are treated, especially keeping in mind the South Asian strategic complexities. So far, these delivery systems are not included in any CBMs between India and Pakistan. The reported miniaturisation of nuclear weapons by Pakistan and its acquisition of Tactical Nuclear Weapons (TNWs) and the short-range nuclear capable Nasr missile are "inherently destabilising" the regional security discourse.[47] Of course, Pakistan views India's BMD capability as equally destabilising and, therefore, it is in the process of acquiring Multiple Independently Targetable Reentry Vehicle (MIRV) capability.[48] This, coupled with submarine-launched, nuclear-tipped cruise missiles, ensures for Pakistan the survivability of its nuclear deterrent and enhances the effectiveness of its missile force to beat any Indian defence. To a certain extent, Indian missile defence is one option to counter Pakistan's nuclear blackmail. However, that does not seem to have effectively deterred Pakistan from striving to sustain its 'parity' strategy. Probably, a diplomatic strategy to bring in some kind of understanding between both countries and initiate a dialogue on the gravity of cruise and short-range missiles, and the blurred line between nuclear and conventional forces in a nuclear overhang, would help.

Towards a Cruise Missile CBM

One needs to ponder on whether there is any tactical, strategic, or logical reason as to why India and Pakistan cannot come together to agree upon a CBM addressing the cruise and short-range missile threats. As China is a major factor in India's nuclear and missile strategy, any consideration for CBMs in the domain of missiles with Pakistan has to accommodate India's China concerns, and its convenience. A number of ideas on missile CBMs have been proposed, though not directly related to cruise missiles. The Colombo initiative at the Track-2 level to start a CBM on the basis of the idea that the first generation Short-Range Ballistic Missiles (SRBMs) like the Prithvi-I and Hatf-1 are obsolete, and a verified phased approach to their retirement can be undertaken,[49] is a recent attempt. However, taking India's China concerns and the state of affairs in South Asia into account, this proposal seems unrealistic.

First, the Prithvi I and II are still in service while the Hatf-1 has already been withdrawn – its new version, the Hatf-1A, had been inducted in the year 2000. From the operational point of view, since the Prithvi has been inducted in large numbers during the last few decades, it would remain the mainstay in India's 150-km range category missiles till the Brahmos and Prahar are inducted in large numbers. Given the level of distrust and suspicion between India and Pakistan, an outright proposal to verify and withdraw inducted armaments from service is easier said than done. Also, there have been occasions when the exchanged list of nuclear facilities (as a provision of the agreement on non-attack on each other's nuclear facilities) has not been wholly accepted by the two sides – with one side doubting the authenticity of the other's list.

Secondly, unlike Pakistan, whose security concerns are India-centric, India's potential challenge also emanates in a big way from China. Therefore, any disarmament/arms control measure between India and Pakistan goes beyond bilateral terms.[50] Thirdly, if so-called obsolete missiles are to be replaced by some other systems in both countries – and they have already embarked on this process – what purpose is the proposed CBM going to achieve?

It would be prudent, therefore, to focus on more imminent threats like cruise missile spread and the safety-security of nuclear weapons rather than investing energy on issues that have no future implications. Initiating a separate CBM on cruise missiles alone would involve many bilateral procedural hassles. Extending the existing ballistic missile CBM to include cruise missiles would do much in the form of quelling regional security fears in South Asia. Pakistan had earlier proposed to include cruise missiles in the Indo-Pak CBM on ballistic missiles to which India had objected. Will India give a second thought to the issue? Since Bangladesh is a new entrant in the South Asian missile discourse, it is in the best interest of all to have rethink on the issue, and a proposal in this regard may be made at the highest political level in each country.

Notes

1. C Uday Bhaskar quoted saying at an Asia-Pacific security seminar on India's Maritime Security Challenges at the East-West Centre on May 7, 2013, "Taking a leaf from China, Pakistan seems to be investing in cruise missiles. This has lowered the index of stability in the region". http://indiatoday.intoday.in/story/cruise-missiles-china-pakistan-stealth-capabilities-uday-bhaskar-india-maritime-security/1/269879.html, accessed on October 05, 2013.
2. Sitakanta Mishra, *Cruise Missiles: Evolution, Proliferation and Future* (New Delhi: KW Publishers, 2011.)
3. Adam J Herbert, "Cruise Control", *Air Force Magazine*, December 2002, p. 43.
4. *FY 99 Air and Missile Defence Master Plan*, "Chapter 2 – Threat", http://www.fas.org/spp/starwars/docops/amd99/chapter2.pdf, p. 2, accessed on October 05, 2013.
5. Dennis M Gormley, *Missile Contagion: Cruise Missile Proliferation and the Threat to*

International Security (Westport: Praeger Security International, 2008).

6. Dennis Gormley, "Winning on Ballistic Missiles but Losing on Cruise: The Missile Proliferation Battle", http://www.armscontrol.org/print/3983, accessed on October 05, 2013.
7. David J Nicholls, "Cruise Missiles and Modern War" (Maxwell AFB: Occasional Paper No. 13, Center for Strategy and Technology, Air War College, May 2000), http://www.au.af.mil/au/awc/awcgate/cst/csat13.pdf. p. 12, accessed on October 06, 2013.
8. "Cruise Missile Proliferation Heats Up in South Asia", *WMD Insights*, February 2006, http://wmdinsights.com/I2/SA1_CruiseMissile.htm, accessed on October 01, 2013.
9. Mark Williams, "The Missiles of August - Part II: The Democratization of Cruise Missile Technology", http://www.technologyreview.com/business/17374/?a=f, accessed on October 6, 2013.
10. Duncan Lennox, "China's New Cruise Missile Programme 'Racing Ahead'," *Jane's Defence Weekly*, January 12, 2000, p. 12.
11. Hans M Kristensen and Robert S Norris, "Pakistan's Nuclear Forces, 2011," *Bulletin of the Atomic Scientists*, 67(4), 2011, p. 97.
12. "Hatf-7 (Babur)", Offensive Weapons/Pakistan, *Jane's Strategic Weapon Systems*, Issue 55, 2011, pp. 128-9.
13. "LO Contagion Spreads: Search for Antidote Underway", *Aviation Week & Space Technology*, September 3, 2007, p. 32.
14. ISPR, Press Release No. PR40/2011-ISPR, February 10, 2011, www.ispr.gov.pk/front/main.asp?o=t-press_release&date=2011/2/10, accessed on October 7, 2013.
15. ISPR, Week View No. PR104/2011-ISPR, April 29, 2011, http://www.ispr.gov.pk/front/main.asp?o=t-press_release&id=1732, accessed on October 07, 2013.
16. "China's Missile Exports and Assistance to Pakistan", http://cns.miis.edu/archive/country_india/china/mpakchr.htm, accessed on October 8, 2013; Bill Gertz, "Pakistan-China Deal for Missiles Exposed: Nuclear Ambitions Spur US Concern", *The Washington Times*, September 7, 1994.
17. Muhammad Javed Iqbal, "India: Bangladesh Missiles Part of China's Encirclement – Experts", http://newsgroups.derkeiler.com/Archive/Soc/soc.culture.pakistan/2008-09/msg00170.html, October 8, 2013.
18. John Grevatt, "Malaysia Plans to Buy Cruise Missiles, Confirms Deputy Defence Minister", *Jane's Defence Industry*, August 1, 2007.
19. Gormley, n. 5, p. 70.
20. "Air Launch Weapon System", http://www.brahmos.com/content.php?id=19, October 10, 2013.
21. Doglas Barrie, "Indian Air Force Proceeds with Test Plans for a Supersonic Land-Attack Program", *Aviation Week & Space Technology*, February 27, 2006, p. 36.
22. Gormley, n. 5, p. 71.
23. Dilip Kumar Mekala, "Breathing Fire", http://www.forceindia.net/BreathingFire.aspx, accessed on October 10, 2013.
24. Ibid.
25. Vladimir Radyuhin, "Brahmos Gains Sub-strategic Super Weapon Capability", *The Hindu*, October 13, 2012.
26. "Cruise Control: Missile Deal Can Boost Tech Capability", *The Tribune*, September 7, 2006.
27. "BrahMos Hypersonic Cruise Missile", http://www.brahmos.com/content.php?id=27, accessed on October 10, 2013.
28. Gormley, n. 5, p. 73.
29. Pravin Sawhney, "A Babur for BrahMos", *Force*, April 1, 2007.
30. Gormley, n. 5, p. 69.

31. Vishal Thapar, "Pakistan Flaunts N-Missile, Catches India Unawares", *CNN-IBN*, April 5, 2006.
32. Shane A Mason, "Pakistan's Babur and Ra'ad Cruise Missiles: Strategic Implications for India", Article No. 3681, July 18, 2012. http://www.ipcs.org/article/india/pakistans-babur-and-raad-cruise-missiles-strategic-implications-for-india-3681.html, accessed on October 10, 2013.
33. Kalyan Kemburi, "Cruise Missiles in Southern Asia: Strategic Implications for China, India, and Pakistan", in *Project on Nuclear Issues*, CSIS, August 2012, pp. 55-70.
34. Ibid.
35. "Land Attack Cruise Missiles", http://www.fas.org/irp/threat/missile/naic/part07.htm, accessed on October 01, 2013.
36. Daniel L Zajac, "The Best Defense is a Good Offense: Preemption, Ramifications for the Department of Defense", USAWC Strategy Research Project, April 7, 2003.
37. Carlo Kopp, "Defeating Cruise Missiles", Technical Report APA-TR-2007-0402, *Air Power Australia*, http://www.ausairpower.net/Analysis-Cruise-Missiles.html, accessed on October 1, 2013.
38. Merrick E Krause (Lt. Col., USAF), *Attack Operations for Missile Defense* (Maxwell AFB: Occasional Paper No. 28, Centre for Strategy and Technology – Air War College, Air University, May 2002), pp. 1-7.
39. "Small Arms Defense Against Air Attack", http://www.fas.org/man/eprint/sad.pdf, accessed on October 11, 2013; "Passive Air Defense Measures", http://www.globalsecurity.org/military/library/policy/army/fm/44-8/ch4.htm, accessed on October 11, 2013.
40. "Première en Europe: Interception d'une cible supersonique évoluant au ras de l'eau", http://www.defense.gouv.fr/dga/actualite/premiere-en-europe-interception-d-une-cible-supersonique-evoluant-au-raz-de-l-eau, accessed on October 11, 2013.
41. John Liang, "DoD Finds Cruise Missile Defense 'Gaps'", http://military.com/features/0,15240,110199,00.html, accessed on October 11, 2013.
42. Ibid.
43. Ben Iannotta, "Progress Cited on Cruise Missile Defense", *Defense News*, May 07, 2012.
44. Robert Wall, "Sketching the Future: Developers Mull Upgrading USAF Bombers with Laser Weapons", *Aviation Week & Space Technology,* vol. 160, issue 23, June 7, 2004.
45. Kalyan Kemburi, "China, India, and Cruise Missiles", http://csis.org/images/stories/poni/110707_Kemburi.pdf, accessed on October 15, 2013.
46. Former Pakistani President Gen Pervez Musharraf quoted saying this in an interview published in April 2002 in the German magazine, *Der Spiegel*. Peter R Lavoy, "Pakistan's Nuclear Posture: Security and Survivability", http://www.npolicy.org/article_file/Pakistans_Nuclear_Posture-Security_and_Survivability.pdf, accessed on October 15, 2013.
47. Gurmeet Kanwal, "India-Pakistan and Tactical Nuclear Weapons: Implications of Hatf-9", *IPCS Debate*, #4169, November 11, 2013, http://www.ipcs.org/article/india/pakistan-is-hatf-9-inherently-destabilising-4169.html, accessed on October 16, 2013.
48. Usman Ansari, "Pakistan Seeks to Counter Indian ABM Defenses", http://www.defensenews.com/article/20110321/DEFFEAT06/103210303/, accessed on October 20, 2013.
49. "Enhancing Strategic Stability in South Asia through the Transparent Elimination of Obsolescent Ballistic Missiles", Article No.: 1925, August 10, 2011, http://www.claws.in/index.php?action=details&m_id=926&u_id=36, accessed on October 25, 2013.
50. Prakash Nanda, "Time to Say Goodbye to Prithvi Missiles?", http://udayindia.in/english/content_06october2012/right-angle.html, accessed on November 1, 2013.

7

Mainstreaming Environmental Security and Cooperation in South Asia

Nishant Gupta

Introduction

The most recent cloudburst in Uttarakhand, termed as the *Himalayan Tsunami*, witnessed enormous destruction and loss of life. Various authorities quote different figures, but the estimated death toll is expected to be around 10,000, though only a few bodies could be recovered and the remaining are expected to be buried under the debris. Additionally, there are reports that the tragedy was not limited to the state of Uttarakhand, as it spanned eastern Himachal Pradesh and western Nepal.[1] Indeed, in the 21st century, extreme weather events in South Asia[2] ranging from the 2005 Kashmir earthquake, the Indus floods of 2010, the Siachen avalanche of 2012, to the seasonal water shortages and droughts have caused severe economic damage and loss to human life (and not the inter-state wars, terrorism or ensuing conflicts which are generally believed to be the biggest threat to national security).

The phenomenon of extreme weather incidents is not peculiar to South Asia—the whole world is facing this harsh reality. As this piece is being written, Chicago in the US is witnessing record polar temperatures and the coldest weather in the last 106 years with temperature recorded below minus 50^{0}C. On the other extreme, in the Southern Hemisphere, heat records are being set in Australia with temperature recorded above 50^{0}C. Europe is also uncomfortable as Oslo experienced its warmest Christmas since records began in1937[3]. For better appreciation of these extreme weather events, and to develop suitable mechanisms to address them, there is a need to study and understand numerous dimensions of environmental change and related matters. The linkages among environmental change, national security and the military are important elements that require critical analyses and greater understanding.

This chapter is broadly divided into five sections. The first section traces the journey of environmentalism and flags the important milestones at the global level. The second section brings out the environmental stresses in South Asia and the major anxieties for India. The third part deals with the environmental security debate. This section also brings out the linkages between the environment and the military, and highlights the positive contribution of the Indian military towards the environment. The fourth section brings out the urgency of environmental cooperation, highlighting regional cooperative initiatives in South Asia. The last section deliberates on the way ahead.

Environmental Change: Global Discourse

Climate change, water scarcity and degradation, land degradation, deforestation and biodiversity loss, impacts on the maritime environment, atmospheric pollution, deficient urban infrastructure and natural disasters are the primary global environmental challenges. The causes of the environmental stress in the developed and developing nations may differ but the increasing population, along with rising disparity, excessive consumerism and inadequacy in policy response are the prominent concerns.

Climate change is considered as the most important constituent of environmental change. Climate change can exacerbate existing environmental crises – like droughts, water scarcity and soil degradation, intensify land-use conflicts and trigger environmentally induced migration. Secondly, climate change may lead to new kinds of conflicts such as over climate-induced degradation of fresh water resources, decline in food production, increase in storm and flood disasters, and environment induced migration. Thirdly, unabated climate change could lead to large-scale changes in the Earth system like the glacial retreat of the Hindu Kush/ Himalayan region, the loss of the Asian monsoon or the dieback of the Amazon rainforest.

The phenomenal social impact of the environmental changes can be broadly categorised into the following five heads[4]:

- Possible increase in the number of weak and fragile states.
- Risks for global economic development.
- Risks of growing international distributional conflicts between the main drivers of climate change and those most affected. There is a major difference between the per capita emissions of the developed nations and the developing/newly industrialised nations, which is commonly termed as the **'equity gap'.** Increasing industrialisation would lead to greater damage in the South and the worst affected countries would obviously strengthen their demand that **'polluter pays'**.
- Triggering and intensification of migration. Environmental changes would increase the migration hotspots across the globe and the associated conflict potential is phenomenal. 'Climate change refugee' is becoming a popular term.[5]

- Overstretching of the classic security policy.

The subject of environmental problems started gaining prominence in the West in the 1960s. This was the era when nations were gaining independence from their colonial rulers and were embarking on the journey of development through various means, including industrialisation, resulting in the increasing appetite for natural resources and energy. This process of expansion of industrialisation and ever increasing demand for resources resulted in environmental stress. The problem of environmental stress was further heightened with the rising population. In Western literature, *Silent Spring,* authored by scientific researcher Rachel Carson in 1962, is considered as a 'game changer' in the field of environment. This monumental work initiated the contemporary environment movement and, thereby, secured a place in the league of classics like *Das Capital* by Karl Marx, *The Wealth of Nations* by Adam Smith and *The Origin of the Species* by Charles Darwin.[6]

In order to address the associated challenges, the West saw the emergence of green activism and enactment of environment related laws. The UN General Assembly conference in Stockholm in June 1972 was the first international recognition of the green awareness. The significant outcome was 109 recommendations, and the creation of the UN Environment Programme (UNEP). The 1987 World Commission on Environment and Development Report titled "Our Common Future (1987)" commonly known as the Brundtland Report, is another milestone. The report expanded the notion of security – traditionally understood as political and national threats to sovereignty – and included the growing impacts of environmental stress – local, national, regional and global. However, the Cold War politics had other priorities and did not allow sincere follow-up on the emerging concepts and declaration principles. At the same time, the realists did not attach much significance to the environment related problems as they believed that natural resources were no more than another relatively stable factor.

The end of the Cold War changed this perception and renewed the focus on the environmental dilemma staring at the world. Since the disastrous effects of global warming, sea level rise, desertification, land degradation, rise in population, poverty and decline in the economy posed threats to the survival of the people, degradation and scarcity of resources underscored the need to increase the focus on the environment and even redefine security. The June 1992 UN Conference on Environment and Development at Rio de Janeiro, Brazil (commonly known as the Earth Summit), was an unprecedented landmark. The conference, attended by 172 states and 2,400 representatives of Non-

Governmental Organisations (NGOs), was one of the largest congregations of state officials, non-officials, activists and other non-state actors on environmental diplomacy. Agenda 21 emerged out of the conference primarily consisting of recommendations for good environmental practices. The conference galvanised the term "sustainable development" and, for the first time, development related predicaments and the question of sovereignty over natural resources were intensely debated upon.

Since 1996, the Millennium Project has been annually listing out the top 15 global challenges for humanity and the top three challenges in the 2011 Report are directly related to the environment. They are: **sustainable development and climate change; clean water; and population and resources.**[7] As per the **State of the Future 2012** report, "**environmental viability for our life support is diminishing ... climate change continues, and the gap between the rich and poor continues to widen dangerously.**"[8] 'Sustainable development' and 'inclusive growth' are essentially the core concerns of the 21st century. UN Secretary-General Ban Ki-moon said during the "Global Warming: Confronting the Crisis" Conference in New York on March 1, 2007, that "in the coming decades, changes in the environment—and the resulting upheavals, from droughts to inundated coastal areas—are likely to become a major driver of war and conflict."

The 1997 United Nations Framework Convention on Climate Change (UNFCCC) also known as the Kyoto Protocol, is generally seen as the first significant step towards a truly global emission reduction regime to stabilise greenhouse gas concentrations. The central feature of the Kyoto Protocol was the requirement for countries to limit or reduce their greenhouse gas emissions. In this process, emission reductions assumed economic value. To help countries meet their emission targets, and to encourage the private sector and developing countries to contribute to emission reduction efforts, negotiators of the Protocol included three market-based mechanisms: Emissions Trading, Clean Development Mechanism (CDM) and Joint Implementation.

The CDM allows emission-reduction projects in developing countries to earn Certified Emission Reduction (CER) credits, each equivalent to one tonne of CO_2. These CERs can be traded and sold, and used by the industrialised countries to meet a part of their emission reduction targets under the Kyoto Protocol. The mechanism stimulates sustainable development and emission reductions, while giving the industrialised countries some flexibility in how they meet their emission reduction limitation targets. The CDM is the main source of income for the UNFCCC Adaptation Fund, which was established to finance adaptation projects and programmes in the developing countries party to the Kyoto Protocol that are particularly vulnerable to the adverse effects of climate change. The Adaptation Fund is financed by a 2 percent levy on CERs issued by the CDM. The ascendency of international focus on climate change can be adjudged from the fact that the Intergovernmental Panel on Climate Change (IPCC) was awarded the Nobel Peace Prize in 2007.

The 2002 World Summit on Sustainable Development (WSSD), a special summit held in Johannesburg to review the implementation of Agenda 21, brought out differences between the developed and developing countries and their inability to arrive at any agreement on targets and a time-table for installation of renewable energy. The 2009 United Nations Climate Change Conference, commonly known as the Copenhagen Summit, also brought out the differences and divide between the North and the South.

Environmental Stresses in South Asia

In May 2011, the Secretary General of the South Asian Association for Regional Cooperation (SAARC), while presenting a draft SAARC Agreement on Rapid Response to Natural Disasters to the inter-governmental meeting in Colombo, pointed out that over the past 40 years, South Asia faced as many as 1,333 disasters that killed 9,80,000 people, affected 2.4 billion lives and damaged assets worth $105 billion. Further, this loss is by far the highest among the recorded disasters in various geographical regions. Jawaharlal Nehru, in his seminal work, *The Discovery of India*, has also stated that climate change was the probable cause of the end of the mighty Indus Valley Civilisation.[9]

In South Asia, there is substantial pressure on natural resources. South Asia occupies just about 5 per cent of the world's landmass, but is home to about 20 per cent of the world's population (1.5 billion). Three-quarters of the South Asian population lives in rural areas, with one-third living in extreme poverty (on less than a dollar a day). South Asia's vulnerability to environmental change has been observed in many ways. Land degradation, deforestation, water scarcity, air pollution, water pollution, degradation of the marine and coastal ecosystem, rise in temperature, rise in sea level, are amongst the most significant environmental problems in South Asia. Climate change, as mentioned earlier, could further lead to large-scale changes in the Earth systems like glacial retreat in the Hindu Kush/Himalayan region, sea-level rise and loss or reduction of the Asian monsoon.

Multiple stresses in South Asia, including accelerating population growth rates, expanding economy and consumption, rising inequality, large scale rural to urban migrations and dwindling resource base are exacerbating environmental fears.

Environmental risks staring at South Asia can be identified into three types[10] :

- **Growth related risks** resulting from processes like uncontrolled release of industrial pollutants into the air, soil and water bodies; excessive use of pesticides, etc.

- **Poverty related risks** resulting from inadequate access to potable water, absence of adequate sanitation, and indoor air pollution by burning freely collected biomass for cooking.
- **Policy-induced environmental risks.**

Environmental degradation and conflicts have a critical relationship in India as well as South Asia. Though the underlying cause of environmental degradation induced conflicts is scarcity of renewable resources, it can be divided into three broad categories: development induced conflicts; environmental migration and conflicts; and water sharing conflicts.[11]

Further, nations and regions with political instability, weak governance structures, and low economic performance will be more vulnerable to climate change amplified conflicts. Limited resources, lack of mitigation and adaptation capabilities and non-availability of effective public institutions reduce the national capability to address the environmental challenges. This increases the dissatisfaction amongst the masses and increases the rift between the government and the governed. Crisis and conflict management in such areas would be more challenging. Moreover, there is always a risk of spillover of the crisis to the neighbouring countries, transcending borders.

Major Concerns for India

South Asia has the world's highest mountain range (the Himalayas) and the largest riparian delta system (the Ganges-Brahmputra). These glaciers form a unique reservoir that supports perennial rivers such as the Indus, Ganges and Brahmaputra, which, in turn, are the lifeline of millions of people in the South Asian countries (Bangladesh, Bhutan, India, Nepal, and Pakistan). The glacier retreat in the Hindu Kush/Himalayan region is one of the prime causes of nervousness. This will exacerbate the challenges of poverty reduction and improving access to safe drinking water, two of the important Millennium Development Goals. There is a growing unease about forecasts that by 2050, increasing temperatures may reduce grain yields in Asia by 15 to 20 percent.[12]

Fresh water, whose consumption is increasing with the rising population, would continue to be a crucial resource and its importance in the calculus of the security dynamics is bound to enlarge. There is humongous international source interdependence on water as about 40 percent of humanity gets water from sources controlled by two or more countries.

As per the UN World Water Development Report, the society is close to approaching the global limit of sustainable availability of water. It also brings out that present global consumption is about 26,000 KM^3/year and some assessments suggest that consumption of 'blue water' should not cross 4,000 KM^3/ year, as the ecosystem would not be able to sustain the supply. Whatever may be the case, there is no denial that some regions, including the Indus basin in Pakistan and India have already crossed their sustainable water extraction limit.[13]

Pakistan: The Kashmir dispute also has its roots in water distribution and environmental survivability. As per some experts, Pakistan wanted Kashmir primarily to strengthen its survivability since all the rivers providing canal irrigation to West Punjab flowed through Kashmir. Religion is another dimension and the face of the problem. It has been reported that in 1990, Gen Pervez Musharraf had argued as a young brigadier, that the Kashmir dispute was dependent on the distribution of the Indus river water between Pakistan and India, and if one were resolved, the other would not exist. He contended that from the Pakistani perspective, fair distribution of water is a prerequisite for resolving the Jammu and Kashmir (J&K) conflict.[14] Under the World Bank mediated 1960 Indus Water Treaty (IWT) the eastern rivers—the Sutlej, Beas and Ravi—were allocated to India while the western rivers—the Jhelum, Chenab and Indus—were allotted to Pakistan (barring their use by India under specified conditions in J&K), with limited consumptive rights over these to India. Despite three wars and several conflicts with Pakistan over the last five decades, India has been abiding by the treaty (though the Tulbul navigation project and the Baglihar, Kishanganga, and Salal hydroelectric power projects continue to be contentious matters revolving around the treaty between the two countries). During Operation Parakram, to end the stalemate and to pressurise Pakistan, in the summer of 2002, the Cabinet Committee on Security (CCS) had discussed the possibility of preventing water supply to the Pakistani deployments,[15] but India finally decided in favour of abidance by the treaty and, thus, maintained the tradition of holding the high moral ground.

The Kashmir valley greatly depends upon the glaciers for its water supply as the rivers feeding the valley draw water from the Himalayan glaciers and climate change induced drying up of the glaciers will turn Kashmir from a *water surplus* state into a *water deficit* one.[16] According to some climate change scenarios, following an initial period of high flows caused by accelerated glacial melt, it is predicted that the amount of water flowing into the Indus river system may decrease by as much as 30 to 40 percent within the next two decades. Additionally, the effects of climate change and siltation may reduce the already low reservoir capacity in the basin by 30 percent. The overall reduction in water availability may have a potentially serious impact on irrigation. This, in turn, may affect food security.

Bangladesh: Cross-border migration from Bangladesh is a grave challenge for India. As per a 2013 Report of the UN Department of Social and Economic Affairs (UN-DSEA), 3.2 million Bangladeshis are living in India and it is termed as "the single largest bilateral stock of international migrants".[17] Eighty percent of the land in Bangladesh is less than 12 metres (m) above sea level, therefore, sea level rise will pose immense challenges. Flooding and cyclones also pose regular threats: 40 per cent of total land area gets flooded every year. Annually, river erosion washes away one per cent of arable land and displaces more than 1,00,000 people. Also trans-boundary rivers keep changing their course and creating fertile islands like the New Moore Island. The islands, like the charlands emerging in mid-river at the international border, are claimed by the border forces of both nations.[18]

Sri Lanka: The proposed Sethusamudram canal project in the sensitive region of the Gulf of Mannar may impact the coastal zone adversely. Increasing shipping activities in the region would also provide an easy target for rival groups conflicting over resources. Rise in sea level is another challenge as it would change the base line and, thereby, alter the maritime boundaries, resulting in change in fishing, mineral and marine rights along the maritime borders.

The Maldives: The Maldives has a fragile, low-lying small ecosystem that is highly vulnerable to climate change. It has been estimated that a two-metre rise in sea level will submerge virtually all the coral islands scattered over 850 km across the equator, forcing its population of 3,00,000 to evacuate. India, being the nearest neighbour, with long-time cultural and political proximities, would be expected to help the nation in rehabilitation and resettlement of environmental refugees. The Maldives has strategic importance for India as a military presence in the Maldives would be instrumental in safeguarding its maritime interests.

Nepal and Bhutan: The aforementioned Himalayan glacial retreat due to climate change and rise in temperature would severely impact water resources and agriculture in Nepal and Bhutan, the landlocked nations. There are questions about the Ganga-Mahakali catchment area. In Nepal, there are anxieties about the dams and hydro projects on the inter-state river systems, including the Mahakali and Karnali. Difference of opinion between India and Nepal over the role of the Indian Dhauliganga dam in Nepal's floods in the 2013 monsoon has been reported. Cooperation between India and Nepal in terms of building of dams, reservoirs and hydroelectricity projects on the trans-border river systems like the Karnali, Narayani and Kosi needs to be explored further.[19]

Environmental Security

The concept of security is inherently controversial, and international relations politics is no different. The interpretation and context of security can vary, but it is undeniable that generally every individual, group, institution and nation-state strives for greater security. Security, in the post World War II era of international relations politics, generally connotes territorial integrity of a sovereign nation-state within the system of international laws, as represented by the United Nations. Thus, in the 'classic' sense, the concept of security is confined to preservation of the integrity of a state in the face of an external threat in an anarchic international system; and the military is seen as the ultimate guardian of security.

In the post Cold War era, the contours of security have been changing and expanding to include other dimensions. It is now universally accepted that increasing globalisation is changing the security dynamics. It is generally recognised that insecurity, instability and violence are not due to external military aggression alone; rather, they may have complex political, economic, socio-cultural and ecological origins. The concept of national security has now been broadened to include other threats like threats to individuals and threats to the interests of the state. Thus, terms like human security, food security, water security and energy security came into existence. After the end of the Cold War, environmental degradation and environmental security have received increased attention. In the past 12 years, almost 50 million hectares of land have been bought by foreign governments.

Comprehensive Security: In the West, the North Atlantic Treaty Organisation (NATO) and Germany follow a concept of comprehensive security according to which military capability is not considered an adequate instrument; rather comprehensive security calls for the ability to defend political and socio-economic crises that threaten to cross the threshold of violence, and to do so as early as possible, using non-military means, and, if necessary, even military means may be considered. Thus, comprehensive security explicitly includes interests in securing strategic resources, which serve to safeguard affluence in the industrialised countries, and relates non-military areas with national security. And, slowly, problems like environmental degradation and poverty, earlier known as '*soft*' policy fields, have been accorded greater importance and there are increasing linkages between military and non-military policy.[20]

Environmental dilemmas are increasingly attracting the attention of political leaders. In 1989, **Jessica Tuchman Mathews**, in her seminal work *Redefining Security*, advocated that the 1990s will demand the need to broaden the definition of national security to include resources, environmental and demographic dimensions. As in the 1970s, the US had realised that its economy was no longer the independent force it had once been, but was powerfully affected by the economic policies of other nations, she brought out that, it was time to redefine constituents of national security and include environmental and other issues.[21]

Human Security: The popularity of the concept and definition of the term 'human security' also pertains to the beginning of the post Cold War period. In 1994, the UN Development Programme (UNDP) articulated the concept wherein the individual's security was given priority; ever since, security needs are being reconceptualised in the international security discourse, shifting the focus from **'security of the state'** to **'security of the people'**. Resources and environment are amongst the primary issues covered under the ambit of human security.[22] In the human security perspective, environmental security is not to be viewed through the prism of nation-states, rather it has to be perceived as an ecosystem in which human beings as users and polluters are themselves the real threat to security. Emerging trends in defining security are definitely leading to the emergence of non-conventional security threats wherein environmental security is gaining prominence in no uncertain terms.

The UN Environment Programme (UNEP), having established the linkages between environment and security, has initiated an inter-agency initiative known as the Environment and Security Initiative (ENVSEC).

But, as per the critics, the concept of human security plays down the security risks like war; trivialises the importance of the state in dealing with such security threats; and blurs the boundaries between human development and human security. They opine that the concept of security should be confined to *"freedom from direct physical violence"*. Even then, there is a danger of enhanced militarisation due to the legitimacy of using the military in traditionally non-military conflicts. The critics point to the vagueness of the enlarged concept of security. Enlargement of the concept of security, as per critics, includes a variety of concepts which make identification of security risks, responsibilities and appropriate responses harder. As a result, it increases the scope and extent of militarisation and military intervention in non-military conflicts. Thus, critics claim that diffusion of the concept of security would increase militarisation.

There is, indeed, a number of ways in which acts of omission or commission pertaining to environmental change in one area or country can have serious consequences in another area or country. However, whether a divergence of interests between countries in these matters would necessarily lead to military conflicts or wars is debatable. Therefore, the political landscape on the subject of securitisation of the environment is deeply divided. There are two distinct approaches towards linking the environment with conflicts and national security. Some argue that environmental stresses are likely to lead to conflict and violence, thus, environmental issues have security implications, and, hence, translate into redefining security. While others opine that environmental changes relate to peace and development, and not to security.

The developed countries and the least developed countries generally subscribe to the former approach. This group feels that globally, emerging environmental changes have the potential to cause conflicts. Environmental changes have already forced people to leave their traditional lands and homes. 'Environmental refugees' is an accepted term. And, historically, migration and refugees have remained a considerable source of conflict between nations. Environmental threats are generally trans-boundary. Therefore, it is logical to link environmental threats with national security policies.

Amongst other environmental challenges, there are fears that 'water' could be the the future 'oil'. At least in the limited context of international competition, water security in future is projected to be akin to the present day's oil (read energy) security. According to the 2002 United Nations World Water Development Report, during the previous 50 years, there were 507 conflictive events over water. Amongst these, 37 involved violence, of which 21 consisted of military acts. This obviously suggests linkages between the environment and national security. Therefore, this school of thought advocates that the issue of climate change and environmental security should be dealt with by the United Nations Security Council (UNSC).

On the other hand, fast developing countries, including India and China, consider environment and climate change a development issue, rather than a security threat. They argue that it is the post Cold War era America, and other developed nations, that are linking environmental issues with national security for their own national interests. The developing nations fear that the developed countries might use the UN Security Council as a tool to influence the development strategies and, thus, impact their state sovereignty.

There are opinions that the threat-based approach to environmental problems may deter the resolution of conflict and prove ineffective. Thus, for enhancing peace and economic stability, in place of securitising the environment, policy-makers must look for framing long-term, proactive environmental strategies that emphasise environmental preservation. Therefore, it is felt that environmental degradation issues, including climate change, should be dealt with by other UN bodies like the UN General Assembly or the UN Economic and Social Council or the UN Commission on Sustainable Development; and not by the UN Security Council (UNSC).

Nevertheless, the transition from environmental conflict to environmental security is perhaps justified by the desire to widen the horizon to issues concerning military establishments. It is important to sensitise militaries to newer forms of dissension and tension so that they are not limited by the conventional security definition and are able to appreciate inter-country relations and politics on environmental changes in all their complexities.

National security experts in India have also started considering environmental security as an important element of the national security paradigm.[23] The increasing importance given by the policy-makers to environmental issues like food security, energy security and climate change can be assessed from the fact that one of the eight verticals initiated at the National Security Advisory Board (NSAB) is dedicated to these issues.[24]

Environment and Military

Generally, the environment and the military are perceived to be at divergence. The military is considered an institution in the profession of arms, and employment of arms leads to pollution and environmental degradation. The ecological destruction caused by nuclear weapons is well documented. Therefore, the military is generally regarded as a one of the largest polluters. But this projection of the military, though partially true, is too simplistic and doesn't put across the complete picture. The actual relationship between the environment and the military is much more complex and needs greater and careful analyses. In a reference to climate change, Stephen Emmott, a scientist heading a laboratory in Cambridge, UK, working on climate change and other issues, emphatically brings out that military leadership is now part of virtually all the scientific conferences on climate change.[25]

Essentially, there are direct linkages between environmental stress and the military, at least at four levels. First, due to limited resources, the developing nations cannot afford to create and sustain a dedicated infrastructure to exclusively handle exigencies emerging out of environmental stresses. Therefore, national militaries invariably find themselves involved in operations arising out of environmental distresses, including disaster relief and humanitarian assistance operations. And the current environmental trends suggest that such requirements are bound to increase with time. Second, the environmental changes may have a direct impact on military operations. For example, increase in temperature would have a direct bearing on aircraft operations and flying capabilities. Rise in sea levels would affect the navy's coastal infrastructure and operations. In the 1980s, fighter operations at the Hindon Air base near Delhi were abandoned because of increased bird activity due to improper waste disposal of carcasses by the meat industry. Third, international treaties and mandates on climate change may have a direct bearing on the military operations. Management of Ozone Depleting Substances (ODS) under the Montreal Protocol of 1987 is a classic example. Militaries had to realign their approach towards the use of ODS substances like halons and chlorofluorocarbons (CFC).[26] Fourth, the mandate to align the peace-time role of the military, including training and exercises, with national, regional and global environmental policies and practices is likely to enhance. In 1988, the US Government Accounting Office (GAO) criticised the Department of Defence (DOD) for giving environmental compliance a low priority. In 1991, for the first time, the US included the issue of the environment in its National Security Strategy (NSS). Similarly, in the future, regional focus on environmental practices followed by the South Asian militaries may also increase. Emphasis on simulators, resource efficiency and renewable resources would also enlarge. Hence, militaries should be alive to these issues and military doctrines, strategies, policies, force structure and training should anticipate (and be prepared for) such mandates.

There are several international treaties/conventions/protocols that prohibit militaries from environmental degradation. The Environmental Modification Convention (ENMOD), formally the Convention on the Prohibition of Military or Any Other Hostile Use of Environmental Modification Techniques is one such treaty that came into force in the late 1970s and prohibits the military or other hostile use of environmental modification techniques having widespread, long-lasting or severe effects. The substance of this treaty was reasserted in the UN Framework Convention on Climate Change (UNFCCC) signed at the 1992 Earth Summit in Rio.

At the same time, these treaties are unable to deter leading governments of the world from pursuing research towards 'weather warfare'. The US government routinely conducts experiments on weather modification, and has been doing so for at least half a century. The US Department of Defence commenced research on weather modification in the late 1940s when the Cold War tensions were significantly high. Weather modification—previously classified under names such as "Project Cirrus" (1947) and "Project Popeye" (1966) is no longer a secret. In 1947, the US military attempted cloud seeding through the use of silver iodide to seed a hurricane, which later hit the Georgia coast near Savannah.[27] During the Vietnam War, under Project Popeye, cloud-seeding techniques were used with an objective to prolong the monsoon season and block enemy supply routes along the Ho Chi Minh Trail. It has been reported that the High-frequency Active Auroral Research Programme (HAARP) at Gakona, Alaska, primarily overseen by the US Air Force, through the Defence Advanced Research Projects Agency (DARPA), is an advanced scientific research programme with high-power radio frequency transmitter facility towards the exciting limited area of the ionosphere and analysing its effects. There are deep-rooted apprehensions that this facility has a capability that enables selective alteration of weather patterns and is an attempt to create a weapon of mass destruction through modification/change in weather that may result in earthquakes, floods, change in the monsoon pattern, etc. A 1996, the USAF report titled "Air Force 2025" recommends weather modification and weather intervention in warfare.[28] Weather detections and modification in terms of interventions in precipitation, storm, space weather, fog and cloud, etc have been recommended.[29] The endeavour is towards owning the weather and exploiting it as a force multiplier by capitalising on emerging technologies and focussing the development of these technologies to war-fighting applications.

As far as India is concerned, environmental sensitivities are ingrained in its culture and traditions. The Indian lifestyle is characterised by the tradition of self-denial and abstinence. Terms like 'three Rs of the environment—Reduce, Reuse and Recycle'—and 'sustainable development' have been coined in the present times, whereas the Indian culture inherently maintains frugality, and its leanings towards sustainability and conservation are well known.[30] India, as a nation, believes in the policy of peaceful coexistence and non-alignment, without holding any expansionist or revisionist designs. It follows the concept of defensive defence, and accordingly, the role of the military is largely reactive to external military threats. It has never initiated a war, rather all the wars have been thrust upon it. The Indian military has also been playing a significant role in 'aid to civil agencies', including Humanitarian Assistance and Disaster Relief (HADR). There is no evidence of India nurturing any intention to develop any kind of Weapon of Mass Destruction (WMD).

The military's sensitivity towards environmental degradation and its capabilities to preserve the environment would have a direct bearing on the national potential of addressing environmental challenges, in the hinterland as well as the border areas. The Indian military, the second largest employer in India, with about 14 lakh personnel (after the Indian Railways) and the largest landholder, maintains about 8.5 million hectares of land. There are about 27 lakh ex-Servicemen and, including families, there are more than two crore citizens in the military community.[31] Therefore, because of its sheer size, the actions of the Indian military can have a huge environmental impact. The greenery maintained at the military estates, including cantonments, is well known. Secondly, the Indian military operates in ecologically susceptible areas since most of our land borders with China, Pakistan, Bangladesh, Nepal and Bhutan are ecologically sensitive. India's maritime borders have their own challenges. Thirdly, in dealing with international and cross-border disasters, and in handling environmental issues near the border areas, military deployments would be the natural choice of response.

The Indian Army, being aware of its environmental obligations, has constituted a special establishment known as the 'Environment and Ecology Cell'. This cell works closely with the Ministry of Environment and Forests (MoEF) on environmental issues and conservation aspects. A 2006 Report of the National Forest Commission under the chairmanship of Justice BN Kripal brought out that the organisational structure, training, motivation, discipline, inter-communications and mobility of the Indian Army make it ideally suited for environmental protection.

With effect from 1981, the Eco Task Force (ETF), a successful model of a joint venture among the Indian Army, Territorial Army, MoEF and the state government, has been doing a commendable job in the field of eco-conservation and restoration through afforestation, soil conservation, restoration of the watershed, etc. There are eight ETFs working in different parts of the country, including the border areas and other regions of Uttarakhand, Rajasthan, Himachal Pradesh, Assam and J&K.

Table 7.1: ETF Deployments in India in 2008[32]

ETF (Regimental Affiliation)	State/Year of Raising	Tasks	Remarks
127 Infantry Battalion (TA) Ecological (Garhwal Rifles)	Uttarakhand/1982	a) Accomplished soil conservation in area Mahand of Siwalik ranges b) Restoration of Agar Watershed north of Mussoorie hills	- Two Company ETF till 2008; - Two additional companies sanctioned in April 2008
128 Infantry Battalion (TA) Ecological (Rajputana Rifles)	Rajasthan/1983	a) Completed afforestation in Area Pugal till Indira Gandhi Canal and creation of Amarpur Lake b) Converting Mohangarh, in Jaisalmer District, into green fields	Three Company ETF
129 Infantry Battalion (TA) Ecological (Jammu and Kashmir Light Infantry)	Jammu and Kashmir/1988	a) Restored catchment and watershed in Samba b) Afforestation and soil conservation in Bahu Jindra mountain range	One Company, with affiliated forest department personnel
130 Infantry Battalion (TA) Ecological (Kumaon Rwegiment)	Uttarakhand/1994	Restoration of forest wealth in Kumaon region in area Pithoragarh	Two Company ETF; Two additional companies sanctioned

132 Infantry Battalion (TA) Ecological (Rajput Regiment)	Union Territory of Delhi/ First Company in 2000 and second in 2005	a) Converting barren and mined land of Bhatti mines to a thick forest and park b) Compensatory plantation in area Ujawa near Najafgarh	The only ETF to claim Carbon Credits through the Clean Development Mechanism (CDM) under the Kyoto Protocol (through German sponsorship)
133 Infantry Battalion (TA) Ecological (Dogra Regiment)	Himachal Pradesh/2006	Ecological restoration of Sutlej basin	One Company ETF
134 and 135 Infantry Battalions (TA) Ecological (Assam Regiment)	Assam/2007	Afforestation in Rangia and Tamalpur	Both units are Three Company ETF

Additionally, there have been umpteen examples of ex-Servicemen and war veterans doing yeomen service in the field of eco-conservation. The eenvironmental and ecological contributions of Mahatma Gandhi, a war veteran of the Boer War, the Great European War and the Zulu 'rebellion' of Natal in 1906,[33] are splendidly acknowledged. Anna Hazare, a staunch Gandhian and war veteran of the Indian Army, has also made significant contributions to the development and ecological restoration of the town of Relagan Siddhi, which are globally recognised.[34] In the early 1980s, Air Chief Mshl Idris Latif, the then governor of the state of Maharashtra and the former chief of the Air Staff, successfully steered the cloud seeding project for afforestation in Maharashtra state.[35] Further research would certainly bring out more such instances of the Indian military's positive contribution towards the environment in many other ways. But is there a focus on this dimension of the Indian military?

Urgency of Environmental Cooperation

Globally, scientists have largely come to a consensus that the extent of environmental change is certainly being amplified by anthropogenic factors; and without resolute counteraction, this change will overstretch the natural ecosystem to a point of no return. It has been accepted that life support systems of the Earth cannot be replaced completely by technology and that uncompensated anthropogenic environmental risk to future generations is unacceptable. Towards this context, optimists opine that environmental change is a slow process and international initiatives and agreements will work, at least fast enough to avert further deterioration in the environment 2050 onwards. Whereas, the pessimist discourse warns that the limits of environmental change have already been reached; and by 2050, growing instability in the biosphere may result in the catastrophic collapse of the human population.

Failure to institutionalise fruitful environmental cooperation would deepen the lines of division in international relations. It would also increase conflict and tension within and between states over resources, especially water and land; and other related issues like management of migration, compensation payments between the countries mainly responsible for the environmental degradation and the countries that are most affected by its destructive effects. Environmental stresses could also result in destabilisation, conflicts, violence and even war, jeopardising national and international security in an unprecedented manner. The increasing tensions and conflicts within and between states may flare up unless concrete steps are taken at all possible levels—local, national, regional and global – to check the environmental degradation.

The global environmental challenges should be viewed as a crucial reason for the global community to unite and coordinate counter-actions. The international community must find reasons to unite and recognise environmental degradation as a threat to humankind and should make efforts to formulate a dynamic and well coordinated global environmental policy. Amongst several global initiatives, the United Nations Environment Programme (UNEP) and the Intergovernmental Panel on Climate Change (IPCC) are the prominent ones.

Regional Initiatives

The environment, a trans-national entity, cannot be compartmentalised according to political boundaries. Regional systems of environmental management are essential components of global environmental governance, complementing governance efforts at the national and global levels. It is a known fact that the environment is global but the world political structure requires that responses to it are to be enforced nationally.

In South Asia, several regional environmental cooperation initiatives, including initiatives by SAARC, South Asian Cooperative Environment Programme (SACEP), Bay of Bengal Initiative for Multi-Sectoral Technical and Economic Cooperation (BIMSTEC), International Centre for Integrated Mountain Development (ICIMOD), South Asian Network for Development and Environmental Economics (SANDEE) are in place.

SAARC, established in 1983, with its headquarters in Kathmandu, includes the countries of Bangladesh, Bhutan, India, Maldives, Nepal, Pakistan, and Sri Lanka (Afghanistan joined later). SAARC has a particular focus on economic cooperation, nevertheless, it also covers many aspects of regional cooperation, including the environment. SAARC has set up several technical committees in many fields. In 1992, the Committee on Environment was given the status of a Technical Committee. The implementation of the recommendations of the Regional Study on Greenhouse Effects has also been mandated to this committee. In 2009, in association with UNEP, SAARC brought out the South Asian Environment Outlook (SAEO), a comprehensive document on environmental issues and challenges in South Asia. Climate change was the main theme of the sixteenth SAARC summit held in Thimpu, Bhutan, in April 2010. In order to emphasise the focus on environmental issues, the summit declaration of this meeting was subtitled "Towards a Green and Happy South Asia".

SACEP's members include Afghanistan, Bangladesh, Bhutan, India, Iran, Maldives, Nepal, Pakistan, and Sri Lanka, and since its inception in 1982, it has initiated a number of projects for building national capacity to manage environmental issues. The overall focus of SACEP's activities includes capacity building and institutional strengthening; conservation and sustainable use of biodiversity; ecosystem conservation and management; environmental information and assessment; and education and awareness-raising. Some of the major programmes are: the SACEP South Asian Regional Seas Programme; Improvement of the Legal and Institutional Framework; Private and Public Cooperation Initiative.

A number of other trans-boundary environmental cooperation initiatives are also in place. The South Asia Development Initiatives is one such initiative that seeks to improve regional cooperation in the poorest parts of South Asia (Bangladesh, Bhutan, Nepal and eastern India) in water resource management, energy development and trade, and transport and commerce.

However, despite numerous initiatives and considerable inputs, the effectiveness of the framework and results in terms of mutual cooperation in real terms are questionable. Therefore, a study of regional cooperative mechanisms elsewhere is desirable.

Globally, several regional environmental initiatives are in place. Amongst them, the European Union (EU) and Association of Southeast Asian Nations (ASEAN) deserve a special mention. The EU has placed itself as the international agenda setter in climate change mitigation. It has adopted a number of policies towards this end. The EU can be seen as both an arena for member states to negotiate with each other and an actor in its own right in the international climate change negotiations. ASEAN is distinct in its "ASEAN Way" of regional cooperation, with a distinct collaborative approach with dimensions of non-interference in the domestic affairs of other nations and pursuance of the consensus building approach rather than legally binding treaties. Preference is for national implementation of programmes rather than reliance on a strong regionwide bureaucracy.

The 2005 ASEAN Regional Forum (ARF) seminar highlighted environmental degradation as one of the non-traditional security issues (Chair's Summary Report.

ASEAN Regional Forum Seminar on Enhancing Cooperation in the Field of Non-Traditional Security Issues, March 7-8, 2005, Sanya, China). The 2004 Indian Ocean tsunami caused 2,25,000 deaths in eleven countries, and since then, HADR has become an important element of the ASEAN Defence Ministers' Meetings (ADMM) and the ASEAN Chiefs of Defence Informal Meetings (ACDIFM), wherein use of ASEAN military assets and capacities in HADR is one of the priority agendas. A regional HADR standby force has also been suggested.

India is part of the ASEAN Defence Ministers' Meeting-Plus (ADMM-Plus), an official framework established in 2010 to bring together defence ministers from 18 countries – 10 ASEAN countries and eight 'plus' countries, including Australia, China, India, Japan, New Zealand, the Republic of Korea, Russia, and the United States.[36] This body appears to be emerging as a pillar of defence diplomacy and cooperation in the region, and deals with several regional security issues, including climate change and environmental degradation.

The IISS Asia Security Summit: The Shangri-La Dialogue (SLD) is another regional initiative. This inter-governmental security forum dialogue is held annually under the aegis of the International Institute for Strategic Studies (IISS), an independent think-tank. It is attended by defence ministers, permanent heads of ministries and military chiefs of 28 Asia-Pacific states. This dialogue considers environmental degradation as one of the major security challenges in Asia. Examining such dialogues would facilitate better understanding of current regional cooperation mechanisms.

The Way Ahead

The developed nations are better equipped to provide economic and health assistance and aid in managing the natural resources and environment of the country. Hence, their population groups are more likely to have a sense of belonging and thereby they seek national identity which mitigates the potential for internal conflicts. But developing countries have more prominent social and economic challenges as the available resources are much less than the national requirements. Thus, in economic/environmental difficulties, citizens are bound to be exposed to greater stress and, therefore, the domestic national/ethnic groups would observe, and resent, uneven and unfair treatment. Therefore, their governments are more prone to accusations of unfair distribution of resources, and the potential to exacerbate the political instability is much higher. Hence, it is more important for the developing nations to mainstream environmental issues and strive for sustainable development through mutual cooperation.

Confronting environmental change, mitigating its effects and adapting to the associated challenges indeed call for a multi-level and multi-disciplinary approach. Viable solutions for anthropogenic climate change can only be found by thinking afresh, outside the mainstream framework. The starting point has to be change in the mindset and behaviour of individuals. The Gandhian concept of addressing a crisis by stepping outside the framework of mainstream thinking and pondering afresh should be followed. Against the prevailing global craze of wars, arms and *giganticism*, Gandhi exhibited preference for 'non-violence', 'non-cooperation' and 'small-scale models'. Against consumerism, he opined that "the world has enough for everyone's need, but not enough for everyone's greed". For maintaining harmonious relations with nature, he would say that "for my material needs, my village is my world but for my spiritual needs, the whole world is my village". The need of the hour is to follow the path shown by Gandhi. For addressing such long-standing issues arising out of (and affecting) generations, patience and optimism must be the cornerstones. The Gandhian concept of being an "irrepressible optimist" with a strong belief in building a new world order, should be the guiding principle.

However, the Gandhian approach is generally discarded by the policy-makers and practitioners as somewhat idealistic. It is understandable that, *prima facie*, in many ways, the Gandhian philosophy appears to some as outdated and impractical, but a deeper understanding would reflect that his concepts are absolutely practical and stand the test of time. As a matter of fact, in the wake of increasing population and climate change, the relevance of his philosophy has only increased. For addressing environmental distresses, in his recent book, Stephen Emmott has also suggested that rather than technological breakthroughs, radical behavioural change appears to be the answer.[37]

The distrusts, ongoing political irritants and conflicts are undermining the prospects of environmental cooperation in South Asia. In such a geopolitical scenario, making headway in politically sensitive 'hard-core' issues like border conflicts is always difficult. Nevertheless, it is essential to keep exploring areas where regional countries can be engaged in mutual cooperation for strengthening of ties and reducing the trust deficit. Environmental stresses certainly belong to a category of issues which are politically less sensitive, yet exceedingly significant for promoting peace and sustainable development and avoiding conflicts. The Indo-Pak Indus Water Treaty of 1960 validates this reasoning, as the treaty has not been violated despite three wars and innumerable conflicts between the two countries. The bonhomie and cordial relationship achieved in the field of natural environment can be further harnessed to enhance cooperation in the more sensitive issues and reduce the general trust deficit. The cooperation and trust, thus, generated would also be helpful in resolving long-standing territorial disputes, especially between India and Pakistan. The possibility of transforming the LoC from the Line of Control to the Line of Cooperation should be explored. Involvement of the military in environmental stresses, and securitisation of the environment appear desirable to effectively address the environmental challenges and inter-state conflicts in South Asia.

Mainstreaming environmental issues in the military, and at other government levels, would be in the national and regional interest. Expertise gained through the technological, policy and procedural initiatives undertaken by the Indian military can be further leveraged for the larger national good. The history of application of military specific research in other fields is well documented. The Indian military, being a highly disciplined and well organised force, generally operating close to the natural environment, is an appropriate instrument of choice for eco-restoration. More ETFs should be created with a right blend of serving personnel, ex-Servicemen, the MoEF and the state government.

Despite several environmental cooperation initiatives in South Asia, the trust deficit amongst countries of South Asia continues. There is a need to strengthen cooperation and develop policy mechanisms that are mutually beneficial, implementable, and *monitorable*. The regional initiatives like the EU, ASEAN and Shangri-La Dialogue (SLD) have exhibited better results. Though, the ground realities in every region are unique, a deeper study of the various successful elements of these initiatives is desirable.

Conclusion

Environmental change may not lead to 'classic' 'force on force' inter-state wars, but environmental conflicts would certainly place greater non-conventional demands on the security and defence forces. In politically and economically overstretched states and societies, the challenge for the military and security forces would be to handle failing states and regions marred by diffused conflict structures. The failure of disaster management systems after extreme weather events and increasing environmental migration would pose unprecedented challenges to the national security framework. There is a need to mainstream environmental security and remodel and transform the military forces so that they are suitably equipped, trained and prepared to meet the emerging non-conventional environmental security challenges domestically, at inter-state borders as well as in overseas areas, away from international borders. In the wake of limited resources and pressing social and economic requirements in South Asia, military-military and civil-military cooperation is a necessary requirement. Effective and mutually beneficial cooperation would also be instrumental in reducing the prevailing trust deficit amongst the regional countries. Towards this cause, South Asia requires quality intellectual inputs and material resources that can strengthen existing mechanisms and undertake additional initiatives, if so required. Regional environmental cooperation pursuits can facilitate an atmosphere that would promote India's cultural ethos of peaceful coexistence, and further its national interests of economic and social growth in a peaceful manner.

Notes

1. Gyanu Adhikari, "Human Encroachment Caused Floods Disaster", *The Hindu*, July 23, 2013, accessed at http://www.thehindu.com/news/international/south-asia/human-encroachment-caused-floods-disaster/article4942030.ece?css=print on January 10, 2014.
2. There have been several attempts to define South Asia by numerous geographers, political scientists, strategists and even students of international relations. However, institutionally, the South Asian Association for Regional Cooperation (SAARC), established about three decades ago with seven member states – India, Pakistan, Sri Lanka, Nepal, Bhutan, Bangladesh and the Maldieves – is the only actual embodiment that is self-consciously South Asian, with regional parameters and perimeters. This chapter also follows this definition of South Asia. Afghanistan, though part of SAARC, has not been discussed primarily because of the prevailing uncertainties and flux.
3. "North and South Reel Under Weather Woes", *The Times of India* (New Delhi), January 10, 2014, p. 24.
4. *Climate Change as a Security Risk* (London: Earthscan, 2008) p. 5.
5. "Kiribati Man Seeks to Become the World's First Climate Change Refugee", *The Times of India* (New Delhi), October 19, 2013.
6. Rachel Carson, *Silent Spring* (London: Penguin, 1962), p. 258.
7. *The Millennium Project: Global Future Studies & Research,* accessed at http://www.millennium-project.org on June 12, 2013.
8. *The State of the Future 2012*, Executive Summary, accessed at http://www.millennium-project.org/millennium/SOF2012-English.pdf on June 25.
9. Jawaharlal Nehru, *The Discovery of India* (New Delhi: Penguin Books, 2004), p. 68.
10. VS Ganesamurthy, *Environmental Status and Policy in India* (New Delhi: New Century Publication, 2011), p. xix.
11. PR Chari, "Environmental Degradation and Conflicts in South Asia" in PR Chari, ed., *Alternative Approaches to Security* (Delhi: Samskriti, 2006), pp 331-425.
12. "The United Nations World Water Development Report 4" (Paris: UNESCO, 2012), ch 44, p. 822.
13. Nishant Gupta, "Environmental Stresses and Regional Cooperation: A Perspective", *Defence and Diplomacy*, vol. 2, n. 4, pp. 23-32.
14. Sundeep Waslekar, *The Final Settlement: Resurrecting India-Pakistan Relations* (Mumbai: International Centre for Peace Initiatives, 2005), pp. 47-48. And Nitin Pai, "Climate Change and National Security: Preparing India for New Conflict Scenarios", *The Indian National Interest Policy Brief,* No 1, April 2008.
15. Aditi Phadnis, "A Water Conflict in Kashmir", *Business Standard*, May 16, 2005, accessed at http://www.strategicforesight.com/sfgnews_122.htm, on May 13, 2013.
16. "How Green was my Valley?: Climate Change Will Only Intensify Problems in Kashmir" *The Economist*, Asia Edition October 23, 2008, accessed at http://www.economist.com/node/12480378 on March 18, 2013.
17. "Bangla Migration to India Largest in the Developing World", *The Times of India* (New Delhi), September 13, 2013.

18. Uttam Kumar Sinha, Sreedha Datta, Sunil Chauhan and PK Gautam, "Impact on India's Bilateral Relations with Neighbouring Countries" in *Report of the IDSA Working Group: Security Implications of Climate Change for India*, (New Delhi: Academic Foundation, 2009), pp. 127-141.
19. India, being the largest partner in South Asia, has greater responsibility towards playing a lead role in strengthening partnerships with its South Asian neighbours since a cooperative atmosphere created by environmental cooperation would also further the cause of regional security.
20. n. 4, ch. 2, pp. 19-23.
21. Tuchman Mathews, "Redefining Security", *Foreign Affairs* 68, pp 162-177.
22. *Human Security Initiative,* official website, accessed at http://www.humansecurityinitiative.org/definition-human-security on September 13, 2013.
23. Jasjit Singh, *India's Security: In a Turbulent World* (New Delhi: National Book Trust, 2013), p. 27.
24. Shyam Saran, chairman NSAB and special envoy to the PM, during the inaugural address at a round-table discussion on India's nuclear strategy held on December 19, 2013, at Air Force Auditorium, Subroto Park, New Delhi.
25. Stephen Emmott, *Ten Billion* (London: Penguin, 2013), pp 148-149.
26. Air Mshl AK Singh, Wing Cdr Manoj Kumar, Atul Bagai, *Ozone Protection and National Security: A Military Perspective* (New Delhi: UNEP, 2009).
27. "The US Government Routinely Conducts Experiments on Weather Modification", accessed at http://www.globalresearch.ca/the-u-s-government-routinely-conducts-experiments-on-weather-modification/7139, on January 14, 2014.
28. Prof Michel Chossudovsky, "Weather Warfare: Beware the US Military's Experiments with Climatic Warfare", *The Ecologist,* December 2007, accessed at www.globalresearch.ca/weather-warfare-beware-the-us-military-s-experiments-with-climatic-warfare/7561, accessed on March 14, 2013.
29. Col Tamzy J. House et al, "Weather as a Force Multiplier: Owning the Weather in 2025", Paper presented to "Air Force 2025" in 1996, Executive Summary, p. vi.
30. Though in the recent past, especially post liberalisation, it is felt that consumerism is making inroads in a big way.
31. NN Vohra, "Civil-Military Relations: Opportunities and Challenges", *Air Power,* vol. 8, no. 4, October-December 2013, p. 1.
32. PK Gautam, *Environmental Security: New Challenges and Role of the Military* (New Delhi: Shipra Publications, 2010) , p. 28; and "Eco-Task Forces Raised in Several States", Press Information Bureau, Government of India, Ministry of Environment and Forests, Rajya Sabha, April 24, 2008 accessed at pib.nic.in/newsite/PrintRelease.aspx on January 11, 2014.
33. Gandhian Institutes Bombay Sarvodaya Mandal & Gandhi Research Foundation website, accessed at http://www.mkgandhi.org/momgandhi/chap93.htm, on January 11, 2014.
34. "Ralegan Siddhi : A Model of Sustainable Development" accessed at http://www.annahazare.org/ralegan-siddhi.html, on January 11, 2014.
35. Bilkees I Latif, *The Ladder of His Life* (New Delhi: KW, 2013), pp 281-284.
36. ASEAN official website accessed at http://www.asean.org/communities/asean-political-security-community/category/asean-defence-ministers-meeting-admm, on January 14, 2014.
37. Emmott, n. 25, p. 193.

8

China's Defence Spending

Raj Mongia

On December 20, 2013, China's military lashed out at Japan's plans to boost defence spending, accusing Tokyo of raising regional tensions under the pretext of safeguarding national security, saying it "resolutely opposes" the five-year defence plan adopted by its rival earlier that week. Japan "continues to deny its history of World War II aggression, challenge the post-war order, and harm the feelings of the people of those victimised nations," China's Defence Ministry spokesman Geng Yansheng said in a statement posted on the ministry's website. Japan will raise defence spending by 5 percent over the next five years to purchase its first surveillance drones, more jet fighters and naval destroyers, and set up an amphibious unit similar to the US Marines. Other outlets have reported that Japan will increase its military spending by 2.6 percent. To achieve that spending increase, Japan will reportedly use streamlining measures to cut costs at other places. China's strongly worded statement marks the latest salvo in the ongoing string of accusations over who is responsible for a sharp rise in tensions in the East China Sea. Broader defence programme guidelines also adopted on December 17, 2013, say Japan is "gravely concerned" about China's growing maritime and military presence in the East China Sea, and its lack of transparency and "high-handed" approach. In late November 2013, China said all aircraft entering a vast zone over the East China Sea must identify themselves and follow China's instructions.[1]

China's military has taken an increasingly hawkish stance amidst a bitter dispute that has erupted with Tokyo over the uninhabited islands in the sea controlled by Japan but claimed by China. Japan's nationalisation of the islands in September 2012 sparked violent demonstrations in several Chinese cities. In the months since, Chinese patrol vessels have routinely confronted Japanese ships in the area, sparking fears of an incident.[2]

Around a year ago, a statement justifying the country's stand was issued by the top leadership of China.

> Building a strong national defence and powerful armed forces that are commensurate with China's international standing and meet the needs of its security and development interests is a strategic task of China's modernization drive...
>
> — Hu Jintao, in a speech to the Party Congress, November 8, 2012.

Perhaps this justification was a precursor to the defence budget which was to be unveiled four months later. The release of China's defence budget is an annual event watched keenly by defence analysts the world over. Surprisingly, some established practices were done away with this year. The procedure of declaring the figures a day prior to the National People's Congress (NPC) convention was also changed, in keeping with the ongoing change in leadership. The defence budget figures were released on March 5, 2013, just before Wen Jiabao's 'work report' to the 12th NPC. The figures neither evoked surprise nor caused a flutter because they were along expected lines—a 10.7 per cent increase over 2012 to RMB 720.2 billion ($117 billion; the figure varies between $114 and 117 billion in various sources). In the past, China's defence budget had increased at an average 15.9 per cent from 1998 to 2007, 14.5 per cent from 1988 to 1997, and 3.5 per cent from 1978 to 19 87. In 2012, it increased by 11.2 per cent to RMB 670.2 billion ($106.4 billion) over the 2011 figures of RMB 602.6 billion ($95.4 billion). In terms of percentage of the Gross Domestic Product (GDP), this year's budget was pegged at 1.3 per cent of the GDP, a marginal increase from 1.28 per cent in 2012, but below the 1.33 per cent registered in 2008.

Zhao Xiaozhuo, deputy director of the Academy of Military Sciences, a think-tank of the People's Liberation Army (PLA), had justified the continued double-digit growth in China's defence spending thus: China's vast land and maritime frontiers, four nuclear neighbours, and the four disputed areas in its proximity have exacerbated tensions in the region. Falling back on the cliché of the "century of humiliation", he asserted that it was essential to modernise, to avoid being attacked again. Finally, Zhao emphasised that "diversified military tasks" have increased the multifaceted roles of the PLA. All these necessitated a double digit increase in military spending.[3] Zhao also criticised the Western media as having "made it their wont to criticize China's defense budget" without taking into account the fact that "China's per capita expenditure on defense is only 3.46 percent of the US, 8.29 percent of the United Kingdom and 18.45 percent of Japan, according to the *SIPRI Yearbook 2012*, published by the Stockholm International Peace Research Institute, an international defence think-tank."[4]

At the official level, the Parliament spokesperson Fu Ying was quick to state, "It's not good news for the world that a country as large as China is unable to protect itself....China's peaceful foreign policies and its defensive military policies are conducive to security and peace in Asia."[5] And as if to give the budget acceptability, the *Global Times*, in a poll conducted the same day, stated that as many as 50.1 per cent people agreed that the budget was 'reasonable' and 28.7 per cent wanted it to be increased. Only 12.7 per cent said that it should be cut while 8.5 per cent had 'no opinion'.[6]

It is no secret that the actual figures of China's budget lack transparency. In its 2012 report on China's military, the US Defence Department estimated actual spending of $120 to $180 billion in 2011, well above China's official figure that year of $91.5 billion.[7] This year, using the average variation factor of 1.6 times of the last year, it could be assessed to be approximately $187 billion. The final expenditure also tended to vary from the budgeted amount. In 2012, actual spending reached RMB 691.3 billion compared with the budgeted RMB 670.3 billion,[8] an increase of almost 3.5 per cent which led to an overall increase of 14.7 per cent over the 2011 figures!

Hidden Spending

John McCreary, a veteran defence intelligence analyst, was quoted in the *Washington Times* as saying, "The announced figure does not include Chinese spending on defence research and development, arms procurement and defence industrial activities."[9] Nor are procurements of weapons from abroad, expenses on paramilitaries, nuclear weapons and strategic rocket programmes, state subsidies for the military-industrial complex, some military-related research and development, and extra-budget revenue included in the budget. The other major exclusion in the budget is the proceeds from the sale of weapons and equipment manufactured at the armament factories owned by the PLA.[10]

Correlation Between Defence Budget and the Economy

A study of China's previous national defence papers reveals that the country links the defence budget to its economy.[11] In the last three years, the rise in the defence budget has been proportional to the growth rate of the economy (see Fig 8.1). This is an indicator that the PLA has limited influence in demanding budget raises with the Party. In a sense, it also sanctifies the relationship between the PLA and the Communist Party of China (CPC)—clearly, the PLA being subservient to the Party. In 2010, China's economy grew by 10.4 per cent over the previous year. In 2011, it dropped to 9.3 per cent and further to 7.8 per cent in 2012. There has been a corresponding decrease in the rate at which the defence budget grew: 12.7 per cent in 2011-12, 11.2 per cent in 2012-13, and now 10.7 per cent for 2013-14.

On the other hand, it would be interesting to note the actual budget expenditure after adjustment for inflation. Last year, China had set a target of containing inflation at 4 percent and achieved an actual inflation rate of 2.6 per cent.[12] Thus, the net increase of China's defence budget in real terms was 12.1 per cent.[13] This year, China has set its inflation target at 3.5 per cent.[14] Hence, one can conclude that the minimum increase in real terms will be over 7 per cent, which is in line with the projected economic growth rate of 7.5 per cent for the coming year, adjusted for inflation.

Fig 8.1: China's GDP and Defence Budget

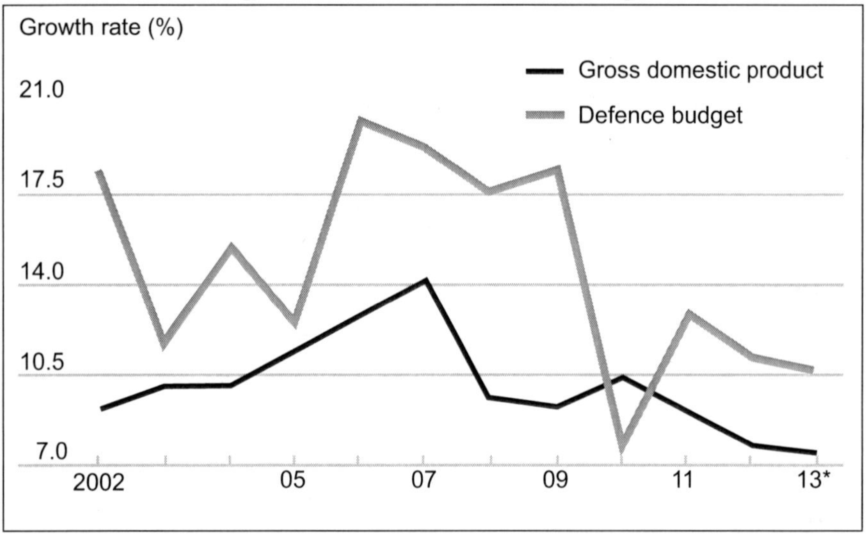

* Official forecast
Source: Ministry of National Defence, Nation Bureau of Statistics of China

Internal Security

Addressing the 12th People's Congress on March 5, 2013, Premier Wen Jiabao listed "maintaining social harmony and stability" as one of the government's priorities for this year. He said: "We should improve the mechanism for assessing potential risks major policy decisions may pose for social stability....The purpose of this work is to preserve law and order and promote social harmony and stability."

For the third year in a row, the internal security (also called public security) budget has exceeded the defence budget. Last year, it stood at RMB 701.8 billion ($111 billion) and this year, it has marginally increased by 8.7 per cent to RMB 769 billion. In 2011, expenditure on public security was RMB 624 billion, an increase of 13.8 per cent over the 2010 figure and almost RMB 23 billion more than that year's defence budget of RMB 601 billion.

China projected bigger spending on internal security than on defence in 2011-12. Perhaps the government tightened physical and technological controls to quash calls for a "Jasmine Revolution" like the one shaking the Arab world. On the first day of the 2011 annual meeting of China's legislature, a Finance Ministry budget report showed that actual spending on law and order last year was RMB 548.6 billion ($83.5 billion), slightly more than what was budgeted for the year. That compared with the officially reported military expenditure of RMB 533.5 billion ($81.2 billion) in 2010. The same report showed that spending in the year 2011 on police, state security, armed civil militia, courts and jails would total to RMB 624.4 billion ($95 billion), an increase of 13.8 percent over 2010.

China's 2011 military budget, by comparison, is RMB 601.1 billion ($91.5 billion), representing a rise of 12.7 percent over last year, a government spokesman announced. That meant that China's internal security spending was growing faster than its defence spending. Actual spending on defence was probably far higher as the official budget omits key items such as arms imports, according to foreign analysts, but they say the same was also true of the public security budget, which did not include all covert surveillance, for example. The report did not detail what exactly the internal security budget would be spent on, but Premier Wen Jiabao suggested in his annual work report that some of the internal security budget would be channelled towards Internet controls. "We will strengthen and improve the system of public security," he said. "We will improve the contingency response system, and enhance society's capacity to manage crises and withstand risks. We will intensify our information security and secrecy, and improve management of information networks."

The increase in the headline figure for law and order perhaps reflected the Chinese leaders' concerns about the potential for the kind of unrest which has wracked the Middle East and North Africa over the previous month, analysts said.

It reinforced concerns among some Chinese scholars that China's immense internal security apparatus is diverting funds away from welfare and other public services that might address the root causes of social unrest. China's security services are engaged in an intense and prolonged crackdown on dissent triggered by anonymous online calls for silent "strolling" protests in dozens of Chinese cities every Sunday. There have been few signs of actual protests since the appeals began circulating two weeks ago on Twitter and other sites which could only be seen in China by wealthier urbanites, who use proxy servers or virtual private networks to circumvent web filters. But China has responded with a massive show of force, detaining or confining to their homes dozens of political activists, and tightening Internet controls, especially on hugely popular Twitter-like micro-blogging sites.

The Chinese police had also reimposed some of the restrictions on foreign journalists that were lifted in the run-up to the Beijing Olympics in 2008, and warned them that they would have their visas revoked if they violate those restrictions. Police summoned dozens of foreign reporters to video-recorded meetings in which many were told they were no longer permitted to go to the places where the protests were supposed to happen. The *Beijing Daily* newspaper, which is the mouthpiece for the Communist Party in the capital, issued one of the loudest public warnings against people taking part in anti-government protests. "Everyone knows that stability is a blessing and chaos is a calamity," it said in a commentary. "Those people intent on concocting and finding Middle East-style news in China will find their plans come to nothing."[15]

Analysts continue to cite a larger domestic security budget as an indication of growing unrest, instability and protests within China. But they ignore the fact that social stability through public security measures, also called 维护社会稳定（*Wéihù shèhuì wěndìng*）, or *Wéiwěn* in short, is the responsibility of the Central Political and Legislative Affairs Committee. Public security spending is distributed among four ministries in China: the Ministry of Public Security, the Ministry of Railways, the Ministry of Justice, and the General Administration of Civil Aviation. Within each ministry, the expenditure on public security may be just 50 per cent while the rest goes to diplomacy, education, etc. According to a European Council on Foreign Relations (ECFR) report, the "Chinese government uses this complex situation to blur the distinction between spending that is dedicated to the maintenance of social stability and that which is not."[16] The report also states that 77 per cent of the public security budget goes to the People's Armed Police (PAP) whose responsibilities have been increased by the implementation of the "six forces" policy in 2012. The "six forces" policy envisages converting the PAP into a "modern, integrated and multi-tasking force" comprising counter-insurgency forces, anti-terrorism forces, emergency first aid and rescue teams and forest fire-fighting forces.[17]

In fact, on March 14, 2013, the government announced a restructuring of some ministries, one of them being the Ministry of Railways, which is being divided into two: operations under a newly created state-owned enterprise, the China Railway Corporation, and administration under the Ministry of Transport. Thus, it might be prudent to conclude that while social unrest and protests might continue to be prevalent in China, the main reason for the sudden and sustained increase in the public security budget is the revamping of the entire public security apparatus and the ongoing reform process in China. Once the structures are in place, we may see a reversal in expenditure trends in the defence budget in China.

Reactions from Various Quarters

According to Japan's senior-most government spokesman and chief Cabinet Secretary, Yoshihide Suga, "Growth has been in double digits for three years running.... China must enhance the transparency of both its defence policy and regarding its military forces."[18] Defence officials said, "The modernization of fighter jets, an aircraft carrier, destroyers and other weaponry presents a threat to us."[19] Japan's own budget was proposed to be raised for the first time in 11 years, and was awaiting approval.

When Japan announced its plans to significantly increase its defence spending over the next five years to acquire surveillance drones, fighter jets, naval destroyers and amphibious vehicles to counteract China's growing military activity in the region, China obviously did not like the reference. New defence and security strategies ordered by Japan's conservative Prime Minister, Shinzo Abe, and approved on December 17, 2013, include the creation of a new amphibious unit modelled on the US Marines, which would be called on to retake islands captured by an enemy – a clear response to Chinese naval and aerial activity near the disputed Senkaku Islands. Relations between Japan and China have sunk to their lowest point in decades over the East China Sea islands, which are administered by Japan but also claimed by China.

Over the past year, Chinese surveillance ships have made regular incursions into waters near the islands, and last month, Beijing increased the pressure on Tokyo when it declared an air-defence identification zone across a wide area of the East China Sea that includes the Senkakus, known in China as the Diaoyus. The islands' location makes them strategically important, and they are thought to lie amid potentially huge natural gas deposits. Abe said the new guidelines did not mark a departure from Japan's post-war pacifism or the strictly defensive posture of its armed forces. "The strategy is designed to make our foreign and security policy clear and transparent both at home and abroad," he said. "We will do our part in contributing to global peace and security further."

Allusions to China's military spending, however, and its increasing naval activity in the region signal Japan's intention to bolster its military in the face of an "increasingly tense" security environment. In a clear reference to Chinese activity near the Senkakus and Beijing's recent insistence that foreign aircraft identify themselves before using the air-defence zone, Japan accused China of ignoring international norms.

"China is attempting to change the status quo by force in the skies and seas of the East China Sea and South China Sea and other areas, based on its own assertions, which are incompatible with the established international order," the country's first national security strategy, launched on the same day as the defence guidelines, stated. China's stance toward other countries, and military moves, coupled with a lack of transparency regarding its military and national security policies, represent a concern to Japan and the wider international community and require close watch.

The defence guidelines said, however, that Japan would *"promote security dialogues and exchanges with China and develop confidence-building measures to avert and prevent unexpected situations"*. On a visit to both countries, US Vice-President Joe Biden said he was deeply concerned by China's imposition of the air-defence zone, saying it has increased the risk of accidents and miscalculations that could quickly spiral into an armed conflict.

"We will continue to explain ourselves by sending people directly to the surrounding countries, starting with China," Japan's Foreign Minister Fumio Kishida, said. China responded by accusing Japan of indulging in "big-power geopolitics" aimed at its increasingly powerful neighbour. "If Japan really hopes to return itself to the ranks of a 'normal country', it should face up to its aggression in history and cooperate with its Asian neighbours instead of angering them with rounds and rounds of unwise words and policies," the state-run Xinhua news agency said.[20]

The *Taipei Times* was muted in its comment, with no official government statement. There was no major comment from *The Jakarta Post* or *The Jakarta Globe. The Washington Post* noted, "The higher military spending may be an important tool for Xi as he moves to shore up personal relations with China's generals and consolidate his power." Quoting Maj Gen Luo Yuan, deputy secretary-general of the Military Science Society and an outspoken officer, the paper said, "Our foreign policy goal is peaceful development and strengthening defensive abilities rather than growing our ability to plunder others."[21] Overall, the world's view on the budget appeared subdued and acquiescent. This is in contrast to the anxiety and concern expressed by various countries on China's budget presented in March 2012.[22]

In India, there was no official comment from the government. *The Times of India* reported that "China significantly upped its defence spending by over 10 %, a rise that will be watched nervously in India. Particularly, since India's own defence budget is constrained not only by decreased funding, but also by a distinct lack of strategic planning."[23] The *Deccan Chronicle* quoted well-known defence analyst Cmde C. Uday Bhaskar (Retd.) as saying, "China is taking its national security requirements in a very serious, focused and determined manner which is a contrast to the Indian example. China is focusing on its trans-border military capability and this is of very deep strategic import."[24] The UPI's headline read, "Increasing Chinese Defence Budget Alarms India", but aside from that had little content to justify the alarm.[25] In short, the budget did not draw much attention of the Indian government or media.

Unravelling China's Defence Spending Mystery

With China once again announcing a major expansion in its defence spending, outside observers are again left to debate what all this could mean. Unfortunately, the planned 10.7 percent increase for 2013 posed more questions than it answered: is it a sign of a more assertive China that wants to pursue regional dominance? Is it an indication of a country seeking to redress long-term weaknesses in its military? Or is it a sign of a domestic leadership that can't say no to the military at a time of political transition? The fact is that it's a bit of all of these.[26]

Chinese Point of View

China's limited transparency concerning its defence spending harms strategic trust, but foreign analysts often lose sight of important realities. Specific details remain unclear, but China's defence spending overall is no mystery: it supports PLA modernisation and personnel development as well as its announced objectives of securing China's homeland and asserting control over contested territorial and maritime claims, with a focus on the Near Seas (the Yellow, East, and South China Seas). The succeeding paragraphs offer a greater context and wider perspective for Chinese and Western discussions of China's rise and its concomitant military build-up, through a nuanced and comprehensive assessment of its defence spending and military transparency.[27]

Whatever the exact size of the defence spending of the People's Republic of China (PRC), it is now the world's second largest. Its rapid increase over the past two decades is a development of considerable significance to the world, yet it remains poorly understood. Many analysts have a tendency to focus on the most unsettling aspects of China's military strategic and budgetary opacity while overlooking the context in which relevant policy choices are made. The result is often an oversimplistic narrative about China's rise and long-term strategic intentions. A salient example of the problematic, decontextualised discourse about China's defence spending is the charge of Donald Rumsfeld, then US secretary of defence, at the June 2005 Shangri-La Dialogue: "Since no nation threatens China, one must wonder: Why this growing investment [in defence]? Why these continuing large and expanded arms purchases? Why these continued deployments?"[28] As the succeeding paragraphs will demonstrate, however undesirable to foreign observers the PRC's military build-up may be, the trajectory of the People's Liberation Army (PLA) is increasingly amenable to external analysis: it is focussed primarily on explicitly identified contingencies and is not particularly surprising. To be clear: to say that China's military trajectory is not as mysterious as is commonly believed is not to say that the PLA's growing capabilities should not be an issue of concern to other states or that China's military has achieved a sufficient level of transparency; nor is it to deny that some of China's recent rhetoric and behaviour toward its neighbours in East Asia has had a deleterious effect on regional stability. Nevertheless, inferences about China's strategic intentions and judgments about the appropriate policy response should be based on a full consideration of the available data, rather than focussed only on the concerns raised by what some might term the "known unknowns" about China's military trajectory.[29]

Although many of these and other specific criticisms raised about China's defence spending are valid, the conclusions about the broader strategic uncertainty surrounding China's short-term military development that many observers reach based on those criticisms are often overwrought. While China's official defence budget does not capture all defence-relevant spending, it is not exceptional in this regard: estimates of any country's total defence-related spending, to the extent that they are possible at all using open sources, are contingent on a subjective judgment about what constitutes "defence-related spending." Despite perennial limitations in China's budgetary transparency, the information currently available about China's priorities and investment is sufficient to develop a good sense of its broader military trajectory. A more complete understanding of the drivers of, and trends in, China's military development and defence spending and the international context in which China's rise is occurring, as well as a forecast of likely developments in the future, are necessary to ensure appropriate policy responses from the international community.

Here it is argued that what open-source data reveal *in aggregate* about the broader trends in China's defence spending is significant. The growth in spending over the past two decades is driven primarily by a desire to modernise and professionalise the PLA after decades of neglect and military backwardness. Throughout much of the post-1978 reform era, the real-world effects of China's nominal defence spending have been mitigated heavily by rampant inflation. Even during recent periods of relatively low inflation, rapid defence budget increases have been roughly consistent with overall GDP growth and outpaced by the growth in total state financial expenditures. Beijing's official defence budget increasingly captures actual PLA funding, and the PLA's widely criticised opacity is improving gradually; it is not as exceptional among countries at its stage of economic development as is widely believed. Defence spending growth over the past two decades has led to significantly improved military capabilities, the most significant of which are designed primarily to address contingencies in the Near Seas and their immediate approaches rather than further afield. Recent defence spending increases are sustainable, at least in the near term, and could be augmented considerably and directed to support selected overseas contingencies. However, in the medium to long term, worsening economic and demographic pressures may impel China's leaders to shift budget resources elsewhere and thereby limit further military spending growth.

Defence Spending Trends

Beijing announces a single overall figure for its official defence budget for the year during the annual March session of the National People's Congress. This figure is usually revised at a later date to reflect routine adjustments to actual spending during the course of the year.

Although it is common knowledge that China's official defence budget has increased in nominal terms at an average annual rate above 10 per cent since 1990, our analysis of a wide spectrum of the publicly available data reveals that several less known, but important, qualifications should be included in any discussion of the topic. First, throughout much of the post-1978 "reform and opening up" period, rampant inflation has mitigated the real-world impact of nominally large budget increases (see Table 8.1). Calculations of China's defence budget at constant prices (which account for the effect of inflation) show that in many years, the effective growth rate of China's defence spending is much lower than the widely cited current price ("nominal") figures suggest. The differences between the nominal (current price) and real (constant price) average annual growth rates are remarkable: 1.6 per cent vs. -3.2 per cent (1980-89); 15.7 per cent vs. 7.8 per cent (1990-99); 16.5 per cent vs. 12.5 per cent (2000-09); and 10.4 per cent vs. 3.1 per cent over the 2010-11 period. In other words, when calculated in real terms, the average annual increases in the budget exceeded 10 per cent during only one of the ten-year periods in Table 1: 2000-09. This suggests that unqualified statements along the lines of "China's official defence budget has increased by double-digits since year 1990," while in most cases technically true in nominal terms, may exaggerate the real-world effects of these budget increases.[30]

Table 8.1: PRC Defence Spending-Related Comparative Statistics, 1980-2011

Defence budget growth rate	1980-1989 (annual average)	1990-1999 (annual average)	2000-2009 (annual average)	2010-2011 (annual average)
at current prices	1.6 %	15.7 %	16.5 %	10.4 %
at constant prices	-3.2 %	7.8 %	12.5 %	3.1 %
GDP growth rate	9.8 %	10.0 %	10.3 %	9.8 %
State financial expenditures (*guojia caizheng zhichu*) growth rate aggregate				
at current prices	8.6 %	16.8 %	19.3 %	19.5 %
at constant prices	3.5 %	8.8 %	15.1 %	11.6 %

Second, throughout most of the post-1978 period, the rapid growth in China's official defence budget has been outpaced consistently by even *faster* increases in overall state financial expenditures, both of which, it should be emphasised, coincide with China's surging GDP (see Table 8.1). And in all periods, the rate of increase in aggregate state financial expenditures (which includes both central and local spending) has exceeded that of the defence budget. For example, the official defence budget has decreased (near-monotonically) from 9.5 per cent of total state financial expenditures in 1994 to 5.5 per cent in 2011.[31] To the extent that these official figures reflect trends in actual spending, these data suggest a very important point: with each passing year, China's military forces receive – on average – a *declining* percentage of the government's largesse. In other words, China's investment in its military development, while increasing at a rapid rate, has been outpaced by the government's overall spending, and does not come close to dominating national priorities – in stark contrast to that of, say, the former Soviet Union. Official data are, thus, consistent with official government statements that defence modernisation (i.e. spending) is subordinate to, but coordinated with, China's principal national objective: economic development.

Nevertheless, there is no denying that the recent surge in China's defence spending is remarkable, no matter how it is calculated and despite the fact that it began from a very low base (see Table 8.2). Over the past decade (2002-11), China's defence budget increased at a rate far exceeding that of any other major power, albeit roughly consistent with GDP growth. At 11.2 per cent, the expected annual increase in the nominal 2012 official defence budget to RMB670.2 billion (approximately US$106.4 billion)[32] makes China's official defence budget almost thrice that of similarly sized India and second only to that of the United States.

Extrabudgetary Sources, Western Criticisms, Budget Reforms, Omitted Inclusions, and Transparency Trends

After Beijing announces its annual defence budget each March, copious Western analyses criticised China's low transparency and the exclusion of major defence-related spending from its official defence budget. Many analysts claim (implicitly or explicitly) that China intentionally underreports actual military spending. As described in the following paragraphs, major items not included in the official defence budget that become targets of Western censure include: the budget of the 660,000-strong People's Armed Police (PAP); some domestic procurement and Research and Development (R&D) expenses; overseas purchases of major weapons and platforms; contributions from regional and local governments; extra-budgetary revenues and resources from a limited number of military commercial enterprises (e.g. hotels, hospitals, and strategic infrastructure); and militarily relevant portions of China's space programme budget. Other extra-budgetary resources, some of which have attracted less scrutiny, include central and local government defence mobilisation funds, one-time entrance bonuses for college students, authorised sales of land or excess food produced by some units, providing personnel for motion pictures, and donations of goods, services and money by local governments and enterprises to units and demobilised personnel.[33]

Table 8.2: PRC Official Defence Budget Annual Data, 2002-2011

GDP growth rate	2002	2003	2004	2005	2006	2007	2008	2009	2010	2011
at current prices	9.1%	10.0%	10.1%	11.3%	12.7%	14.2%	9.6%	9.2%	10.4%	9.2%
Defence Budget (RMB Billion)										
at current prices	170.8	190.8	220.0	247.5	297.9	355.5	417.9	495.1	533.3	602.7
at 2002 constant prices	170.8	186.0	200.6	217.1	251.8	279.1	304.4	362.9	366.6	385.3
as % of GDP	1.42%	1.40%	1.38%	1.34%	1.38%	1.34%	1.33%	1.45%	1.33%	1.28%
Defence Budget growth rate										
at current prices	18.4%	11.7%	15.3%	12.5%	20.4%	19.3%	17.6%	18.5%	7.7%	13.0%
at 2002 constant prices	18.4%	11.4%	14.0%	11.0%	17.2%	15.2%	12.8%	13.6%	5.3%	8.3%

Perhaps the largest alleged exclusion from the official defence budget is the budget of the PAP. Distinct from the PLA, however, the PAP's primary focus is domestic: its responsibilities include routine guard duties, fire-fighting, public emergency response (e.g. natural disaster relief), counter-terrorism and border security. In peace-time, the PLA does not routinely support PAP domestic stability operations. In the event of war, the PAP's secondary mission is to support the PLA in local defence. Because of these disparate roles, the PRC government categorises the PAP budget under expenditures for public security, while the PLA budget is under expenditures for national defence – separate line items in publicly available government statistical yearbooks.

The PRC does not release any information publicly about the specific costs of procuring weapons and equipment built by the domestic defence industry; nor does it publicise how defence-related R&D funds are allocated to PLA armament research institutes and civilian defence contractors. Defence-related R&D funding may come from several parts of the government (e.g. the State Administration for Science, Technology and Industry for National Defence and the Ministry of Science and Technology) or defence firms.

Although most PLA procurement is domestically sourced, a significant percentage (by cost) of its most advanced weapons technology and some weapons platforms is acquired overseas. In addition to purchases of complete systems (e.g. Kilo-class submarines and Sovremenny-class destroyers), many of China's most advanced defence technologies originate from foreign-assisted development (officially authorised or otherwise) and/or licensed production and reverse-engineering of existing foreign platforms. These include the PLA Air Force (PLAAF) Jian-11B fighter, based on Russia's SU-27, and the Jian-15 fighter, based on Russia's SU-33. The money spent on these imports is believed to come from special accounts controlled by the State Council (not the PLA) that are not included in the official defence budget.[34] Although arms imports have declined as China's domestic defence industry has become more capable, continued difficulties in developing key technologies, such as mass-producing modern high-performance aero-engines, suggest that China will continue to rely on imports from Russia for at least several more years. Meanwhile, the volume of Chinese weapon exports remains relatively small, but is growing rapidly; exports increased a total of 95 per cent between the 2002-06 and the 2007-11 periods. China is now the sixth-largest arms exporter by volume.[35]

China's defence budget is frequently criticised for not including provincial defence-related spending, such as the cost of operating military bases, and demobilisation and resettlement funds resulting from major force reductions since 1997. These are thought to come from the Ministry of Civil Affairs and local governments.[36] Local governments also contribute to reserve and militia expenses, including personnel costs for local civilian cadres working in grassroots People's Armed Forces departments. According to 2010 government statistics, only 2.94 per cent of defence expenditures was covered by local governments.[37]

China's general lack of transparency about how its official defence budget is calculated makes judging the validity of these Western criticisms very difficult. However, the potential significance of the above exclusions for assessing the size of China's actual defence budget is suggested in three important studies conducted by the International Institute for Strategic Studies (IISS). In 2006, IISS estimated that including the costs of foreign weapons purchases, subsidies, R&D spending, new product expenditures, arms exports and PAP funding revealed a 72 per cent gap (in RMB terms) between China's Financial Year (FY) 2005 official defence budget and "actual" (i.e.IISS-estimated) defence spending.[38] In 2010, IISS estimated a roughly 39 percent difference between the FY2008 official defence budget and "actual" (i.e. IISS-estimated) defence spending.[39] In 2012, the estimated gap for the FY2010 budget was 41per cent.[40] It should be noted that, although large, the disparity between the official budget and the IISS estimates declined significantly over the initial three-year period before stabilising. As argued in the next section, this shrinking gap, which is consistent with similar trends in estimates by the

US Department of Defence, suggests that in recent years, an increasing percentage of "actual" PLA funding has been placed "on the books"; that is, officially reported figures increasingly reflect actual spending.

The Impact of Reforms on Budget Assessments

Longitudinal comparisons of China's defence spending are complicated by a number of factors:

- Prior to 1998, the only information publicly released about China's official defence budget was the single aggregate figure of total spending announced in an annual yearbook; and
- Since 1998, the content of the official defence budget has changed because of various budget reforms. This section focusses on the latter.

One important consequence of defence budget reforms since the mid-1990s has been a substantial reduction in the gap between the PLA's official government-distributed budget and the amount of aggregate funding it actually receives. Major reforms include:

- Divestiture of the PLA's commercial assets, and reimbursement to the PLA (for a few years) of some of the funds that used to come from the businesses;
- Regularisation of accounting and auditing;
- Marketisation of defence procurement; and
- The creation of the General Armaments Department in 1998 to oversee a new procurement bidding system and implement a zero-based budgeting initiative.[41]

For example, with regard to the first reform, before 1998, various commercial enterprises, in-kind subsidies and revenue- sharing practices were significant sources of income for PLA entities. However, in the late 1990s the President at the time, Jiang Zemin, ordered the PLA to exit most of its commercial businesses and to "eat imperial grain" (i.e. increasingly rely on state funding). Because of this commercial divestiture, over the past 15 years, an increasing percentage of the PLA's total funding has come directly from the central government and is, therefore, "on the books." One implication of this development is that a sizable percentage of the defence budget increases since 1998 may be attributable to more accurate, systematic and transparent government accounting practices, together with reduced corruption, rather than actual increases in the PLA's funding stream.[42] Perhaps the best evidence that recent defence budgets more accurately reflect actual PLA funding can be found by comparing estimates by the US Department of Defence in 2002 (~3.25-4 times China's official defence budget for

2002)[43] and 2010 (~2.14 times the announced 2009 budget).[44] While in recent years, the Pentagon has not itemised publicly what it includes in its calculations, these data show that the department now estimates China's "actual" defence spending to be much closer to the officially announced figure.

Nevertheless, an unwieldy defence economy and budgeting process continues to inhibit both insiders' and outsiders' ability to determine China's actual military spending. As the US Department of Defence assesses, "What little public information China releases about defence spending is further clouded by a multitude of funding sources, subsidies, and cut-outs at all levels of government and in multiple ministries. Real spending on the military, therefore, is so disaggregated that even the Chinese leadership may not know the actual top line."[45] Even the PLA recognises problems concerning inefficiencies and coordination stemming from a lack of centralised administration of various funding streams, lack of oversight, lack of competitive bidding, and the absence of departments tasked with analysis of procurement demands.[46]

Overlooked Inclusions

Although the exclusion of major items from China's official defence budget is undoubtedly an issue of concern, less widely known is that the budget also *includes* some items that are *not* included in those of its Western counterparts. For example, the PLA still engages in some infrastructure construction projects, although many are designed to be dual-use and paid for from local and national non-defence funds. It provides some medical help to civilians in remote areas and provides some support to domestic security operations (e.g. during the 2008 Olympics). The PLA also engages in disaster relief, such as the dispatch of over 200,000 personnel in response to the 2008 Wenchuan earthquake—the largest deployment of Chinese armed forces since the 1979 War with Vietnam.[47] There are legal provisions for it to be reimbursed for these operations, but the processes, delays and extent of such reimbursements remain unclear.[48] In the Western countries, such tasks are assigned primarily to non-military organisations. The PLA also provides perquisites for retired senior officers (offices, assistants, cars, drivers, cooks, caregivers, and special hospital facilities) that their better-salaried Western counterparts do not receive.

What Official Documents Reveal About China's Defence Spending

Salutary developments of direct relevance to China's military transparency include

China's publication of biannual national defence White Papers since 1998 and its annual submission of a "Simplified Reporting Form" to the United Nations (UN) since 2008. This sub-section presents a brief overview of budget-related information included in each of these two types of documents.

China's national defence White Papers separate the PLA's official budget into three main categories: personnel, training and maintenance, and equipment; each of these has reportedly been consistently allotted roughly 33 per cent of the defence budget. The first category, *personnel expenses,* covers salaries, allowances, food, clothing and bedding, insurance, welfare benefits and pensions for officers, non-ranking cadres, enlisted personnel and contracted civilians. It also apparently includes family housing. The second category, *training and maintenance expenses,* covers troop training, institutional education and the running and development of "daily work and activities." In contrast to the US budget's operations and maintenance category, the category of "training and maintenance expenses" in China's defence budget includes only the maintenance of facilities; it does not include maintenance, transportation and storage of equipment. Rather, the latter item falls into the Chinese defence budget's final category, *equipment,* which covers R&D, procurement, maintenance, transportation and storage of weaponry and other hardware. According to one group of US experts who have queried Chinese government officials extensively about China's defence-related spending, China is most transparent about the first category of defence spending and least transparent about the third. For example, very little is known about the costs of weapons and equipment produced by the Chinese defence industry or the amount of money allocated to weapons research and development.[49]

Since 2008, China has submitted the Simplified Reporting Form on military expenditures annually to the UN Secretary General. This form contains previously unreleased information about the relative shares of China's defence budget allocated to its active forces, reserve forces and militia. Although China's submission of this form is a step toward greater transparency, it is important to note that the "Simplified" form contains much less information than the "Standardised Reporting Form" submitted by most advanced industrial democracies.[50] For example, neither the Simplified Reporting Form nor any other publicly available official document includes a breakdown – even top-line figures – of China's defence budget by branches and Services.[51]

In sum, trends in China's defence budget transparency, when examined holistically, are mixed. Recent major budget reforms suggest that more spending is accounted for: the official budget, therefore, increasingly reflects *actual* PLA funding. Furthermore, although excluding various major items from China's defence budget limits transparency, and instances of overreporting do not compare to underreporting in terms of magnitude or importance, China's official budget does include several categories of spending that are not included in Western defence budgets. At the same time, more informative defence White Papers and the submission of defence budget data to the UN manifest a gradual shift toward greater military transparency, albeit with major gaps, the most basic being lack of information about spending for each Service. Trends in China's defence spending and military development over the past two decades admittedly remain uncertain in specifics, but are no mystery in aggregate. Increases in the official defence budget are roughly consistent with GDP growth and constitute a declining percentage of central government expenditures. This suggests that, generally speaking, investment in military modernisation – aside from specific capabilities considered exigent for Party leadership continuity, national survival and defence of critical national interests – remains a lower priority overall than economic development for Beijing's leadership. While it would, of course, help foreign analysts to know more specifically **where** and **how much** China is spending to improve its capabilities, especially when it comes to future defence spending priorities, Beijing's leaders have boosted military spending for precisely the reasons that they have stated consistently: to compensate for inflation and past neglect, consolidate funding into a unified budget, and improve capabilities to address outstanding territorial and maritime claims. Many decisions about defence spending and military transparency are driven at least partially by relatively predictable security concerns and evolving interests, as well as a distinctly "non-Western" – though hardly unique – perspective on the value of budgetary transparency. That said, even some PLA experts have called for China to reduce suspicion about its defence budget by releasing more information. [52]

Implications for India

- China's military modernisation programme would in all likelihood continue as per schedule. The Indian defence budget, on the other hand, at one-third that of China ($37 billion) with an increase of 5 per cent over the previous year hardly caters for inflation. In real terms, it may have even been lower than in 2012. Undoubtedly, this will impact fresh defence acquisitions adversely.
- The Y-20 long range strategic lift capability, Type 094 nuclear submarines, DF-41 and JL-2 ballistic missiles, J-20 and J-31 fifth-generation fighter programmes, etc will continue to be on schedule. Almost all the PLA's programmes will be able to meet the deadlines.[53]
- It can be logically extrapolated that China's military budget will continue to increase

by double digits in percentage terms each year all through during the three phases of its military modernisation. The funds provided for national security will be commensurate with the country's economic development and growing GDP and the Central Military Commission's (CMC's) perception of China's defence needs.

- China's overall objective is to reduce the wide military gap between the PLA and the world's leading military powers, particularly in hardware designed to provide strategic outreach capabilities. This aim will continue to be pursued with utmost fervour. The achievement of this aim will automatically lead to a still greater gap between the military power of India and China. Consequently, India ought to enhance its investment in modernising its armed forces so that they are not found wanting in case of another conflict in the Himalayas, both in terms of the adequacy of force levels for carrying the conflict into Tibet and the military hardware [firepower, crew-served weapons and Command, Control, Communications, Computers, Intelligence, Surveillance and Reconnaissance (C4ISR)], that is necessary to fight at altitudes above 11,000 feet on the Tibetan plateau.

Notes

1. "China Irate Over Japan's Plan to Beef up Defence Spending", Aljazeera America, December 21, 2013, available at http://america.aljazeera.com/articles/2013/12/21/china-irate-overjapanplantobeefupdefensespending.html, accessed on December 23, 2013.
2. Ibid.
3. Zhao Xiaozhuo, "What China's Defence Budget Growth Means", *China-US Exchange Foundation*, March 7, 2013, available at http://www.chinausfocus.com/peace-security/what-chinas-defense-budget-gr..., accessed on March 8, 2013.
4. Zhao Xiaozhuo, "Increased Defense Spending Justified", *China Daily*, March 7, 2013, available athttp://www.china.org.cn/china/NPC_CPPCC_2013/2013-03/07/content_28158516, accessed on March 16, 2013.
5. John Ruwitch and Ben Blanchard, "China Hikes Defense Budget, to Spend More on Internal Security", Reuters, Beijing, March 5, 2013, available at http://www.reuters.com/article/2013/03/05/us-china-parliament-defence-id..., accessed on March 10, 2013.
6. "Overwhelming Public Support for 2013 Defense Budget Rise: GT Poll", *Global Times*, March 6, 2013, available at http://www.globaltimes.cn/NEWS/tabid/99/ID/766415/Overwhelming-public-su., accessed on March 8, 2013.
7. "China Defends Massive Growth in Military Spending", *Associated Press*, March 4, 2013, available at http://news.yahoo.com/china-defends-massive-growth-military-spending-040..., accessed on March 8, 2013. The variation factor is 1.3 to 1.9 times the actual declared figure. The average guess estimate would be 1.6 times.
8. Ruwitch and Blanchard, n. 5.
9. Shaun Waterman, "Red Alert: China's Defense Spending Increases While US Cuts Back", *The Washington Times*, March 5, 2013, available at http://www.washingtontimes.com/news/2013/mar/5/chinas-defense-spending-i., accessed on March 9, 2013.
10. Mandip Singh and Lalit Kumar, "China's Defence Budget 2012: An Analysis", *IDSA Issue Brief*, March 28, 2012, available at http://www.idsa.in/issuebrief/ChinasDefenceBudget2012_

MandipLalit.

11. Ibid.
12. "China Boosts Military Budget to Uphold 'Sovereignty, Security, Territorial Integrity'", *South China Morning Post*, March 5, 2013.
13. Total increase in the budget was 11.2 per cent plus 3.5 per cent additional expenditure, totalling 14.7 per cent. A deduction of 2.6 per cent inflation leaves a net increase of 12.1 per cent.
14. Wen Jiabao's speech to 12th NPC on March 5, 2013, at Beijing.
15. "Internal Security Tops Military in China Spending", *China Real Time*, March 5, 2011, available at http://blogs.wsj.com/chinarealtime/2011/03/05/internal-security-tops-military-in-china-spending/, accessed on December 23, 2013.
16. David Peneau, "Enforcing Stability by Managing Social Conflicts", *China Analysis*, ECFR Report, June 2012, p. 3.
17. Emmanuel Puig, "The Challenges of Transforming People's Armed Police', *China Analysis*, ECFR Report, June 2012, pp. 7-9.
18. "Japan Urges China to Open Up Over Military Spending", *Asahi Shimbun*, March 6, 2013, available at http://ajw.asahi.com/article/asia/china/AJ201303060064, accessed on March 9, 2013.
19. Ibid.
20. "Japan Increases Defence Budget Amid Tensions With China", *The Guardian,* December 17, 2013, available at http://www.theguardian.com/world/2013/dec/17/japan-increases-defence-budget-tensions-china, accessed on December 2013.
21. William Wan, "China Makes Increased Military Spending a Top Priority as People's Congress Meets", *The Washington Post*, March 5, 2013, available at http://articles.washingtonpost.com/2013-03-05/world/37448996_1_military, accessed on March 9, 2013.
22. Singh and Kumar, n. 10.
23. "10% Boost in China's Defence Budget Gives India Jitters", *The Times of India*, March 5, 2013, available at http://articles.timesofindia.indiatimes.com/2013-03-05/india/37469245_1, accessed on March 10, 2013.
24. Sridhar Kumaraswami, "Chinese Defence Budget 3 Times More than India", *Deccan Chronicle*, March 6, 2013, available at http://54.251.40.25/130306/news-world/article/chinese-defence-budget-3-t, accessed on March 13, 2013.
25. "Increasing Chinese Defense Budget Alarms India", *UPI*, March 5, 2013, available at http://www.upi.com/Top_News/Special/2013/03/05/Increasing-Chinese-defens, accessed on March 8, 2013.
26. Scott Warren Harold, "China's Defence Spending Mystery", RAND Commentary on CNN, March 12, 2013.
27. Adam P. Liff and Andrew S. Erickson, "Demystifying China's Defence Spending: Less Mysterious in the Aggregate', *The China Quarterly*, March 2013, pp 1-26.
28. Richard A. Bitzinger, "Just the Facts, Ma'am: The Challenge of Analysing and Assessing Chinese Military Expenditures.", *The China Quarterly* ,173, 2003, pp. 164-175.
29. Dennis J. Blasko, Chas W. Freeman, Jr., Stanley A. Horowitz, Evan S. Medeiros and James C. Mulvenon. n.d. Defense-Related Spending in China: A Preliminary Analysis and Comparison with American Equivalents. The United States-China Policy Foundation, http://www.uscpf.org/ v2/pdf/defensereport.pdf.
30. Dennis J. Blasko, *The Chinese Army Today: Tradition and Transformation for the 21st Century* (New York: Routledge, 2012).
31. Bingfu Chen, "*Xifang guojia dui Zhongguo guofang zhichu de cesuan: chayi yu wenti*" (Estimates of China's national defence expenditures by Western countries: differences and problems). In *Zhongguo guofang jingjixue*: 2004 (China Defence Economics: 2004), (Beijing:

Jingji kexue chubanshe), pp. 83-94.

32. Sean Chen, and John Feffer, "China's Military Spending: Soft Rise or Hard Threat?" *Asian Perspective,* 33 (4), 2009, pp. 47-67.
33. Weifeng Chen, chief ed., *Junfei guanlixue,* (Military expenditure management), (Beijing: Jiefangjun chubanshe, 1997).
34. Chinanews, com. 2010. "*Guofangbu guanwang: Zhongguo guofangfei kexue heli wanquan gongkai touming*" (Ministry of Defence official website: China's scientific and rational defence spending completely public and transparent"), March 5, 2010, http://www.chinanews.com/gn/news/2010/03-05/ 2154879.shtml.
35. Information Office of the State Council (PRC), China's National Defense in 2006. english.chinamil.com.cn/site2/special-reports/2007gfbps/index.htm, accessed on September 12, 2012.
36. Information Office of the State Council (PRC), 2009, China's National Defense in 2008, available at http://www.china.org.cn/government/whitepaper/2009-01/21/content_17162799.htm.
37. Keith Crane, Roger Cliff, Evan Medeiros, James Mulvenon and William Overholt, *Modernizing China's Military: Opportunities and Constraints* (Santa Monica, CA: RAND Corporation, 2005).
38. M Taylor Fravel, "Why 'Non-Combat' PLA Operations are Vital for China's Regime Stability." *Global Asia,* 6 (2), 2011, pp. 46-49.
39. John Garnaut, "Rotting From Within," *Foreign Policy*, April 16, 2012 http://www.foreignpolicy.com/ articles/2012/04/16/rotting_from_within, accessed September 20, 2012.
40. Jianyi Gu, and Chen Bingfu, "*Yonghao guanhao junfei: quanmian tigao junfei shiyong xiaoyi*" (Use and manage military spending well: increase the effectiveness of military spending comprehensively), *Caijingjie*, 8, 2006, pp. 51-54.
41. Da Guo, "*Jiedu Zhongguo 2010 nian guofangfei yusuan*" (Deciphering China's FY2010 defence budget), *Xinmin wanbao*, March 18, 2010, available at xmwb.news365.com.cn/jjlw/201003/t20100318_2651453.htm, accessed on September 20, 2012.
42. Angang Hu and Liu Taoxiong, "*Zhongguo guofang jianshe dada zhihou yu jingji jianshe*" (China's national defence construction lags far behind its economic construction), *Zhongguo guo-fang jingji*, 2, 2003, pp. 2-5.
43. Ruixin Huang, and Zhang Xibin, "*Dui woguo junfei zengzhang xingzhi de zairenshi*" (Understand anew the nature of the growth of China's military spending), *Jiefang junbao*, February 26, 2008.
44. IISS (International Institute for Strategic Studies), *The Military Balance 2006* (Oxford: Routledge for IISS, 2006).
45. IISS, *The Military Balance 2010* (Oxford: Routledge for IISS).
46. Ibid.
47. IMF (International Monetary Fund), "World Economic Outlook Database April 2012," http://www.imf.org/external/pubs/ft/weo/2012/01/weodata/index.aspx, accessed on September 29, 2012.
48. Jane's.com, "China Defence Budget," Jane's Defence Budgets (Jane's Information Group), July 2, 2012, www.janes.com, accessed on July 26, 2012.
49. Luming Jiang, and Wang Weihai, "*Ruhe kandai Zhongguo guofangfei zengzhang*" (How to view the growth of China's national defence expenses), *Guangming ribao*, March 20, http://theory.people.com.cn/GB/136458/17433560.html, accessed on September 15, 2012.
50. Isaac B Kardon, "China's Emerging Debate on Military Transparency," *China Brief,* 10 (18), 2010, pp. 8-10.
51. Michael Kiselycznyk, and Phillip C Saunders, *Assessing Chinese Military Transparency* (Washington, DC: Institute for National Strategic Studies, 2010).

52. Donald Rumsfeld, "The Hon Donald Rumsfeld." Speech at 6th International Institute for Strategic Studies (IISS) Shangri-la Dialogue, Singapore, June 4, 2005, available at http://www.iiss.org/ conferences/the-shangri-la-dialogue/shangri-la-dialogue-archive/shangri-la-dialogue-2005/2005- speeches/first-plenary-session-the-hondonald-rumsfeld, accessed on September 12, 2013.
53. Mandeep Singh, "China's Defence Budget: 2013-2014", *IDSA Comment*, March 18, 2013.

9

India-China Relations in 2013: An Assessment

Sana Hashmi

Introduction

Ever since the independence of India in 1947 and establishment of the People's Republic of China (PRC) in 1949, the trajectory of their relations has been unpredictable. The year gone by, 2013, was another year that demonstrated this trend. High-level power packed diplomatic visits of policy-makers and top political leaders, intense boundary standoffs, including one that brought the two countries to the verge of a military conflict, attempts towards their peaceful and diplomatic resolution, initiation of a number of Confidence-Building Measures (CBMs) and mutual attempts to address bilateral trade issues marked the year 2013 in the context of India-China relations.

This paper gives an account of India's relationship with China in the year 2013, and attempts to analyse the events against the bigger and broader canvas of the India-China relationship.

High Level Diplomatic Visits

In one of the most interesting and positive moves, in May 2013, Chinese Premier Li Keqiang made India his first foreign destination after assuming his new responsibilities in the Chinese government. The visit attracted a lot of international attention and in some ways attempted to inject new vigour into the idea that the two major powers of the world – India and China – can not only live together but also work towards making the Asian region more peaceful, prosperous and advantageous for the two Asian giants. The Prime Minister of India, Dr. Manmohan Singh, reciprocated Li Keqiang's visit in October 2013. During his visit, Dr. Singh raised a number of issues, which in their essence, were meant to put a reality check on the bilateral relationship, while keeping the enthusiasm alive.

Premier Li Keqiang's India Visit

Premier of the State Council of the People's Republic of China (PRC), Li Keqiang visited India from May 19-22, 2013, soon after assuming his position in the Chinese government. A lot of symbolism was attached to the visit, which captured the media's attention both before and after the premier's visit. With the aim to focus more on trade and economic ties, Premier Li brought a huge business delegation along. During the visit, Premier Li emphasised on the importance of good relations between India and China. To be sure, the visit was an attempt to show India and the rest of the world that China's new leadership attaches great importance to its southern neighbour. Premier Li's statement, which he made during his meeting with Prime Minister Singh, showed keenness on his part to inch closer to India. He said, "The two countries have the will, wisdom and capability to jointly nurture new bright spots in cooperation among Asian countries, create a new engine of the world economy, provide huge growth potential and market demand for Asia and the world, and push forward the China-India strategic cooperative partnership for peace and prosperity."[1] During his brief stay in India, Li Keqiang held meetings with Dr. Singh and Indian President Pranab Mukherjee to discuss issues of bilateral concern and mutual benefit. The main purpose of the visit, as stated by Li Keqiang himself, was to increase mutual trust, intensify cooperation and join hands in facing the future together.[2] China views India as a potential economic partner and a huge market, which is evident from the fact that the primary focus of the visit was, more or less, restricted to trade and investment aspects.[3] Depicting the true spirit of the aim of the top leaders, the joint statement issued declared,

> The two sides attached great importance to the active role of the Strategic Economic Dialogue in promoting macro-economic policy coordination and pragmatic cooperation in various fields between the two countries…, strengthening cooperation in the areas of energy and environmental conservation, new and renewable energy and high-technology and in the railway sector, including heavy haulage and station development.[4]

During the visit of Premier Li, both sides underlined that the India-China relationship is of critical importance and, therefore, demands more careful attention by policy-makers from the two sides. Naturally, therefore, it was agreed that regular exchange of visits between the heads of state/government of the two countries is of immense importance and is necessary for smooth bilateral relations. The leaders of the two countries reiterated that they will continue to meet on the sidelines of important multilateral forum meetings.[5] Assessing the Chinese premier's visit, one may argue that it was a moderate success.

Though it was full of rhetoric and symbolism, the visit did break new ground in terms of smoothening India-China relations, which had gone sour in the aftermath of the Depsang incident. In essence, "it covered a profusion of convergent ideas while leaving many more areas of divergence untouched".[6]

Prime Minister Dr. Manmohan Singh's China Visit

In a reciprocal gesture, Prime Minister Manmohan Singh visited China from October 22-24, 2013, where he met President Xi Jinping, Chairman of the National People's Congress Zhang Dejiang and Premier Li Keqiang. As per the joint statement,

> The two leaders discussed political and economic issues of regional and global significance, including those with a potential to affect the growth and development prospects of their respective nations. They agreed to further strengthen coordination and cooperation in multilateral forums, including Russia-India-China, BRICS, and G-20 to jointly tackle global issues such as climate change, international terrorism, food and energy security, and to establish a fair and equitable international political and economic system. They encouraged the various mechanisms and dialogues covering relevant issues to meet regularly to ensure a proper appreciation of each other's concerns and interests.[7]

Clearly, the visit was much appreciated by the Indian and Chinese media and the diplomatic community alike. For instance, as reported in the Chinese news agency Xinhua, "Chinese Premier Li Keqiang hailed Indian Prime Minister Manmohan Singh's visit to China as a 'landmark' event in bilateral relations, which will inject new impetus to ties between the two countries."[8]

"This is another high-level visit between China and India after my visit to India in May, and it is the first time since 1954 that the Chinese premier and Indian prime minister visited each other in the same year," Premier Li is reported to have said to Prime Minister Singh. For the record, it may be noted that after a long gap of 59 years, an exchange of visits by the Indian prime minister and Chinese premier occurred in the same calendar year. The last time this had happened was in 1954 when Zhou Enlai and Jawaharlal Nehru had exchanged visits in the same calendar year and, this, in 1954, had led to the signing of the landmark Panchsheel Agreement.[9]

However, there are contradictory views about the visit also which find Manmohan Singh's visit a case of flawed timing.[10] Explaining the reason for such an argument, Ambassador R. S. Kalha, former secretary, Ministry of External Affairs, India says,

> The Chinese would be aware that there are about six months left in the life of the UPA-II government, with general elections in India imminent. They would have also no doubt taken cognizance of various 'surveys' as well as soundings of the political scene that would indicate that it is entirely possible that there would be a change of government following the elections. The Chinese Embassy in Delhi would be seriously remiss if it did not report back to Beijing the internal scene in India. Even if the UPA were to come back to power, the picture of who would lead the government would only become clear after May 2014.[11]

But not many scholars agree with such a view, as the matters of internal politics do not have as big an impact as is suggested. Nevertheless, the prime minister's China visit achieved considerable success.

Economic Cooperation: Challenges and Opportunities

Both India and China are mindful of the fact that a strong bilateral relationship depends on the strength of the overall nature of trade and economic ties. While the two sides aim to reach new heights vis-à-vis their economic relations, the trade imbalance, which is in favour of China, also needs to be addressed. The point was underscored during the visits of the leaders from both India and China. During Li Keqiang's visit, amongst other things, issues of macro-economic coordination, prevention of protectionism, and an open multilateral trading system, the Doha Development Round and the Regional Comprehensive Economic Partnership (RCEP) figured prominently in the agenda. In one of the major initiatives to pump up bilateral trade and investment ties, the first meeting of the India-China Chief Executive Officers' (CEOs') Forum was held during Li Keqiang's visit to India. There is indeed a realisation on the part of the governments of the two countries that without the active participation of the private sector, the trade and economic potential of the ties cannot be utilised to the fullest. The CEOs' Forum was set up keeping that vital aspect in mind. It is expected to come up with a detailed set of recommendations to further enhance bilateral trade and investment. This is important for two reasons:

One, India's trade ties with China have reached commanding heights in the recent past, to such an extent that China has become India's biggest trade partner. India-China trade reached US$ 66 billion in 2012 and the two sides are now aiming to realise a trade turnover target of US$ 100 billion by 2015.

Two, notwithstanding the volume of bilateral trade, there is a significant trade imbalance, which is tilted in favour of China. China remained the largest exporter to

India in the year 2013 and its exports to India include machinery, electrical and electronic equipments, organic chemicals, fertilisers, articles of iron and steel and plastic. In contrast, ores, slag and ash and cotton are China's main imports from India. India's share in China's total import of major items is still trivial and this huge trade deficit of US$ 40 billion with China has the potential to be the biggest challenge for the leadership of India. In order to deal with this, India has been raising the issue with China, asking for a detailed discussion. As one of the positive outcomes of the visit, China has finally agreed to take measures to address the issue of the trade imbalance, which is by all means a welcome move.

Additionally, there are other issues that will not only help increase trade but will also address the trade imbalance issues. The list includes "cooperation on pharmaceutical supervision, including registration, stronger links between Chinese enterprises and Indian IT industry, and completion of phyto-sanitary negotiations on agro-products, willingness on the part of Chinese enterprises to invest in India and participate in India's infrastructure development. Project contracting cooperation between the businesses of the two countries would also be enhanced."[12] An agreement regarding the establishment of industrial zones to enable conditions that provide platforms for cluster-type development of enterprises of the two countries as well as strengthen cooperation between their financial regulators, and support their banking institutions in setting up representative offices, branches or subsidiaries, and carrying out business activities subject to relevant laws and regulations will also help the two countries reap the benefits of trade and economic ties.[13] A significant chunk of India's overall bilateral trade architecture comes from border trade, and to enable border trade to give its optimal contribution to India-China trade relations and make it one of the very important components, the two sides have to find ways for deep-rooted institutionalisation of the border trade mechanism. In that regard, the two sides agreed to "consider strengthening border trade through Nathu La Pass. China has also agreed to provide greater facilitation to Indian pilgrims for the Gang Renpoche and Mapam Yun Tso Pilgrimage (Kailash Manasarovar Yatra), which will only facilitate greater tourism and people-to-people contacts."[14] There are no two views on the point that a lot needs to be done to shape up India's trade and investment relations with China. More intense discussions on the services sector and border trade are required to reap the benefits of the two fastest growing economies in the world.

Major Initiatives for Stronger Bilateral Ties

'Panchsheel' and the 'Year of Friendly Exchanges'

Sixty years ago, in 1954, India and China agreed to the Five Principles of Peaceful Coexistence which are popularly known as Panchsheel in India. The year 2014 will witness the 60th anniversary of the agreement, and to mark the anniversary, India and China have agreed to designate it as the "Year of Friendly Exchanges".

Highlighting the importance of Panchsheel for both India and China, Professor Surjit Mansingh, of the American University, Washington D. C., says that Panchsheel "jointly offered to the world by former Indian Prime Minister Jawaharlal Nehru Nehru and Chinese Premier Zhou Enlai as a more ethical and less destructive code of international conduct than power politics is underlined as the basis of China's foreign policy in statements by its present leader."[15] The statement holds true even today and in a way binds India and China, at least at the rhetorical level.

Both India and China have a huge percentage of youth in the overall population, a constituency that will shape bilateral relations. Exposure of the youth of India to the Chinese people and their culture will be helpful in understanding the common Chinese psyche – an essential tool to analyse one's neighbour in times both good and bad. In this regard, an annual exchange of 100 youths from each side has also been agreed to. Additionally, during Li's India visit, Hanban, the Chinese National Office for Teaching Chinese as a Foreign Language, and CBSE (Central Board of Secondary Education) on the Indian side were instructed to work in tandem to build up Chinese language teaching and learning in India. Furthermore, the Programme of Cultural Exchange for the years 2013-15 which includes art and culture, cultural heritage, youth affairs, education and sports, media, publications and mass communications, was also signed. This would be supported by sister-city relationships, which will be on a pilot basis to start with.[16] The sister-city relations are to be established between Delhi and Beijing, Bengaluru and Chengdu, and Kolkata and Kunming, to foster people-to-people ties.[17] The sister-city agreement will undertake exchanges involving delegations, interactions between institutions and sharing of experiences in areas of mutual interest. According to reports, prior consultation with the respective national agencies, namely, India's East Asia Division of the Ministry of External Affairs and the China International Friendship Cities Association (CIFCA) will be undertaken before commencing exchange activities.[18]

Another critically important aspect of India-China bilateral dynamics is the role of the media. The media has been playing a key role in shaping the relationship between the two Asian giants. Interestingly, a commentary issued by China's official Xinhua news agency in July hit out at the Indian media for "hyping" the situation along the disputed border, following the incursions in Depsang valley by Chinese troops.[19] But, the fact of the matter is that India is a vocal democracy where the media takes its right to free speech very seriously. China, in contrast, is typically a closed society, with authoritarian rulers who work to curtail press freedom and political rights. While both sides have divergent ways of handling the media, they are aware of the vitality of the role played by the media in influencing bilateral relations. Therefore, during Li's visit to India in 2013, both agreed to hold a Media Forum for mediapersons from the two countries. The event provided an opportunity to the Indian minister of external affairs and minister of foreign affairs of the PRC to work together. In addition, both have also agreed to simplify the visa application and issuing process for media personnel.

Sub-Regional, Regional and Multilateral Cooperation

Apart from the bilateral interplay of actions, sub-regional, regional and multilateral fora also play a crucial role in shaping the India-China relationship by providing both countries with opportunities to interact with each other. As Ashley Tellis, senior associate at the Carnegie Endowment for International Peace, and Sean Mirski, editor, *Harvard Law Review* point out,

> The two countries are united by certain acknowledged aims: recovering the preeminence they once enjoyed as international entities of consequence; establishing a multipolar world with themselves as constituent poles; avoiding the costs of contributing to global public goods on the grounds that their vast developmental challenges are not yet overcome; and protecting their hard-won sovereignty in the face of new principles justifying foreign intervention in the internal affairs of states.[20]

So far as the sub-regional dynamics is concerned, both India and China are mindful of the fact that their landlocked areas – the seven northeastern states of India and the Chinese province of Yunnan – are underdeveloped in terms of connectivity, infrastructure, and easy access to resources. Regional cooperation is perhaps the most suitable way to deal with the issue of lack of connectivity and infrastructure as well as the problems posed by underdevelopment. In that regard, a regional initiative has been undertaken, called the BCIM (Bangladesh, China, India, Myanmar) Regional Forum, which includes not only India and China but also their two neighbours – Bangladesh and Myanmar. A BCIM Car Rally between Kolkata and Kunming was also organised in February 2013. Later in the year, India and China agreed to consult member countries of BCIM to set up a Joint Study Group for strengthening connectivity in the BCIM region for closer economic, trade, and people-to-people linkages and to initiate the development of a BCIM Economic Corridor.[21] The recently proposed and accepted idea of making Kolkata and Kunming sister-cities is certainly a great move, which has the potential to enhance connectivity at all levels. So far as mutual understanding and bilateral cooperation at multilateral fora is concerned, India and China have been working in coordination, though not regularly and systematically, at a number of fora, including the World Trade Organisation (WTO). China and India have also been working with each other on climate change issues, while there are some issues on which they do not find it convenient to work with each other. Highlighting the achievements and underscoring the concerns, the joint statement issued during Li's India visit, notes,

> As developing countries, India and China share common interest on several issues of global importance like climate change, Doha Development Round of WTO, energy and food security, reform of the international financial institutions and global governance. This is reflected in the close cooperation and coordination between the two sides within the BRICS and G-20 frameworks. The two sides agreed to enhance coordination in the follow-up process of the United Nations Conference on Sustainable Development and in discussions on the post-2015 development agenda as well as international negotiations on climate change.[22]

Clearly, there are numerous fora that demand that India and China work closely for mutual benefit and growth.

The Association of Southeast Asian Nations (ASEAN) has been one of the major success stories of the developing world, showing countries of the Southern Hemisphere the way to regional cooperation and economic harmonisation. For years, both India and China have been trying to inch closer to ASEAN and get in sync with the goals and vision that ASEAN has been advocating. For instance, the RCEP has emerged as one of the most important aspects of an Asia, which is getting more and more interconnected. The RCEP is likely to realise a comprehensive economic partnership by 2015 among the ASEAN member-states and its partners: Australia, China, India, Japan, New Zealand and South Korea. The agreement encompasses trade in goods and services, economic and technical issues, intellectual property and investments, and dispute settlement mechanisms. Like several other ASEAN propelled organisations, ASEAN will be in the "driver's seat" of this regional trade arrangement. It is important to note here that the idea of the RCEP was first given by Japan, but it decided to bring ASEAN on board and let it take the initiative. As far as India and China are concerned, they have always been supportive of the move. However, according to reports, China was not in favour of including India. Rather, it supported the idea of involving only ASEAN and its three external partners, namely, China, Japan and South Korea.

However, apart from emphasising the "ASEAN centrality" in the emerging regional economic architecture, ASEAN itself has been working on involving as many external powers of the neighbourhood as possible. Thus, ASEAN not only found it impractical but also against its own goals to not include India in the RCEP. Clearly, the RCEP is an ambitious project, which, for the first time, intends to bring in Asia's three biggest economies – China, India and Japan – into a regional trade arrangement. Naturally, the proposed trade area will be the largest in terms of population covered and will have a combined Gross Domestic Product (GDP) of around US$19 trillion. When fully established, it will become one of the largest trade blocs in the world.[23] The RCEP promises to be a group wherein lies the future of regional economic cooperation, as well as a more positive role for both India and China.

Several members of the proposed RCEP already have bilateral Free Trade Agreements (FTAs) with one another. However, numerous and varied terms of agreements for the FTAs and the different rules of origin have created a "spaghetti-bowl" situation, thereby impeding the harmonisation and effective use of the FTAs.[24] When the RCEP comes into force, it will certainly bring in simpler conditions and strengthen the trade relations between the members. As a result, the trade costs are also likely to go down. India, which has been quite supportive of the RCEP, naturally looks upon it as a way to achieve the goal of integrating with the economies of the East Asian region. However, "concerns regarding China have to be assuaged to realise the RCEP on time, and China has to do its bit on that count. Finding ways and means to arrive at a bilateral trade agreement with China is not going to be an easy task for India."[25] As per the joint statement, even during the meeting between the top leaders of the two countries, the two sides agreed to look into the prospects of a bilateral Regional Trade Arrangement (RTA) as also attempt to review the state of the negotiation on the RCEP. Efforts to conclude a framework agreement for the establishment of industrial zones to provide platforms of cluster type development for enterprises of the two countries would be expedited. Economic agreements signed at the conclusion of the talks reflect the progress made since May 2013.[26]

Clearly, India's and China's interests converge at the global level to a great extent, thus, strengthening the idea that the two countries should work together and strengthen bilateral relations. The ASEAN Regional Forum (ARF), ASEAN Defence Ministers

Meeting (ADMM) Plus, Shanghai Cooperation Organisation (SCO), G- 20, the grouping of Brazil, Russia, India, China and South Africa (BRICS) and several other such fora provide India and China ample opportunities to join hands and work together. Sadly, however, the two sides have not been able to systematise their policies to arrive at an understanding. It may also be said that while analysing the Indian and Chinese behaviour, one arrives at the conclusion that the policies of both the countries with regard to each other are marred by ad-hocism.

Border Defence Cooperation Agreement Between India and China

Well-defined boundaries are fundamental for smooth international relations. Clearly, to maintain peace and tranquillity along the borders, avoiding use of force is of the utmost importance. However, in the case of India and China, the protracted border issue has for long troubled their ties. One may find from historical records that China has been highly unaccommodating on the border issues and especially on the McMahon Line. For instance, in 2006, during the term in office of Chinese envoy to India Sun Yuxi, China laid claims of sovereignty over Arunanchal Pradesh in official pronouncements. The statement came just before the then Chinese President Hu Jintao's first ever state visit to India in 2006.[27]

Regardless of what China's earlier position on the status of the India-China border has been, as soon as he took charge in March 2013, Xi Jinping himself stated that, "the resolution of the boundary dispute between the two sides 'won't be easy' and pending its final settlement, 'peace and tranquillity' should be maintained on the border without affecting the overall ties". He further referred to China's ties with India as "one of the most important bilateral relationships".[28] Despite such affirmations from the top leadership, repeated unpleasant incidents of Chinese incursions have caused concerns in India. China's stand on Pakistan Occupied Kashmir, Arunanchal Pradesh, the Brahmaputra river, Tibetan refugees in India, and its stand on the land boundary with India has led to uneasy relations, creating anxieties in India. However, in view of the criticality of border issues and the need to solve the disputes, a mutual understanding in both Beijing and New Delhi seems to be evolving that substantial CBMs are required to maintain peace along the borders between the two countries. Unfortunately, during Li's India visit, the boundary issues did not figure much in the agenda, beyond rhetorical statements. To make matters more mysterious, even the details of the discussion between the Indian and Chinese leaders could not come out in the public domain. One may argue that the visit, which may be termed a lost opportunity for India on the boundary question, did not meet the expectations of those who believe in India-China bonhomie.[29] The issue which should have been given prime importance in the meetings with Li and in the joint communiqué, failed to figure high in the list. Pushing such an issue under the carpet would pose serious challenges to India's national security in the coming years.[30]

However, one possibly cannot overlook some positive signs on the border issue that make us believe that Dr. Singh's visit to Beijing was a success. It is widely believed that amongst all the agreements signed during Dr. Singh's visit, the most important document is the Border Defence Cooperation Agreement (BDCA). With the signing of the agreement, the two countries reached "a comprehensive agreement to avoid border tensions and army faceoffs along the Line of Actual Control (LAC) by deciding that neither side will use military capability to attack the other side nor tail patrols along the border."[31] While the BDCA is a positive step, it should be assessed for its implications for India. It is interesting to note that the proposal was hurriedly put forward by China in March 2013 for the first time, ahead of Li's visit to India. Li seemed sure when he said, "We hope that the seeds we have sowed today in spring will be harvested in autumn".[32] Needless to say, Dr. Singh's visit was successful enough to touch upon the most prolonged issue hindering the relations with the inking of the BDCA. The BDCA will hopefully maintain the status quo by addressing future flare-ups along the border. It is a well-known fact that lack of coordination and understanding between the Indian and Chinese troops worsens the already convoluted border question. Thus, it is hoped that the complete realisation of the BDCA will help the Indian and Chinese armed forces exercise restraint in tailing each other's patrols along the LAC. It is imperative for the stability of India-China relations as the pact has the potential to manage the day-to-day differences along the border, without high-level intervention in the matter. Unlike the 1993 "peace and tranquillity" agreement which, for the first time, suggested "no use of force" by both sides or the 1996 CBMs in the military agreement which specified the interactions between border personnel of the two countries, the current BDCA suggests the possibility of "establishing a hotline between the military headquarters in all the sectors," initiating "small scale tactical exercises along the LAC" and "joint military training exercises" along the 4,000-km-long India-China border.[33]

Nevertheless, the current arrangement, with minor changes, has been, more or less, built on the 1993, 1996 and 2005 agreements; this much needed initiative was largely seen as a consequence of the April-May 2013 Chinese intrusion into India's Depsang Valley and perceived as a reconciliatory measure towards differences stemming from contradictory perceptions of the India-China border. Highlighting the importance of maintaining peace and tranquillity on the India-China border, Dr. Singh stated that the BDCA would strengthen maintenance of stability on the border.[34] He further stated that peace and tranquillity on the India-China border must remain the foundation for growth in the India-China relationship, which would be strategic. Noting their burgeoning cooperation at almost all international fora, the signing of the BDCA was timely and crucial for both India and China.[35]

Additionally, to address the boundary issue in a more systematic fashion through CBMs, the services of special representatives, who are supposed to carry out meaningful and peaceful negotiations, are also utilised. As stated in the joint statement released during Premier Li's visit, "The leaders expressed satisfaction over the work done so far by special representatives of the two countries on the boundary question and encouraged them to push forward the process of negotiations and seek a framework for a fair, reasonable and mutually acceptable settlement in accordance with the Agreement on Political Parameters and Guiding Principles. Pending the resolution of the boundary question, the two sides shall work together to maintain peace and tranquillity in the border areas in line with the previous agreements."[36]

Analysing the Chinese behaviour, Ambassador P. Stobdan argues:

> At the heart of China's engagement with India is economic interest. Even burgeoning trade relations in favour of China could not be leveraged by India, but Beijing showed no sign of compromising on the core boundary issue. The Chinese are only interested in resolving the border issue on their terms: these extend to cover all of Arunachal Pradesh, which appears linked to Beijing's Tibet policy. Should India seek to resolve the boundary issue first, or wait for China to solve its Tibet problem? In any case, the Chinese have nothing to lose in Ladakh. However, in the absence of a more nuanced borderland strategy, we will have to continue to rely on the military mechanisms. One hopes that with BDCA in place, incidents like Depsang will never occur again and the government will spend less time on fire-fighting. Equally important is to fast-track early conclusion of a framework agreement at the special representative level talks for a lasting solution to the boundary issue.[37]

While one cannot deny the points made by Stobdan, the point worth highlighting is that the BDCA is a landmark positive move in the context of the India-China relationship.

Military Exchanges

The scars of the China imposed 1962 War on India and eventual scepticism on the part of both countries have left the militaries of the two sides with very little engagement. For decades, not much was done to address the issue. However, in the past two decades, some attempts have been made in that regard starting from former Prime Minister Rajiv Gandhi's term in office. In 2013, yet another step was taken to enhance bilateral military-to-military contacts and cooperation. In fact, during Li Keqiang's India visit, India and China agreed to enhance military interaction for building greater mutual trust and confidence. It was also agreed that the armed forces of the two sides will hold the next round of joint training exercises. Both sides also decided to increase exchanges among the army, navy and air force of the two countries.[38] Later in the year, a bilateral military exercise was also conducted with the aim to give a fillip to military-to-military cooperation.

In November 2013, so as to highlight the vitality of fighting global threats jointly, a bilateral counter-terrorism exercise was conducted. Code-named "Hand-in-Hand 2013", the joint training session included demonstration of weapons, exchange of tactics and mixed training in the arrest of suspects and rescue of hostages, in which 144 soldiers from each side took part.[39] Held in the Sichuan province of China, the drill was the third joint military exercise between China and India and was revived after a gap of five years. The two countries had conducted their first joint anti-terror training exercise in southwest China's Yunnan province in 2007. Their next joint military exercise was held at Belgaum in Karnataka in 2008. The annual exercises, however, suffered a setback after India called off military exchanges in protest against the denial of a visa to a top Indian general.[40] Apart from initiating closer military-to-military interactions, a number of other military related issues came to the fore during the meetings between the Indian and Chinese sides in 2013. For example, enhancing bilateral cooperation on maritime security, search and rescue at sea, oceanic scientific research and environment protection, working together to tackle increasingly outstanding non-traditional security threats, and strengthening cooperation in naval escort missions in the Gulf of Aden and the waters off the coast of Somalia, earnestly safeguarding security of international sea-lanes and freedom of navigation.[41]

Major Irritants and Bottlenecks in Bilateral Relations

Chinese Incursions in Depsang/ Daulat Beg Oldi [42]

One of the most contentious and provocative issues between India and China in the year 2013 was the Chinese incursion in India's Daulat Beg Oldi area in Depsang valley. Just a month before Li's maiden visit to India, in April 2013, Chinese platoons entered 19 km inside the Indian side of the LAC, put up tents, and remained there for three weeks. The Depsang incident demonstrated how a single event of incursion could derail the India-

China relationship. There are no two views on the point that the Depsang incident once again reminded Indian policy-makers of their weaknesses vis-à-vis China, while for the Indian armed forces, it was once again clear that lack of vigilance and preparedness could lead to disastrous consequences. Interestingly, the increasing Chinese assertiveness and the pattern of their incursions in recent years clearly show how extraordinarily dramatic events like the Depsang incursion have to take place before any high-level visit takes place between India and China.

There are reports indicating that a major general based in the Chengdu Military District, who is close to Jiang Zemin, was responsible for the Chinese forces launching a Chinese version of the Indian policy of the late 1950s/early 1960s, popularly termed as the "forward policy".[43] Such actions by some military personnel who are assumed to be faithful to, and pursuing, the policies of the erstwhile top leadership, even though the current leadership's approach is positive towards a specific country, may be referred to as the "rogue general theory". Nevertheless, the moot question is whether the People's Liberation Army (PLA) has the authority to carry out such a grave action without the consent of the Chinese Communist Party (CCP). The possibility of this seems bleak. The rogue general theory, for the most part, cannot be substantiated vis-à-vis the recent Ladakh standoff.[44]

Interestingly, apart from the abovementioned 2006 incident, when the Chinese envoy to India, Sun Yuxi, in his official pronouncement, laid claims of Chinese sovereignty over the entire state of Arunanchal Pradesh, there have been several instances proving that such activities have become a regular feature preceding the high-level diplomatic visits of the leaders. For instance, in 2008, the Chinese incursion at PangongTso lake as well as Trig Heights in eastern Ladakh was witnessed on September 2, just four days before the visit of former Chinese Foreign Minister Yang Jiechi to India. This typical Chinese behaviour can be seen as an indication of China's rigidly uncooperative stance on the border issues.

It may be noted that the Chinese incursions into Indian territory, by land, sea and air, increased after 2005, with as many as 233 violations in 2008 and more than 500 transgressions from 2010 to 2012.[45] This is clear evidence that the issue of demarcation of their border can lead to precarious relations between India and China. The fact that there was no high level visit from 2010 till 2012, further suggests that there exists a problem between these two Asian giants. Furthermore, the recent standoff contributed to the waning of mutual trust and will take some time to fade away. In this context, Srinath Raghavan, senior fellow, Centre for Policy Research, says, "It is naïve to expect China to drop its claims on Arunanchal Pradesh at this stage. Has India foresaken its claims to

Aksai Chin? Both sides will only relinquish them when a deal is struck. To be sure, India cannot give up any populated areas; but short of this, there is room for compromise. China, too, can accommodate India's interests in the Ladakh sector."[46]

Assessing the Depsang issue, Professor Srikanth Kondapalli, of Jawaharlal Nehru University, says, "Overall, the Chinese transgression will leave its scars for a long time to come on the bilateral equations, even as India will have to learn lessons in statecraft to protect its sovereignty and territorial integrity."[47]

A close study of the India-China border skirmishes and differences reveals that the border dispute will continue to be a major flashpoint in India-China relations. Nevertheless, while a direct confrontation is not on the cards, the resolution of the recent standoff and for that matter, a final settlement of the border conflict can be reached through diplomatic channels only. The likelihood of an early settlement of the border dispute has become all the more problematic, and there is a possibility that while the Chinese may push for a resolution of the border differences along the LAC in Ladakh, the matter of Arunachal Pradesh will remain untouched for a longer time. Given that procrastination and deception are inherent in Chinese foreign and security policies, it is imperative for India to keep pushing for a more transparent approach, and exchange of maps and relevant documents as evidence of the claims of both countries should be accelerated. Given that, as of now, reaching a mutually agreeable solution seems a distant dream for India; making China retain the status quo is certainly in India's favour.

Chinese Incursion in Chumar/Chepzi

In what has been termed as the first such incident along the LAC, Chinese troops detained five Indians in Chumar (Ladakh) inside the Indian territory and took them to their side, in "an apparent bid by the troops to stake a claim on the area."[48] The incident that occurred in December 2013 was preceded by the June 17 incident in which Chinese troops illegally entered the Chumar area. In the December 2013 incident, as per the media reports, Army Headquarters sought to play down the incident, saying that the matter was resolved "amicably" but sources said the Chinese side relented only after the local Indian Army authorities sought a flag meeting on the matter and warned that the issue would be raised at a higher level.[49] It is believed that "unlike a majority of areas along the 4,000-km-long LAC as perceived by India, Chumar is one sector where the Chinese do not enjoy the benefit of access. The reason for that is the lack of road development and terrain, which acts as an impediment for the former. It is not that the Indian side has it all developed but owing to the presence of dirt tracks and a not-so rocky terrain means vehicles can move."[50] It is also believed that "despite the BDCA signed between the two sides, there is no let-up in Chinese transgressions across the LAC. In fact, the number of transgressions has increased in comparison to last year."[51] Clearly, such incursions have only raised suspicions about China's boundary approach vis-à-vis India, which should be a cause of concern for India. In the light of such unfortunate events, one hopes that the BDCA proves worthwhile and prevents the India-China relationship from going on a downward spiral.

Tibet Issue

Notwithstanding the presence of Tibet as a persistent unresolved matter between India and China, India has not done enough in taking up the issue head-on. Rather than dealing with the Tibet issue in a more direct and upfront fashion with China, whose actions have been termed as "the clearest case of overt aggression in the post-war period"[52], and even with the Dalai Lama and the Tibetan refugees, India chose to remain a silent spectator. Even on the diplomatic front, it is only recently that India has started associating the severity of the Tibet issue with the Kashmir issue. Following the same line, India preferred to refrain from mentioning Tibet in the joint statement issued after talks between Manmohan Singh and Li Keqiang. Interestingly, during Wen Jiabao's visit to New Delhi in 2010, India adopted the same stance, by omitting the reference to the "one China policy" from the joint statement. India made the point then that Kashmir was as much a core concern to India as Tibet was to China, and that China's policies of issuing stapled visas and carrying out projects in Pakistan-occupied Kashmir violated this core concern.[53]

Though symbolic, the incident indicates that India is firming up its position on the importance of both Kashmir and Tibet. Nevertheless, there is no doubt that India still approves of China's "one China policy", and is not likely to question it in totality any time soon.

Brahmaputra River

By trying to divert the flow of the Brahmaputra river, and building dams over it, China has been using its position as an upper riparian state to the fullest, leaving the lower riparian states, India and Bangladesh, in a much deprived and disadvantageous position. For years, the Indian media has been reporting instances of massive Chinese activity along the Brahmaputra river and their attempts to build dams, big and small, along the river. China's Zangmu dam has been a cause of concern for India, though India has tried to overlook the matter.[54] India's apprehension has been that China might use such dams to India's detriment in conflict situations, thereby subjecting India to a non-traditional security emergency. Interestingly, the Chinese government, as well as its state-run media agencies have, time and again, denied that it had such a diversion programme. In that regard, Indian policy-makers have also been expressing India's concerns to the Chinese counterparts. A remarkably positive step on that count was taken during the visit of Dr. Singh, when it was decided that the Chinese government would make sincere attempts in sharing data on emergency management of the trans-border rivers twice a day. A Memorandum of Understanding (MoU) on Strengthening Cooperation on Trans-border Rivers was also signed, paving the way for more institutional level cooperation on the matter. The two sides also agreed to other issues, namely, to further strengthen cooperation and, within the expert level mechanism, work together on provision of flood-season hydrological data and emergency management, and exchange views on other issues of mutual interest.[55] However, one must not forget that China does have plans to build dams on the Brahmaputra no matter how India gets affected. What makes the matter worse is that India and China are not bound by any treaty obligations on the Brahmaputra issue. It is, therefore, necessary for India to keep on working closely with China and pursue the matter to arrive at a mutually beneficial way out on the Brahmaputra issue.

Conclusion

A number of contrasting trends that emerged in the year 2013 demonstrated that the India-China relationship is likely to stay like this as the two nations 'rise' to power. Whether to choose full-fledged cooperation or opt for balance of power politics is a question that is difficult to answer at this juncture. Nevertheless, the fact remains that India and China are neighbours and will have to live with each other. So far as the boundary question is concerned, India must deal with China from a position of strength and devise a multi-pronged approach that encompasses cooperation with China on several other fronts, while dealing firmly with it on the boundary issues. Clearly, as it happened in 2013, India and China have to opt for dialogue as much as possible to understand, and live in harmony with, each other.

Notes

1. "China, India to Make New Engine of World Economy: Chinese Premier", Embassy of the People's Republic of China in India, http://in.chineseembassy.org/eng/zt/likeqiang2013/t1043065.htm, May 23, 2013, accessed December 27, 2013.
2. "Li Keqiang on New Delhi Visit Vows to Build Trust with India", *South China Morning Post,* http://www.scmp.com/news/china/article/1241266/li-keqiang-new-delhi-visit-vows-build-trust-india, May 19, 2013, accessed on May 19, 2013.
3. Sana Hashmi, "Li Keqiang's India Visit: Rhetoric Over Results", Rediff, http://www.rediff.com/news/column/li-keqiangs-india-visit-rhetoric-over-results/20130521.htm, May 21, 2013, accessed on December 22, 2013.

4. Ministry of External Affairs of India, Government of India, "Joint Statement on the State Visit of Chinese Premier Li Keqiang to India", http://www.mea.gov.in/bilateral-documents.htm?dtl/21723, May 20, 2013, accessed on May 20, 2013.
5. Ibid.
6. Hashmi, n. 3.
7. Ministry of External Affairs, Government of India, "Joint Statement- A Vision for Future Development of India-China Strategic and Cooperative Partnership", http://mea.gov.in/bilateral-documents.htm?dtl/22379/Joint+Statement+A+vision+for+future+development+of+IndiaChina+strategic+and+cooperative+partnership, October 23, 2013, accessed on October 23, 2013.
8. "Chinese Premier Hails Singh's Visit as "Landmark" Event", Xinhua, http://news.xinhuanet.com/english/china/2013-10/23/c_132823259.htm, October 23, 2013, accessed on October 23, 2013.
9. Sana Hashmi, "Border Defence Cooperation Agreement: A New Beginning?", *In Focus,* http://capsindia.org/files/documents/CAPS_Infocus_SH3.pdf, October 29, 2013, accessed on October 29, 2013.
10. R.S. Kalha, "PM's Visit to China: A Case of Flawed Timing", *IDSA Comment,* http://idsa.in/idsacomments/IndiaPMsVisittoChina_rskalha_251013, October 25, 2013, accessed October 29, 2013.
11. Ibid.
12. n. 4.
13. n. 7.
14. n. 4.
15. Surjit Mansingh, "India-China Relations in the Post-Cold War Era", *Asian Survey,* vol. 34, no. 3, March 1994, pp. 285-300.
16. n. 7.
17. "India-China Agree to Set Up Sister-Cities: Delhi-Beijing, Bengaluru-Chengdu, Kolkata-Kunming", *DNA India,* http://www.dnaindia.com/india/report-india-china-agree-to-set-up-sister-cities-delhi-beijing-bengaluru-chengdu-kolkata-kunming-1907805, October 23, 2013, accessed on December 14, 2013.
18. Prime Minister of India, Government of India, "Agreement on the Establishment of Sister-City Relations between Bangaluru, Republic of India and Chengdu, People's Republic of China", http://pmindia.nic.in/press-details.php?nodeid=1732, October 23, 2013, accessed on October 24, 2013.
19. Ananth Krishnan, "Xinhua Hits Out at 'Indian Media Hype'", *Hindustan Times,* http://www.thehindu.com/news/international/world/xinhua-hits-out-at-indian-media-hype/article4945238.ece?ref=relatedNews, July 24, 2013, accessed July 25, 2013.
20. Ashley J. Tellis and Sean Mirski, eds., "Introduction", *Crux of Asia China, India, and the Emerging Global Order* (Washington DC: Carnegie Endowment for International Peace, 2013), p. 5.
21. Kishan S Rana, "Cooperation with Neighbours Vital for India's Northeast", Rediff, http://www.rediff.com/news/column/cooperation-with-neighbours-vital-for-indias-northeast/20130603.htm, June 3, 2013, accessed November 4, 2013.
22. n. 4.
23. Rahul Mishra, "RCEP: Challenges, Opportunities for India", *RSIS Commentaries*, http://www.rsis.edu.sg/publications/Perspective/RSIS1402013.pdf, July 25, 2013, accessed on August 28, 2013.
24. Ibid.
25. Ibid.

26. n. 7.
27. Hashmi, n. 3.
28. "China Unveils 5-Point Formula to Improve Ties with India," *The Hindu Business Line,* http://www.thehindubusinessline.com/news/international/china-unveils-5point-formula-to-improve-ties-with-india/article4524944.ece, March 19, 2013, accessed March 20, 2013.
29. Hashmi, n. 3.
30. Ibid.
31. "India, China Sign Landmark Border Defence Agreement to Maintain Peace at LAC", *The Indian Express,* http://www.indianexpress.com/news/india-china-sign-landmark-border-defence-agreement-to-maintain-peace-at-lac/1186124/, October 23, 2013, accessed on October 25, 2013.
32. P. Stobdan, "BDCA with China and its Implications for India", *IDSA Comment,* http://www.idsa.in/idsacomments/BDCAwithChinaanditsImplicationsforIndia_pstobdan_291013, October 29, 2013, accessed on October 29, 2013.
33. Srikanth Kondapalli, "Can Chinese be Trusted This Time", Rediff, at http://www.rediff.com/news/report/slide-show-1-can-the-chinese-be-trusted-this-time/20131024.htm, October 24, 2013, accessed on October 29, 2013.
34. Hashmi, n. 3.
35. Ibid.
36. Ibid.
37. Ibid.
38. "India, China Say their Ties Model for Neighbours", *The Dawn,* http://www.dawn.com/news/1012702/india-china-say-their-ties-model-for-neighbours, May 21, 2013, accessed May 22, 2013.
39. "China, India Anti-terror Joint Military Exercise Ends, *The Economic Times,* http://articles.economictimes.indiatimes.com/2013-11-13/news/44030884_1_border-defence-cooperation-agreement-china-and-india-military-exchanges, November 13, 2013, accessed on November 15, 2013.
40. Ibid.
41. n. 4.
42. This section is based on the author's previous work on the same issue. For details, see Sana Hashmi, "India-China Stand-Off in Depsang: Some Observations", Centre for Air Power Studies, *Issue Brief,* vol. 88, no.13, June 10, 2013.
43. Madhav Nalapat, "Jiang Group in Chinese Army Behind Incursions", *The Sunday Guardian,* http://www.sunday-guardian.com/news/jiang-group-in-chinese-army-behind-incursions, April 27, 2013, accessed on May 15, 2013.
44. Hashmi, n. 3.
45. Suman Sharma, "Army Accessed China War-game Plan, Did Not Enhance Security", *The Sunday Guardian,* http://www.sundayguardian.com/news/army-accessed-china-war-game-plan-did-not-enhance-security, April 27, 2013, accessed on May 15, 2013.
46. Srinath Raghavan, "The Case for Restraint on Tibet", *Economic and Political Weekly*, vol. 43, no. 14, April 5-11, 2008, pp. 11-12.
47. Srikanth Kondapalli, "The Fallout of China's Depsang Plains Transgression', Rediff, http://www.rediff.com/news/column/the-fallout-of-chinas-depsang-plains-transgression/20130506.htm, May 6, 2013, accessed on May 15, 2013.
48. "Chinese Troops Detain 5 Indians in Ladakh", *Live Mint,* http://www.livemint.com/Politics/TU68IdHT5f9WOMk85vrEAO/Chinese-troops-apprehend-Indians-in-Ladakh.html, December 15, 2013, accessed on December 27, 2013.
49. "Chinese Troops Net Three Indians in Ladakh", *Hindustan Times,* http://www.hindustantimes.

com/StoryPage/Print/1162882.aspx, December 15, 2013, accessed December 27, 2013.
50. "Why China is Working Overtime to Blunt India in Chumar", *India Today,* http://indiatoday.intoday.in/story/china-working-overtime-to-blunt-india-in-chumar/1/290500.html, July 9, 2013, accessed on December 14, 2013.
51. "Chinese Troops Came into Ladakh on December 19-20", *Hindustan Times,* http://www.hindustantimes.com/StoryPage/Print/1166180.aspx?s=p, December 25, 2013, accessed on December 26, 2013.
52. Cited in Neville Maxwell, "The Threat from China", *International Affairs* (Royal Institute of International Affairs, 1944), vol. 47, no. 1, January 1971, pp. 31-44.
53. Sandeep Dikhsit and Ananth Krishnan, "India Plays Down Omission of 'Tibet' from Joint Statement", *The Hindu* ,http://www.thehindu.com/news/national/india-plays-down-omission-of-tibet-from-joint-statement/article4733709.ece, May 21, 2013, accessed on May 21, 2013.
54. "China Not Reducing Height of Dam on Brahmaputra, Says Intelligence Report", *India Today,* http://indiatoday.intoday.in/story/china-not-reducing-height-of-dam-on-brahmaputra-says-intelligence-report/1/142142.html, June 20, 2011, accessed on September 26, 2013.
55. "List of Agreements/MoUs Signed Between India and China During Prime Minister's Official Visit to China", Press Release, Prime Minister of India, http://pmindia.nic.in/press-details.php?nodeid=1727, October 23, 2013, accessed on December 23, 2013.

10

Tibet: A Historical Perspective till 1950

Simrat Virk

> He who holds Tibet dominates the Himalayan piedmont; he who dominates the Himalayan piedmont, threatens the Indian subcontinent; and he who dominates the Indian subcontinent, may well have all Southeast Asia within his reach, all of Asia.
>
> — George Ginsburgs[1]

Introduction

The issue of the autonomy of Tibet has been in and out of the focus of the world for centuries now. Despite that, any resolution of the issue seems unlikely in the foreseeable future. Tibet, that had for long remained unnoticed by the rest of the world, came into prominence once again in 2008 with the heavy rioting in Lhasa, done on a day the Tibetans marked the 49th anniversary of the uprising in 1949. Several shops and establishments owned by the majority Han ethnic group were targeted by angry Tibetans who had been and continue to be, at the receiving end of China's unequal policies. This unrest came at an uncomfortable time for China which was preparing for the Summer Olympics in Beijing in the same year. With large scale media reports that marred the almost perfect Beijing Olympics, the world became more conscious of a sense of urgency for freedom for the people of Tibet. Since then, China has successfully quashed all freedom of expression by imposing strict media control, yet, despite, that, the world is growing more aware of the issue of Tibet, as is evident in newspaper and media reports.

As international pressure grows on China because of its severe human rights violations in Tibet, it is important to address the issue of Sino-Tibetan relations and how these have played out on the world stage. There is enough evidence to suggest that there is a crisis-like situation inside Tibet (information regarding which is scarce owing to strict Chinese control). One example that demonstrates the extent of Chinese control is that of a Tibetan film producer, DhondupWangchen and his friend being sentenced to six years' imprisonment because their film, "Leaving Fear Behind', showed Tibetans speaking of the Dalai Lama with great fondness.[2]

Keeping the above events in mind, this paper seeks to explore the historical background of Sino-Tibetan relations. It traces the evolution of the institution of the Dalai Lama, as well as the current views across China and Tibet. Also several terms like "Middle Kingdom syndrome"[3] and "loss of face",[4] that are commonly employed in research reports and analytical papers while speaking about China's Tibet policy, will also be discussed.

China's expansionist ideologies are a well-known tenet of its foreign policy. There Chinese are three main characteristics that stand out sharply when reading China's history: first, the Chinese attachment to their land (or what they claim to be their land); second, their obsession with power; and third, the concept of losing face. These three characteristics can perhaps explain most of the Chinese behaviour and form the foundation for understanding China's foreign relations with the rest of the world.

One look at the flag of China and the country's views on the issue of Tibet becomes rather clear. The four smaller stars on the flag denote China's four ethnic minorities that include the Tartars, Uighurs, Mongols and Tibetans; while the large star is representative of the majority Han nationality. For China, therefore, the Tibetans form one of four ethnic minorities, and that Tibet is an integral part of China is a clear principle in China's Tibet policy. Further, the Chinese flag also clearly symbolises China's unquenchable thirst for territorial superiority and its intention to 'integrate' Tibet into the 'motherland'.

The primary reason cited by China for laying a territorial claim over Tibet is that it has been a part of China since the time of the Mongol invasions—and that Tibet became a part of China as a result of the conquests by the Mongol Khans. Their claim that Genghis Khan was Chinese is indeed a misconception and something that cannot be easily explained by the Chinese themselves. During Zhou Enlai's visit to New Delhi in 1960, he proclaimed that Tibet had been a part of China since the 14th century and that the Chinese did not think of it as being a separate state. In fact, the reason for his visit turning out to be unsuccessful was his protest against the perceived political interference by India in the Tibet issue, which it considered to be its internal matter.

Meanwhile, the stated goals of the Central Tibetan Authority(CTA)or what was earlier known as the Tibetan Government-in-Exile (headquartered in Dharamsala in the Indian state of Himachal Pradesh) is "rehabilitating Tibetan refugees and restoring freedom and happiness in Tibet."[5] Tibet has for a long time been viewed as a "vast zone of neutrality"[6]; a sort of buffer zone between the two Asian giants, India and China, it finally came to the forefront and became one of the highlights of the Beijing Olympics in 2008. The view held by the United States of America was that Tibet was a "blank space on the map, void of notable geopolitical significance".[7]

Is Tibet a part of China, as the Chinese claim? Or is it an in independent state, as the Tibetans would like to believe? And what is the role of the Tibetan Government-in-Exile that functions out of Dharamsala, a small hill town in the northern part of India. Although India has granted asylum to the Dalai Lama, why is he treated as a spiritual head and not accorded the status given to other heads of state? And what is his current political status? These are questions that this chapter will attempt to address by examining the history of the Sino-Tibetan conflict and exploring what could be the possible solutions to it, if any. The paper concludes with a detailed discussion on the relevance of the Dalai Lama and presents the prevalent views and analysis on whether the Tibet 'movement' will die down after the death of the Dalai Lama, as is widely speculated.

Historical Background: The Mongol Khans

At the very outset, it is important to note that the Chinese government and the Central Tibetan Administration (CTA)—the erstwhile Tibet Government-In-Exile (TGIE)—offer differing views on Tibet's independence. If one is to believe the Chinese government and accept that Tibet has always been a part of China, what was the reason behind the troops of the People's Liberation Army (PLA) invading Tibet in 1950?Further, what was the need to forcibly seize what were originally Tibetan territories? Although now Tibet is widely recognised as a part of China, there is enough evidence that points to the fact that China indeed exercised force when it came to the issue of Tibet. It is important to note here that the crisis is around the Tibetan Autonomous Region (TAR) and not the eastern parts of Tibet which include Kham and Amdo, that comprised largely Chinese territories even before the invasion in 1950. (Even historically, the Amdo region was never under the direct administration of Lhasa.)

Although in 1906 the British recognised Chinese rights over Tibet after signing an Adhesion Treaty with China in 1913 with the fall of the Qing dynasty, Tibet successfully expelled the Chinese Amban and proclaimed independence. Such an act did not go down well with China, for which the concept of "loss of face", a deep sense of offence, is sacrosanct. Further, most of China's handling of Tibet it seems has been a result of this very notion of "loss of face". One gets the feeling that Tibet has been a matter of national honour and prestige. In fact, even the India-China War in 1962, as mentioned earlier, was a result of the Chinese being insulted by what they perceived as too much interference in Tibet from the Indian side. The fact that China never accepted Tibetan independence is perhaps the foremost reason behind the current dispute. There are mainly two extremely opposite views regarding Tibet and China relations in the academic sphere[8]. One, held by pro-Tibet observers is that Tibet is an independent country and has been wrongfully incorporated into China. The second opinion, held by the pro-China observers, states that Tibet is a part of China and only split from it because of the British 'machinations' , but was 'rightly' reunited with China in 1951. This view is held by the political establishment and a majority of the Chinese, who despite great opposition from the Tibetans, maintain this stance.

It is important here to look into the details of China's historical claims. The Chinese claim over Tibet originates in the 12th century with the invasion of the Mongol Khans[9]. Prior to that period, there is evidence to show that Tibet was primarily an independent state. But what was the status of Tibet before the Mongol invasion? Is there any concrete evidence of any Chinese influence in Tibet prior to the Mongols? Even if the Chinese claim that there is, it is perhaps insignificant.

Tibet that was essentially a feudal society made up of ethnic groups originating along the Sino-Tibetan border, was finally unified somewhere between 600 and 630 AD. Tibet at that time resembled a confederation of various feudal states. It was also around this time that, as a result of the marriage between the king of the Yarlung dynasty, Srongtam Gmapo and princesses from Nepal and China that Buddhism was first introduced in Tibet.(Interestingly, China often gives the example of this alliance between the Chinese princess and the king when it makes it claims over Tibet!)

The void that was left in Tibet with the collapse of the Tibetan Empire in 842 was filled by Monastic Buddhism. Therefore, until the Mongol invasion in the early 12th century, Tibet did not have any central authority. Goden Khan, as we will see in the later section of this chapter, was the first to invade Tibet. It was on his invitation that Sakya Pandita was made the imperial preceptor, which gave rise to the *Choe-Yon*[10]relationship which became the cornerstone of Sino-Tibetan relations. Goden Khan was succeeded by Kublai Khan under whom Buddhism was adopted as a state religion. Sakya Pandita's nephew, Dogon Choegyol Phagpa became the imperial preceptor and the highest spiritual authority of Tibet. So strong was the *Choe-Yon* relationship that, in fact, in the year 1254, Kublai Khan in gratitude to his Tibetan teacher offered Phagpa political authority over all of Tibet.The phrase that needs to be explained at the very outset is the *Choe-yon* relationship, which literally translates into priest-patron since it became the cornerstone of relations between the Tibetans and the Mongols (or China, as the Chinese claim). It was the primary reason for China's claims over Tibet, as it believed that Tibet was its protectorate, since it had been providing protection in return for spiritual guidance.

Why Mongol history is important here is because China fails to make a distinction between the Mongols and itself; this despite the fact that the Mongols themselves clearly state that they ruled China and Tibet separately. In fact, a large part of the evidence that is cited by China goes back to the fact the Tibetan Lamas were bestowed titles by successive Chinese dynasties.

Further, there is not too much factual evidence of deep Sino-Tibetan ties during the Ming dynasty (1368-1644). Reading some of the limited literature that is available on the issue, one gets the impression that China is uncomfortable discussing the ties during this period.[11] What could be the reason behind this? The reason for this caution is perhaps that it was during this period that the Phagmodun kings ruled Tibet. Further, strengthening the Tibetan stand is the fact that for the first time, Tibet required absolutely no foreign protection. Also, during this period, known as the "Golden Period"[12] of Tibetan history, the king challenged the powers of the Sakya Lamas, and emerged as the new king of Tibet.

Another reason that is often cited by China when it makes its claims over Tibet is that historically Tibet sought protection from successive Chinese emperors. For example, the Qing dynasty, which succeeded the Ming, was called upon for help by the eighth Dalai Lama (1758-1804), when the Tibetans were attacked by the Gurkhas in 1788. Only a small Manchu contingent was sent at that time; but by the time of the Second Gurkha War in 1792, the Chinese and the Tibetan soldiers fought under one unified Sino-Tibetan command. The joint forces were successful in pushing back the Gurkhas. China, however, seized this opportunity, and in an attempt to have a more governance-based role in Tibet, issued a 29-point document called "Regulations for Governance". On the basis of this document, the Ambans were given the same status as that of the Dalai Lama, though this was never accepted by the Tibetans who regarded them as mere ambassadors. This was China's way to ensure more direct control over Tibet, but the Tibetans accepted only those parts of the 29-point document that suited them and chose to ignore the rest.

It is important to note here that the Tibetans only sought protection from the Qing rulers by invoking the *Choe-Yon* relationship, and did not realise that the Chinese had intentions of using this at a later stage to strengthen their claim over Tibet.

The Qing's protection that was sought by Tibet, based on the relationship, deteriorated with the decline of the Qing dynasty. (It is important to mention here that the *Choe-Yon* relationship had been weakened tremendously when Qing troops invaded Tibet in 1909). For a large part of the 18th and the early 19th centuries, Tibet managed its own affairs. Lhasa also fought the Dogra invaders (1841-42), the Gurkhas (1855-56) as well as the Younghusband expedition (1903-04).

Finally, in 1912, when the nationalist forces defeated the Qing Army, Tibet too expelled the Qing Amban and declared independence.

Tibet: Post the 1911 Revolution

During the period between the fall of the Qing dynasty in 1912 and the invasion of Tibet in 1950, Tibet enjoyed freedom and fairly less interference from its neighbouring countries. But as we will see clearly in the following section, the Chinese leadership never forgot the strategic importance of Tibet. New China's leader, Mao Zedong, took up the cause of Tibet with renewed vigour. The issue of the integration of Tibet with China now seemed like a personal goal that he had set for himself. However, that will be discussed in the following section.

As we already know, the *Choe-Yon* relationship had weakened considerably. Several advances were made by the Chinese troops into the eastern parts of Tibet, particularly Kham. After subjugating Kham, a force of 2,000 troops was sent to Lhasa, which led to the Dalai Lama leaving Lhasa along with his entourage. The Dalai Lama, who had fled to India as a result, returned only after the revolution and after the last Chinese soldier had left Lhasa. This absence of the Dalai Lama in the years preceding the 1911 revolution was exploited by China which looked to strengthen its political position in Tibet. China, in yet another attempt to achieve its goal, restored the status of the Dalai Lama as "loyal and submissive vice-regent bound by the laws of the sovereign state".[13] However, the Dalai Lama refused to accept any such titles given by the Chinese state, stating that he did not need any Chinese seal to establish his spiritual and temporal role, which the thirteenth Dalai Lama thought was the enough to declare Tibetan independence.

It is also worth noting that following the revolution in 1911, the Manchu Amban was replaced by a Chinese Amban.

By 1914, the Tibetan Army, that had been strengthened at the behest of the thirteenth Dalai Lama, had reorganised itself and resisted a bulk of the Chinese Army from eastern Tibet, further setting up its military line along the watershed between the Salween and Mekong rivers.

Soon after, there was another occasion that brought China and an independent Tibet face to face. This was when the British convened a Tripartite Convention famously called the Simla Convention in order to adopt a more aggressive policy towards Nationalist China which had issued a doctrine stating that Tibet was an integral part of China. The Simla Convention which divided Tibet into Inner Tibet and Outer Tibet (Inner Tibet, which included Kham and Amdo were to be under Chinese control) was rejected by China and, as a result, not signed by the Chinese representatives.[14] This rejection is widely believed to be due to the fact that China had specific problems of being at the same table with Tibet. What stands out here is the oft mentioned concept of "loss of face". The idea of an independent Tibet, of course, didn't go down well with China that was, and remains, concerned with additions to its territory. The claims and counter-claims with regard to Sino-Tibetan boundaries defied a resolution. McMahon had, therefore, devised the concept of Inner and Outer Tibet and related it with the concept of suzerainty. Outer Tibet comprised western Kham, central and western Tibet, while Inner Tibet comprised eastern Kham and Amdo. The British interest lay mainly in Outer Tibet. Owing to China's refusal to ratify the Simla Convention, it stood to lose certain rights. One of the primary privileges that China lost was the recognition by Britain of Chinese suzerainty over Tibet, and the right to station at Lhasa, a Chinese Amban along with a certain number of troops.

As a result of this, we can say that for all practical purposes, Tibet was an independent nation. This was until 1920, when China tried to reestablish ties with Tibet by sending a mission to Tibet to persuade it to align with China in order to keep the British at bay. The Chinese attempts failed, however, because Tibet sought British help, despite the Anglo-Russian Convention of 1907 (which barred negotiations between Tibet and Britain), China, however, did gain an upper hand in Tibet with the flight of the Panchen Lama to Beijing in 1924; China managed, for example, to drastically reduce the influence of the British and also successfully managed to display the Dalai Lama in a poor light, showing Tibet to be a highly feudal state. China also passed a resolution in 1922 whereby, all territories like Tibet, Xinjiang and Mongolia were to be a part of China but could exercise self-determination. In fact, in 1928, China, led by Sun Yatsen, also adopted a resolution which clearly stated that the Chinese minorities had a right to "self-determination" as well as the right to secede from China.

Another momentous year in Tibet's history was 1933. This was the year that the thirteenth Dalai Lama, who played an epic role in rebuilding Tibet, passed away. China, by sending a Condolence Mission headed by Gen Huang (Chiang Kaishek's vice chief of staff), got another opportunity to establish itself in Tibet. Gen Huang, who set up an office in Lhasa, was given an agenda, which included, among several suggestions, the fact that "Tibet must form a part of China" and "obey the Chinese government"[15]. Furthermore, it went on the state that the "Central Government shall grant Tibet autonomy within the framework of Chinese sovereignty."[16] Tibet did accept subordination to China, but agreed to this only within the framework of the Simla Agreement. So the proposals that were made were that Tibet would be a part of China but it would not be turned into a Chinese province; also, that Tibet would allow absolutely no interference from China in its religious and cultural affairs. It is also important to note here that Tibet did not have a strong enough army to fight off the Nationalist Army, but, at the same time, it did not want its entire eastern border to fall with the Chinese. As a result, it adopted a rather reconciliatory approach. This resulted in the Kham area being incorporated into China.

This was also due to the fact that the Kham and Amdo areas were not under the direct control of Lhasa.

Soon after these events, China was too involved with the Japanese War (1937-45) and so Tibet became lower priority. Soon after liberation in 1949, China's new leadership, under Mao Zedong, took up the Tibet issue with renewed fervour, which ultimately led to the invasion of Tibet by Chinese troops.

The Invasion

It is important to note the events leading up to the invasion of Tibet in 1950. For this purpose, it is pertinent to apprise the reader of the situation in Tibet at that time. The fourteenth Dalai Lama was still a teenager and hadn't attained ruler status yet. The government was divided into various factions, the Panchen Lama was in exile and the members of the Kashag, who were meant to be representatives of the Dalai Lama, were divided. Further, the Tibetan Army was no match for the troops of China's People's Liberation Army (PLA).

As stated earlier, Mao lost absolutely no time in his task of "liberation" of Tibet[17]. A year after declaring liberation in China, Mao sent PLA troops into Tibet. Mao clearly used Qing history to justify China's invasion of Tibet. But was he legitimate in going back to Qing history to validate the invasion? The Chinese would perhaps agree with Mao's actions, but when seen from a Tibetan point of view, Tibet had now been free for several years; added to that was their view that Tibet's relationship with China's dynasties in their own eyes was more spiritual in nature. But for Communist China, it was hard to make this distinction. Further, China was also confronted with the problem of its minorities who primarily inhabited the country's periphery like Tibet, Inner and Outer Mongolia, and Xinjiang. Mao, following Stalin's model, chose to refer to these states as "autonomous regions", corresponding somewhat to provinces.

A conflicting question that appears from the above is one that is often asked: what was the need for China to invade Tibet if it considered it part of the Chinese territory? In October 1950, three divisions of China's Eighteenth Army launched an attack at Tibet's Western Kham frontier. The Kham area, as we know, was mainly populated by Khampa nomads, who were not under the direct control of the government in Lhasa. The Khampa soldiers did put up a defence, but this was not enough to defeat the indomitable PLA troops, and soon enough, the Tibetan forces were decimated. The military invasion did not last very long. The PLA troops that had crossed the Jingsha river in eastern Tibet on October 6 and 7, defeated the Tibetan troops by October 19. Western Kham was set up as Chamdo territory, which eventually became a part of Tibet Autonomous Region (TAR), while eastern Kham (previously Xikang) was merged into Sichuan province.

Once the PLA troops had been deployed, China surprisingly did not continue with its military campaign and offered to Tibet a "peaceful" proposal[18]. This famously came to be known as the *Seventeen Point Agreement for the Peaceful Liberation of Tibet*. The Governor of Cham, Jigme Ngabo, who is regarded by some Tibetans as a traitor, was responsible for the Tibetan troops. He, undoubtedly, realised the futility of fighting the PLA troops. As a result, it was soon decided that a group of officials would travel to Beijing to negotiate a deal. It is important to note here that China has used the Seventeen Point Agreement to legitimise its sovereignty over Tibet; but the circumstances under which the deal was signed were entirely illegal. The Tibetan side claimed that it was forced to sign the agreement, despite the fact that it had not been authorised to do so. The instructions given to it were that certain points were to be negotiated on with the Chinese side, but clearly not for signing the document. The Tibetan officials also claimed that they were not allowed communication with their government in Lhasa; further, they were not given permission to make any recommendations or alterations to the document. In other words, therefore, China allowed absolutely no negotiations and simply asked the Tibetans to sign the document. What becomes clear here is that the Seventeen Point Agreement does not in any way legitimise Chinese sovereignty over Tibet since Tibet was made to sign it under duress. Although China claims that it received an authorisation letter from the Dalai Lama, there is no proof of that; further, the Dalai Lama himself has repudiated the agreement on several occasions! (However, this was only after the Dalai Lama went into exile in India.)

On the basis of this agreement, Tibet became a part of China. China was allowed to station its troops inside Tibet; further, all matters relating to defence were now under Chinese control. Tibet's foreign affairs too were to be looked after by China. As a result of this, no country recognises the Tibetan Government-in-Exile (TGIE). In a surprising concession that Mao made (although it is widely believed that this was because he had no local Communist government to look after Tibet when he invaded it), he allowed the authority of the Dalai Lama to continue, and the traditional government to remain in power; further, Tibet's religion would be respected. The Dalai Lama, as is mentioned in the following section, did attempt to work at the agreement through the early 1950s , but soon, there was brewing tension in the eastern part of Tibet, which spread to Tibet main, ultimately leading to the Dalai Lama leaving Tibet for India, where he remains till date.

Several reasons for China's stand on Tibet now come to the forefront. Out of these, the ones that stand out are: firstly, to use Tibet as a 'buffer' between itself and other countries. As we are well aware, in the 'great game' Tibet was used as a 'pawn' in the hands of bigger players. Tibet, as we know, by virtue of its location, has been used as an important barrier between relatively stronger nations. There is no denying that in the early 20th century, the British maintained relations with Tibet in an attempt to counter the growing influence of the Russians. Another factor could possibly be the strategic geopolitical position of Tibet, or further, the fact that 40 percent[19] of China's natural resources are in Tibet. Identifying one reason can be a difficult task. Another rather conflicting reason that is often cited by China is that the intention behind the invasion of Tibet was also to rid it of serfdom that was highly prevalent in Tibetan society. China claims that prior to its invasion of Tibet in 1950, Tibet was 'hell on earth'. In fact, supporters of the invasion suggest that 95 percent of Tibetans lived in feudal serfdom before 1950, and go on to cite cases of severe cruelty and abuse in the traditional Tibetan system. According to the People's Republic of China (PRC), "There was a historically imperative need for progress of Tibetan society and welfare of Tibetan people to expel the imperialists and shake off the yoke of feudal serfdom. The founding of the People's Republic of China in 1949 brought hope for the deeply distressed Tibetan people." To this, the TGIE responds, "The Chinese justifications make no sense. First of all, international law does not accept justifications of this type. No country is allowed to invade, occupy, annex and colonize another country just because its social structure doesn't please it. Secondly, the PRC is responsible for bringing more suffering in the name of liberation."[20]

What best explains the reasons for China's stance on Tibet are the words of George Ginsburg, "He who holds Tibet, dominates the Himalayan piedmont; he who dominates the Himalayan piedmont, threatens the Indian subcontinent; and he who dominates the Indian subcontinent, may well have all Southeast Asia within his reach, all of Asia."[21]

Many pro-China thinkers are of the view that Tibet has repeatedly sought to internationalise the issue; be it through the Dalai Lama's opinions stated at various international forums or even the worldwide protests carried out by various Tibetan groups. China, however, has made all attempts to sweep the issue under the carpet, claiming that Tibet is an internal matter.

China has seen unprecedented growth in the last century, making it the "new great power of the 21st century". But China's meteoric rise has come at a price. Not only has it not been peaceful but, on the contrary, it has been a violent one. In the last century, China has been involved in several border disputes that have arisen due to the unclear demarcation of boundaries with most of its neighbouring countries. China shares its borders with fourteen countries. One of the implications of this has been the continuous border disputes that it has been involved in. This has had a deep impact on its unfolding relations with its neighbours, thus, influencing stability and peace in the region.

No sooner had the new China been established than it swiftly doubled its territorial size by forcibly absorbing Xinjiang and Tibet.

Tibet, as has been mentioned previously, with its population of approximately two million, became a protectorate of China only during the Qing dynasty (1644-1911). After the fall of the last dynasty, the Qing, China lost its initial rule over Tibet, as Tibet now strove to regain its independence. However, the Chinese continued to lay claim over it. In 1949, when the Chinese Communist Party (CCP) founded the PRC, it made Tibet an autonomous region of China. It sent the PLA troops in 1950 and in 1951, signed an agreement with the current Dalai Lama, the 14th, Tenzin Gyatso, allowing the Tibetans to continue with their system, though under Chinese control.

Also worth mentioning here is the Patriotic Education Campaign that was started by China in Tibet in all earnest in 1996. It was started in monasteries and nunneries, and the monks were forced to study four pamphlets. Only on completion of the study and successfully passing the subsequent examination were the monks allowed to remain in the monasteries and nunneries. The first pamphlet comprised the history of Tibet, which in no uncertain terms stated that Tibet had historically been a part of China, and any talk of Tibetan independence was a result of Western imperialism. The second pamphlet while stressing the inevitably of Tibet being a part of China if it wanted to prosper, spoke of the Dalai Lama and his spilittist ways as well as the ills of serfdom in the society. The third pamphlet dealt with the Chinese legal system and how it applied to religious institutions. The fourth pamphlet stated the CCP's views on religion and clarified that religion ought to conform to the socialist society.

For the Chinese, it was a "sacred duty" to liberate Tibet and "to make the east wind prevail".[22] By cooperating with its neighbours, China has successfully created an environment that is conducive to economic growth. An economically strong China could, therefore, effectively supress ethnic and religious uprisings in the future.

The Dalai Lama

The 'institution' of the Dalai Lama is now, more than ever, at the centre of the Sino-Tibetan conflict. Most of the somewhat 'weak' evidence given by China in its claims over Tibet revolves around the ties between the Mongol Khans (clearly failing to make a distinction between them and China) and Tibet, and the bestowing of titles on the Dalai Lama by successive Manchu emperors. Therefore, suffice it to say that there are primarily two main reasons that China cites to legitimise its claim over Tibet; these are, firstly, that owing to the conquest of Tibet by the Mongol Khans in the 13th century, Tibet became a part of the Mongol empire and as a result, a part of the Chinese empire.

(The Mongols, however, claim that they ruled Tibet and China separately). Secondly, and more significantly, the Chinese claim that they played an important role in the selection of the Dalai Lama, and the bestowing of various titles on him. In fact, even the title of Dalai Lama, as the Chinese news agency, Xinhua New Agency states, "was granted by the central agencies of China's dynasties"[23] and not created by Tibetan Buddhism or granted by the old ruling class of Tibetans. However, these attempts by China have been unsuccessful so far as even at present, the 'cult' of the Dalai Lama only seems to be growing and getting stronger. With a sharp increase in the number of self-immolations (since 2009 there have been a total of 125 confirmed self-immolations , 12 in 2009, 86 in 2012 and 27 in 2013) [24] by Tibetans fighting for independence, and the Dalai Lama's return to Tibet, it is hard to overlook the hold that he has over the people of Tibet. A report in the *Tibet Daily* shows that senior Tibetan official, Padma Choling, chairman of the Standing Committee of the Tibet Autonomous regional People's Congress, said in Lhasa, that the Government-in-Exile in India is two-faced because it claims to ban self-immolations, but actually "fans extremism in China".[25]

Further, several remarks by China's top political leadership highlight the tactics that China is trying to employ in order to, what they term, 'expose' the Lama's façade, accusing him of encouraging self-immolations. For example, the newly elected President Xi Jinping is believed to have stressed the need to "fight against the separatist activities by the Dalai Lama group and completely destroy any attempt to undermine stability in Tibet and national unity."[26] The role of the Dalai Lama is central to the conflict because China sees him as one of the biggest hurdles in its ability to integrate Tibet into China. This is mainly due to the support that the Dalai Lama finds with the people of Tibet, who have revered the institution for centuries. Not only this, the Dalai Lama is seen as the face of Tibet's international campaign. It is even conjectured that the Tibetans themselves might lose their commitment to the Tibetan cause, with the death of the fourteenth Dalai Lama.

Keeping this in mind, this section, therefore, seeks to explore how the Dalai Lama has come to be the face of the Tibetan struggle for independence. While doing this, it attempts to trace the historical background of the evolution of the institution, and how the Dalai Lama now, by virtue of the position he holds in the hearts of the Tibetan people, is playing a vital role in Sino-Tibetan relations. An attempt will also be made to highlight the role that the Dalai Lama played in Sino-Indian relations. The conclusion will focus on the future prospects for China-Tibet relations, in a scenario when the present Dalai Lama is no more.

Dalai Lama: Historical Background

Historical evidence has shaped most of China's arguments when it comes to the issue of Tibet or the Dalai Lama who now holds an influential position. Also, it is one of the main arguments that China makes in its ownership claims. Therefore, the historical background of the how the institution of the Dalai Lama came about is tremendously important. Looking at the history of Tibet, or for that matter the relations between Tibet and China or the impact that these have had on the stability of Asia, one cannot ignore the role that the Dalai Lama has played in the events that have unfolded. What was the reason for his escape every time that Tibet faced a crisis? And why was the main concern of the Tibetan people to ensure the Dalai Lama's safety?

Although the Mongols emphasise that they ruled China and Tibet separately, most of the evidence given by China in its claims over Tibet, dates back to the time of the Mongol empire, also known as the Yuan dynasty. Using the Dalai Lama (often as a pawn), the Chinese realised, would add legitimacy to their ploy in the eyes of the people of Tibet.

Goden Khan[27] was the first Mongol to invade Tibet. Tibet was at that time ruled by Songtsen Gampo of the Yarlung dynasty. Buddhism, introduced first into Tibet by Songtsen Gampo, especially under the Gelugpa sect[28] was flourishing at this time. When faced with the dominant Mongols, the Tibetans realised that they were no match for the invading Mongol armies and needed urgently to protect their territories. Spirituality came for their rescue here, as Goden Khan, who recognised the importance of spirituality, invited Sakya Pandita, the nephew of Songsten Gampo, to his court to become the imperial preceptor. This change of heart benefitted the Tibetans the most, since this was the beginning of the long *Choe-Yon*[29] relationship which became the cornerstone of the relations between the Mongols and the Tibetans and something that the Chinese, at a later stage would exploit in their claims of suzerainty. This priest-patron relationship continued to flourish during the 14th century, wherein, in return, for spiritual guidance, the emperors would protect the Sakya Lamas. The Lamas were also given several titles by the Mongol and the Manchu rulers. This bestowing of titles on the Lamas often forms the basis of the rather weak claim of suzerainty. Many Indian scholars have been felicitated by foreign universities, but this doesn't necessarily mean that they've lost their Indian citizenship! So the Chinese claim seems a little weak.

Rise of the Dalai Lama

The institution of the Dalai Lama came into prominence with the further advent of the Gelugpa or the Yellow Hats sect. As mentioned earlier, it was founded at the end of the 14th century and flourished thereon. It was in the 15th century primarily that the sect rose to eminence and its influence spread to central Tibet. Altan Khan, a descendant of Kublai

Khan was the first to give the title of the Dalai (originally Talei) Lama, meaning the 'Ocean of Wisdom' to Sonam Gyatso, who was his guru. The title of the first and second Dalai Lama was given retrospectively to Tsong Khapa and Gedun Gyatso respectively after the death of Sonam Gyatso. Further, with the ascent of the Gelugpa sect, the clerical office of the Dalai Lama also rose, and he began to serve as the head of the Tibetan traditional council. It was during the Ming dynasty (1368-1644) in China when, in order to keep the military threat from the Mongols at bay, there was a surge in the number of titles that were bestowed on senior Lamas from Tibet. The Chinese perhaps thought that through these titles given to the 'priests' they could manipulate the 'patrons'. Two important questions that arise here are: what was the status of Tibet during the Ming dynasty, and why was there a need on China's part to protect itself from the Mongol threat if most of their claim relies on the fact that they were not separate from the Mongols? Isn't it true, that for all practical purposes, Tibet was independent at the time of the Ming dynasty?

It was during the reign of the fifth Dalai Lama, also known as the Great Fifth that the political structure in Tibet became a little more organised and definite. Under the patronage of the Gushri Khan, the Dalai Lama set up a new form of government known as the Kashag[30], with himself as its head. The Dalai Lama remained the head of the Kashag until 1959 and came to be the spiritual and the temporal head of Tibet. The Kashag is still being maintained by the Central Tibetan Authority (CTA) in Dharamsala with Lobsang Sangay as its Kalon Tripaor, the prime minister. This was shortly after the Dalai Lama gave up his temporal role and resigned as the leader of the CTA in 2011.

The thirteenth Dalai Lama who, seizing the opportunity of a weakened Qing dynasty, in 1912, declared an independent Tibet, also expelling the last of the Chinese officials stationed at Lhasa. The Chinese, for whom the idea of 'loss of face' is prime, were deeply angered by this, and part of the anti-Dalai Lama propaganda can be viewed as an attempt to avenge this 'humiliation'

It is true that the Chinese realised, although a little late, that the only way to exert influence over Tibet was through their leader and, therefore, the Dalai Lama. The people of Tibet, as we know, revere the Dalai Lama and look up to him not only for guidance on spiritual aspects but also on all other aspects, although he has given up his temporal role. China knew that once it succeeded in controlling the Dalai Lama, there would be a sense of legitimacy of Chinese rule in the minds of the Tibetan people. So their historical claim on Tibet centred on the history and the origin of the Dalai Lama.

Dalai Lama: Sino-India Relations

It is also worth underlining how the Dalai Lama has influenced bilateral ties between

India and China and thereby impacted the peace and stability of the entire Asian region. The Dalai Lama became the tipping point of the breakdown in Sino-India relations. As we know, that it was the flight of the Dalai Lama, and him being granted asylum by the Government of India, that led to the ultimate breakdown in Sino-Indian relations. As Natwar Singh states in his book, *My China Diary*, "The day the Dalai Lama walked into India in the end of March 1959, the character and content of Sino-Indian relations altered drastically. By the time Zhou Enlai came to India in 1960, the point of no return had almost been reached." [31] The fact that India has provided a safe haven for the Dalai Lama and thousands of other Tibetans hasn't gone down well with the Chinese, and continues to be a bone of contention between the two neighbours. Tibet, under the guidance of the Dalai Lama, established the Central Tibet Administration, previously known as the Tibetan Government-in-Exile, which is said to be the representative of the people of Tibet. This fact irks the Chinese the most, who feel that there is too much interference by India in its internal matters (Tibet being an internal Chinese issue). In fact, one of the primary reasons for the Sino-Indian War in 1962, as experts say, is that China (under the leadership of Mao) wanted to "teach India a lesson." Despite repeated assurances given by successive Indian prime ministers that Tibetan activities will be controlled on Indian soil, there exists a trust deficit between the two countries.

Even China's reaction to the Dalai Lama's Nobel Prize was centred on the claim that there had been too much interference by other countries in its 'internal' issues. All matters relating to Tibet and the Dalai Lama, they claim, are strictly China's concern, and no other country should interfere.

The Panchen Lama

Any talk of the Dalai Lama is incomplete without highlighting the position and the role of the Panchen Lama. The Panchen Lama is considered to be the second highest ranking Lama after the Dalai Lama, and has in the past served as the replacement to the Dalai Lama during the intervening period between the death and the selection of a new Dalai Lama. As a result of this, the Tibetans consider the Dalai Lama and curiously, also the Panchen Lama to be supreme in spiritual matters. This lack of differentiation has been skilfully used by China in their anti-Dalai Lama propaganda. The Dalai Lama and Panchen Lama have been at loggerheads even in the past. For example, the ninth Panchen Lama (1883-1937) fled to Mongolia after a dispute with the Dalai Lama over the issue of taxes. This kind of a strained relationship had been used by China to its advantage. In 1949, when Mao invaded Tibet, the Panchen Lama supported China's claim on Tibet, as a result of which he was appointed acting chairman of the "Preparatory Committee for the Tibet Autonomous Region", a post previously held by the Dalai Lama. More recently, in March this year, the Panchen Lama has been appointed as a member of the Standing Committee of the Chinese People's Political Consultative Conference National Committee, one of China's top political advisory bodies. The eleventh Panchen Lama also came out strongly against the riots that erupted in 2008, stating that the acts "not only harmed the interests of the nation and the people, but also violated the aims of Buddhism."[32] However, it is important to stress on the fact that the present Panchen Lama has been selected by China, and the status of the Dalai Lama's choice is unknown. The Panchen Lama, therefore, is manipulated by the Communist regime in China and more often than not, tows their line. Since the Panchen Lama plays an important role in the selection of the next Dalai Lama, this move has been viewed as extremely calculated. Keeping the Panchen Lama on their side, the Chinese realise, they can influence the next selection. The Panchen Lama, therefore, is seen as a conduit for China in its attempt to win over the confidence of the people of Tibet. The Dalai Lama, however, has strongly disapproved of the fact the Panchen Lama is being used as a puppet in the hands of China.

What is the status of the Panchen Lama who was selected by the present Dalai Lama? While the Chinese claim that he is safe and leading a normal life, there are slight discrepancies in their details of his exact whereabouts, with some presuming that he may be dead.

The Middle Way Approach

The fourteenth Dalai Lama has proposed, what is called the '*Middle Way of autonomy*' to resolve the issue of the independence of Tibet; a solution that he says should be acceptable to Tibet as well as China. The Dalai Lama, as mentioned earlier, pioneered efforts all through the early 1950s to rework the Seventeen Point Agreement, which he claimed was signed under duress. Not achieving much success, he was forced to seek asylum in India. The negotiations for the 'Middle Way' are somewhat analogous to those of the abovementioned agreement. The Middle Way approach was adopted by the Dalai Lama, after talks with Deng Xiaoping who told him rather categorically that, "except independence, all other issues can be resolved through negotiations". The Middle Way approach as proposed by the Dalai Lama does not seek independence for Tibet which, the Tibetans claim is a historical fact. Treading a cautious and middle path, it suggests autonomy for the three traditional provinces of Tibet within the framework of the People's Republic of China (PRC). This autonomy would be governed by an independently and democratically elected legislature and executive. In a clear softening of stand, Tibet, led by the Dalai Lama has agreed that once the above criteria are fulfilled, it will not seek separation, and will work within the framework of the People's Republic of China. While the central government of the PRC will be responsible for the political aspects of Tibet's international relations and defence, the people of Tibet will concern themselves with all matters relating to Tibet such as religion and culture, education, economy, environmental protection to name a few. The Chinese, the approach goes on to suggest, should stop all human rights' violations and the transfer of Chinese nationals to Tibetan areas. The Dalai Lama, it says, will be responsible for all negotiations pertaining to the approach with China. To give an example of the hold that the Dalai Lama has over the Tibetans, nearly 64 percent of the Tibetans were in support of the Middle Way approach and did not feel the need for a referendum. However, the Dalai Lama's Middle Way of autonomy has been rejected by groups such as the Tibetan Youth Congress and the Young Tigers, who are willing to consider violence as an approach.

Conclusion: Emerging Scenarios

There hasn't been much of a shift in China's Tibet policy over the recent years. The continuing protests by Tibetan nationals are seen by China as being encouraged by the Dalai Lama and, what they call his "clique".[33] A report in *The Hindu* newspaper last year stated that China will "resolutely crush"[34] any activities that destabilise peace in the Tibetan areas of western China. Jia Qinglin, a senior Politburo member and the highest official in charge of ethnic affairs in China said, "The clique of the Dalai Lama are trying in vain to continuously create incidents in Tibet and Tibetan occupied areas".[35] Further, he is believed to have said that the conspiracy by the Dalai Lama's clique "to make Tibetan areas unstable, needs to be resolutely crushed". China also claims, as mentioned earlier, that it is indeed the Dalai Lama who encourages self-immolations by Tibetan agitators. Part of their anti- Dalai Lama propaganda revolves around this. They say that the idea of self-immolations goes against the basic tenets of Buddhism, and by encouraging these, the Dalai Lama isn't being loyal to Buddhism.

As has been discussed earlier, China and Tibet are now facing two possible scenarios when it comes to the issue of the future of the Tibetan agitation in the context of the presence of the Dalai Lama. China first: with the death of the fourteenth Dalai Lama, China can possibly promote the Panchen Lama, somebody propped up by the Chinese regime itself and also someone who may be be possibly revered by the Tibetans as he is the second highest Lama. By having an influential figure like the Panchen Lama, China can possibly move a step closer in bringing about a change in the people of Tibet with the further hope that this change in mindset may help in the toning down of the agitation. Also, with the Panchen Lama as a Chinese puppet, they can indirectly have a say in the selection of the next Dalai Lama, thereby influencing negotiations between Tibet and China. Or secondly, although it seems to be an unlikely scenario, given the 'Middle Kingdom Syndrome' and the Chinese obsession with expanding territory, they may accept the Middle Way approach that has been proposed by the present Dalai Lama. For the Tibetans: the death of the Dalai Lama could hold serious and unfortunate repercussions. Firstly, his absence at the helm may lead the agitation to die out, and the fact that Tibet is a part of China, will have to be accepted as a *fait accompli.* Another picture is that the present struggle continuing in the absence of a moderate leader can go out of hand. We have also seen a sharp rise in the number of self-immolations and the fact that the Middle Way approach has been rejected by some Tibetan groups, leads to the possibility of violent clashes resulting in the destabilising of peace in this region.

Therefore, we can conclude that in China, the Dalai Lama faces a formidable adversary. He must push for a peaceful settlement of the dispute through negotiations. The hold that he has over the people of Tibet is unchallenged; therefore, he ought to ensure that the crisis is resolved in his lifetime. Although he has hinted that his successor will not necessarily be from Tibet, it is important that the next Dalai Lama must also push for a peaceful settlement of the dispute; which should have something for the people of Tibet as well as China, and as a result be an important catalyst for the peace and stability of this entire region.

Notes

1. George Ginsburgs and Michael Mathos, *Communist China and Tibet: The First Dozen Years* (The Hague: Martinul Nijhoff, 1964).
2. Jayadev Ranade, *China Unveiled: Insight into the Chinese Strategic Thinking* (New Delhi: Knowledge World, 2013), pp. 267- 269.
3. Middle Kingdom is the traditional translation of China's common name, *Zhongguo.*
4. Loss of face, translation of the traditional *diulian,* is known as shame or the ultimate embarrassment in Chinese culture, and something that at all costs must be avoided.
5. The Central Tibetan Administration, first established in Mussorie, India, in 1959 as the Tibetan Government-in-Exile Administration, was shifted to Dharamsala in 1960 as the continuation of the government of independent Tibet, at http://tibet.net/about-cta/, accessed July 2013.
6. Mikel Dunham, *Buddha's Warriors: The Story of CIA Backed Tibetan Freedom Fighters, The Chinese Invasion and the Ultimate Fall of Tibet* (New Delhi :Penguin Books, 2005), pp. 1-3.
7. Ibid.
8. BhavnaTripathi, "The Tibetan Uprising and Indian Opinion of the Chinese", *Journal of Defence Studies*, vol. 6, issue 4, at http://idsa.in/system/files/jds_6_4_BhavnaTripathy.pdf, accessed on November 21, 2013.
9. Kallie Szczepanski, "Tibet and China: History of a Complex Relationship, Asian History", at http://asianhistory.about.com/*od*/china/a/TibetandChina.html, accessed November 2013.
10. *Choe-Yon* means priest-patron, and roughly corresponds to the guru-disciple relationship
11. For more details, see Diane Wolff, *Tibet Unconquered* (New York: Palgrave Macmillan, 2010),

pp. 74-75; Claude Arpi, *Tibet: The Lost Frontier* (New Delhi : Lancer Publishers, 2008), pp. 38- 39; V P Malhotra, *Tibet Conundrum* (New Delhi: Knowledge World, 2006), pp. 100-101

12. *History of Tibet*, Tibetan Alliance of Chicago, at http://tibetan-alliance.org/nomads/?page_id=21, accessed September 2013.
13. Melvyn C. Goldstein, *A History of Modern Tibet, 1913-1951:The Demise of the Lamaist State* (University of California Press, 1989) p. 49.
14. Nirmal C. Sinha, "The Simla Convention 1914: A Chinese Puzzle", at https//www.repository.cam.ac.uk/bitstream/handle/1810/243068/bot_1987_02_01.pdf?sequence=1, accessed July, 2013.
15. Goldstein, n. 13, p. 238.
16. Ibid.
17. Arpi, n. 11, pp. 165-168.
18. Ibid.
19. Antoaneta Bezlova, "Tibet: China's Little Treasure", Asian Times Online at http://atimes.com/atimes/China_Business/HI19Cb02.html, accessed September, 2013.
20. http://en.wikipedia.org/wiki/Serfdom_in_Tibet_controversy
21 Gingsburgs and Mathos, n. 1.
22 Arpi, n. 11.
23. Liu Wei, "The Origin of the Title of 'Dalai Lama' and its Related Backgrounder", Xinhua News Agency, March 2009, at http://news.xinhuanet.com/english/2009-03/01/content_10921943.htm, accessed July 2013.
24. "Map: Self-Immolations in Tibet from 2009-2013", International Campaign for Tibet, December 19, 2013, at https://www.savetibet.org/resources/fact-sheets/self-immolations-by-tibetans/map-tibetan-self-immolations-from- 2009-2013/, accessed December , 2013.
25. "Tibetan Exiled Government called Two- Faced, China Daily", March 6, 2013, at http://www.chinadaily.com.cn/china/2013npc/2013-03/06/content_16280933.htm, accessed July 2013.
26. Ranade, n. 2, p. 269.
27. Goden Khan was the grandson of Ghengis Khan.
28. Also known as the Yellow Hat sect of Tibetan Buddhism
29. See *Choe-Yon.* Priest-patron.
30. See *Kashag*. The highest executive office of the Central Tibetan Administration.
31. K Natwar Singh, *My China Diary (*New Delhi:Rupa& Co. , 2009), p. 86.
32. "Panchen Lama Takes Higher Advisory Position", Xinhua, March 12, 2013, at http://www.chinadaily.com.cn/china/2013npc/2013-03/12/content_16303296.html
33. "The Dalai Clique's Separatist Activities and the Central Government's Policy", at http://chineseculture.about.com/library/china/whitepaper/blstibet9204.htm
34. Ananth Krishnan, "China: Will Crush the Dalai Lama Clique", *The Hindu,* March 2, 2012. http://www.thehindu.com/news/international/china-will-crush-dalai-lama-clique/article2954854.ece
35. Wang Li, "Jia: Resolutely Crush Dalai Lama Clique's Conspiracy, People's Daily", Online. http://english.peopledaily.com.cn/90785/7745243.htm

11

Separatist Movement in Xinjiang: Implications for the Regional Security Environment

Pravda. P

Introduction

China has been the cynosure of the 21st century world view. It has successfully manoeuvred its emergence by taking paths less trodden in international relations. Seeking to project its rise, not as a threat, but as an asset to other nations, it preferred to project its 'peaceful development' rather than 'peaceful rise'. However, this poses a multitude of challenges on the way for the People's Republic of China(PRC), like promoting its "soft power", projecting its image as a "responsible major power" (*fuzeren de daguo*) and, most of all, maintaining and expanding its international participation through multilateral, regional and bilateral interactions.[1] The separatist struggle of the Uyghur minority in Xinjiang is intertwined closely with these aspirations of China. It presents a precarious picture, something beyond what a mere separatist movement can exemplify.

The Uyghurs are China's fifth largest minority nationality from its northwest province of Xinjiang, with a population of about 8.9 million. The separatist saga of the Uyghurs who seek to break away from the PRC and establish an independent 'Eastern Turkistan' is more than 200 years old. Historically, the Uyghurs were an integral part of Central Asia. The genesis of the relentless struggle of the Uyghurs in Xinjiang for a separate Eastern Turkistan can be traced back to the integration of Xinjiang with China by the Qing rulers in 1759 by defeating the Oirats.[2] Though the Chinese historians would preferably call it a "unification" rather than "conquest",[3] this was not merely a political integration, but the beginning of a systematic suppression of the long held cultural and religious values and practices of the Uyghurs. The Qing rulers exercised effective domination of the native political community of Xinjiang by attaining the decision-making authority and from the late 18th century, began to promote Han immigration to Xinjiang.

However, the administration of Xinjiang under the Qing rulers was shortlived. Through persistent rebellion, the Uyghurs sought autonomy, which they finally achieved with the Yakub Beg rebellion (1864-79) under Yakub Beg, a Khan of Kokand (now a part of Uzbekistan).[4] The Uyghurs enjoyed a brief period of statehood: the first, from 1931 to 1934, and the second from 1944 to 1949. But in 1949, the Communist government annexed the territory back and gave it its present name—Xinjiang Uyghur Autonomous Region (XUAR). Since then, the PRC has maintained firm political control of the region. In 1955, the status of 'autonomous region' was conferred on Xinjiang. However, a strong ethnic identity and Turkic roots persist among the Uyghurs, and catalyse the movement even today. The effort of the government to dilute the ethnic spirit by mobilising the Han population into Xinjiang has aggravated the situation, by causing competition for resources and social space.

Post the demise of the Soviet Union, it was undoubtedly felt in Beijing that with the emergence of the post-Soviet space, Central Asia, with its instability and sudden upsurge of Islamist extremism would have negative consequences on the PRC as a whole and the XUAR in particular. The very fact that their neighbors, ethnically and religiously similar, were granted independence also strengthened the motives of the Uyghurs.

With the high profile security alert announced during the Beijing Olympics of 2008 and the subsequent cooperation with the United States in combating terrorism, the separatist movement in Xinjiang drew the attention of the international community. Further, with the Amnesty International Report "Justice, Justice" on the July 2009 protests in Xinjiang, reporting the violent suppression of peaceful protests, and the arbitrary arrests and human rights violations committed by the authorities against the Uyghurs, Xinjiang has become the focal point of the human rights watch.[5]

The separatist movement is currently active and still figures prominently on China's internal security concerns. In June 2013, dozens died in a violent eruption in Xinjiang on ethnic grounds that have forced the new leadership to adopt extraordinary security measures in the affected districts. Following this, in August 2013, 15 Uyghurs were shot dead in a police shootout during a lightning raid. Three suspected Islamic militants, accused of the June terrorist attack, were sentenced to death in September 2013.

The political leadership constantly issues statements calling for the support of other nations in combating the separatism in Xinjiang. China's top political advisor, Yu Zhengsheng, in September 2013, called for better employment, education and talent to ensure development and stability in Xinjiang at a conference held on September 23 and 24 on other regions' assistance in the development of XUAR. Admitting that Xinjiang still faces many special difficulties in development and stability, he stressed bilingual and vocational education as well as education on ideology and politics to promote scientific knowledge and competence among the local people. He also called on other regions of the country to support Xinjiang, by setting goals and ensuring implementation of projects in the region.[6]China had also recently rebutted the US advocacy for Uyghur separatism by saying that Tibetan and Uyghur minorities enjoyed "unprecedented freedom".

The separatist movement in Xinjiang poses a myriad challenges to the PRC. Given the geographical positioning of Xinjiang, the course of separatism here will have significant implications for the regional actors also. The province houses the 1,300 km Karakoram Highway starting from Kashgar and ending at Hasan Abdal in Khyber Pukhtunkwa province of Pakistan. The artery of the Sino-Pak nexus, the Karakoram Highway witnesses bustling trade and trans-border movement. It has also been the medium for some of the most important arms and missile transfers from China to Pakistan. Chinese nuclear and military equipment, including the MH missiles, reportedly traversed the Karakoram Highway to reach Pakistan.[7] There is also a proposed road leading from Hasan Abdal to further south, extending up to Gwadar port. Notably, the Khushab and Chashma reactors of Pakistan are located along this road, thus, making it a link of utmost strategic importance to China.

Due to the proximity of the region to Pakistan, Afghanistan and Central Asia, it has the threatening potential to evolve as a hub of Islamist terrorism. The PRC also fears that the secession of Xinjiang will strengthen the separatist movements in Inner Mongolia and Tibet. This increases the complexity of the issue. There are other factors too that contribute to the region's importance to China. The separatist struggle, which has led to enormous eruptions of violent incidents, allegedly supported by the terrorist factions of Pakistan, has had a significant impact on Sino-Pak relations. The future of the province will be of special significance to India, which shares long-standing border issues with China. This mainly arises from the geographical positioning of Xinjiang in relation to India and its contested borders. This implies that India's responses to the separatist aspirations of the Uyghur nationalists should not be mere rhetoric in support or denial of the cause of an ethnic group seeking democratic fulfilment, but a calculated response which will have significant and long-term consequences. The stand that India adopts should be a careful one, weighing both negative and positive implications of a break off, without compromising, but rather promoting, the nation's policies and principles. This would be made possible by an analysis of the history and legitimacy of the movement and the strategic choices and chances that await India. Thus, when one views China's rising stature through the prism of the separatist struggle in Xinjiang, it manifests a multitude of implications, not only for the PRC but also for the regional security environment. A holistic analysis of the separatist movement in Xinjiang will bring into the picture, the various facets of China's challenges from the movement that are intrinsically linked with the regional security environment.

Implications for Regional Security

The Xinjiang separatist movement presents concerns not only for the PRC but also for regional security in itself which is inherently embedded in its connections with the regional states and the impact that it will have on the PRC, a major global player. The separatist movement of the Uyghurs and its course of action was initiated and spurred by various regional factors like the independence of the Central Asian Republics (CAR), trade and subsequent cross-border support from Pakistan, and the synergy with the much analogous Tibetan independence movement. The fact that the troubled Xinjiang and Tibet together occupy a major portion of China's total land area, poses a threat to the internal security of China, as mentioned earlier, which, in turn, will have an impact on its defence policies, and economic and energy resources. When one applies the realist paradigm which assumes that statesmen think and act in terms of power, the separation of Xinjiang and Tibet from China will be in the interest of the other competitive nations as this will increase their strength relative to China.

However, deeper intricacies of the separation present contrasting colours. The policy choices that India and the other regional actors would adopt will be essentially by assessing these contrasting factors and acting in terms of their preponderant interests. These policies will be further influenced by the nature of the government in power, its ideological affinity and the nation state's economic and security interests. Xinjiang shares a 5,743 km boundary with eight countries, including Russia, Kazakhstan, Kyrgyzstan, Tajikistan, Mongolia, Afghanistan, Pakistan and India.[8] By circumscribing the term 'regional' relative to Xinjiang, these nations can be taken into consideration. The region houses most of the centrifugal forces that are allegedly promoting the cause of the Uyghur movement. China has been manifesting all aspects of its diplomacy to garner the support of the regional actors to nip the separatist movement.

Central Asia: Xinjiang is sometimes referred to as "Chinese Central Asia", owing to its cultural and political roots. The Central Asian nations that border Xinjiang Uyghur Autonomous Region (XUAR) are Tajikistan, Kyrgyzstan and Kazakhstan. China considers diplomatic relations with these peripheral nations important. This is represented in its 'periphery policy', the core of its external strategy to fortify its sovereignty and relations with the peripheral states. The importance of these nations for China has increased manifold ever since it has been facing separatist struggles in Xinjiang.

China has expressed its fundamental interests in Central Asia as follows on various occasions:[9]

- 1. Establishing peaceful and good-neighbourly relations. For China, Central Asia holds importance in many ways as a neighbour, in terms of natural resources, as a part of the Muslim world and a gateway to the West. It hopes to build long-term and privileged relations with the region.
- 2. Evolving cooperation on the basis of mutual benefit and common prosperity. China-Central Asia relations are an exemplary model of mutually beneficial relations. While the relations with Central Asia help China appear as a peaceful rising power that can engage through multilateral fora, and give it a hold over the natural resources, Central Asia benefits from the transport and pipeline linkages and loans provided by China.
- 3. Giving due respect to the choices of the Central Asian masses and non-interference in the internal affairs of these nations. China aims to be a "responsible stakeholder" through the rhetoric of mutual non-aggression and mutual non-interference in the internal affairs of the Central Asian states.
- 4. Respecting independent sovereignty as well as promoting stability in the region. This is perhaps Chine's primary concern in the region. The challenges of China in its western province of Xinjiang are closely linked with the Central Asian security architecture in this respect.

One of the most pronounced ripples in the relationship between the Central Asian nations and China come from the Uyghur elements of Central Asia, who support, fund and sympathise with the Uyghur nationalists in Xinjiang. After independence from Soviet rule, the Central Asian region emerged as a breeding ground of religious sectarianism and the presence of radical Islamic elements in politics. Though a secular form of government was adopted due to their history under the Soviet rule, the influence of Salafists and Islamic groups is predominant in the Central Asian politics. Pan-Islamism and pan-Turkism as representing a concept, have acquired contagious dimensions in the region, with even some Uyghur organisations accepting them as a theoretical base. Extremist groups in Central Asia—the Islamic Movement of Turkestan (IMT), also known as the Islamic Movement of Uzbekistan (IMU), Hizb at-Tahrir al-Islami (HTI, or Party of Islamic Liberation) and Islamic Jihad Union (IJU) have expanded their activities beyond Central and South Asia to other areas of the globe. Ferghana valley, shared by Uzbekistan, Tajikistan and the Kyrgyz Republic, has emerged as an epicentre of terrorism in Central Asia. The proximity of Xinjiang to Central Asia has bolstered and leveraged the pan-

Turkic identity of the Uyghurs. There has been synergy between Xinjiang's Uyghurs and Central Asia on other aspects also. The Nevada Semipalatinsk Movement started in 1989[10] to ban the nuclear tests in Central Asia had a separate branch to protest against the Lop Nor nuclear tests at Xinjiang which purportedly caused civilian deaths in the area.[11]

The preeminent factor that catalyses the Central Asian connections of the Uyghur separatists is the ill-managed borders permeable to various illegal elements. The downfall of the Soviet Union and the subsequent independence of the five Central Asian states in 1991 led to enormous changes in the security architecture of these states. The nascent regimes proved to be inefficient and unable to manage the national security environment and the national borders efficiently. The border demarcation was made further cumbersome with the mixed ethnic population across the borders and the contradicting interpretation of the Soviet borders. Though China has now settled the border disputes with Central Asia, the borders still remain porous and, thus, safe havens for many illegal activities. The Border Management Programme for Central Asia (BOMCA), initiated by the European Union states had identified that the Central Asian states experience a number of problems along their frontiers that include "trafficking, cross-border terrorism, undocumented migration, and escalation".[12] The opening of the Chinese frontier with Central Asia which was closed for twenty years after the great leap forward led to greater mobilisation of people and ideas. This resulted in increased trans-border trade and traffic. The people of Xinjiang began to traverse freely to Pakistan, Afghanistan and Central Asia which, in turn, has led to trans-migration of radicalisation. After the September 11 event, the NATO forces initiated border management and financing the border policy of Central Asian states, out of the sheer necessity to control cross-border terrorism. But the problem of illegal migration and drug trafficking persists and poses a major threat to regional security. There are also sizeable numbers of the Uyghur communities in Central Asia, with Kazakhstan having the largest chunk. The Uyghur cause has a mass base of sympathisers in Xinjiang, including a prominent Uyghur Association, the Uyghur Association of Kazakhstan (UAK), functioning actively in Kazakhstan.[13] The presence of Islamist radical elements in the Central Asian politics is another matter of concern. The Chinese leadership has recognised these centrifugal forces that shape the ideology of the Uyghurs. The Chairman of the Xinjiang Autonomous Region People's Government Tomur Dawamat, in 1992, had openly charged that the independence of the Central Asian Republics has influenced the politics of Xinjiang. He stated: "The changeable international situation has affected and is still affecting Xinjiang's social stability. Hostile forces from both home and abroad have stepped up their infiltration, subversion and sabotage"[14]

Besides its diplomatic goal of diversifying the energy sources, China's policies towards Central Asia have been guided by factors that shape and transform the separatist movement in its homeland. The formation of the Shanghai Cooperation Organisation (SCO) constituting China, Kazakhstan, Kyrgyzstan, Uzbekistan, Russia and Tajikistan was a major move made by China in enlisting the support of these nations in its fight against "the three evils"—separatism, terrorism and extremism. At a meeting of SCO defence ministers in Bishkek in 2007, Russian Defence Minister Anatoly Serdyukov underlined: "We do not consider the SCO to be a bloc opposing someone. This is an organization created with a completely different task – to combat terrorism and nothing else."[15] China also engages with the Central Asian government through bilateral and multilateral military exercises, joint operations, trade and supply of training aid.

In the current security environment, with Xinjiang separatism fuelled by Central Asian radical groups and Uyghur organisations, it is highly unlikely that China would disengage with these nations. The post 9/11 intervention of the US in the region has also shaped the 'great game' in Central Asia and China's strategies towards the region. The robust presence of the US would prompt China to increase its grip in the region for larger ends.

China's interaction with Central Asia, the separatist movement at Xinjiang and China's energy demands are closely interrelated and deserve special attention. Chinese President Hun Jintao's declaration in 2003 that oil and finance constituted the two most important components of China's national economic security revealed the importance that oil has assumed in China's 21st century economic calculus.[16] This demand is further expected to rise with the country's current pace of growth. China's diplomatic endeavours in all the energy rich nations have been guided by this contingency. Central Asia has received focal attention in China's energy security strategy. It has been investing huge amounts of money in the energy market of Central Asia and has adopted many initiatives in the region, including the construction and securing of oil transport routes, which has helped Central Asia open up to one of the second largest oil importers in the world. China now has increased stakes in the region with the 1,833 km gas pipeline operationalised in 2009, capable of feeding its energy thirsty sectors by providing 85 percent of the gas China currently consumes. [17] This was a giant leap that China made in the 'scramble for resources' in Central Asia that has seen a number of countries participating, including the US and India. As the transit route for China to these natural resources of Central Asia, the PRC would try every move to knit Xinjiang closer to China.

However, the strategic cooperation will be limited by the cautious Central Asian leadership which does not want Chinese intervention in the internal politics. But cooperation on the security level will be robust, mainly due to the presence of the SCO. Besides, as per the Bishkek Declaration, the stability and security of Central Asia can be essentially provided by the regional states, under the "established regional organizations", which intend cooperation with China under the SCO. Besides this, China has been providing military aid to the Central Asian nations to fight against terrorism in their own land. The SCO's anti-terrorist wing, the Regional Anti-Terrorism Structure (RATS) has been instrumental in this context. China was particularly helpful in assisting the Central Asian nations to fight with the Islamic Movement of Uzbekistan. This was because the Islamic Movement of Uzbekistan was suspected to be undertaking the training and recruitment of Uyghur nationalists in their camps in Afghanistan.[18] The Central Asian nations have reciprocated the Chinese efforts by shutting down Uyghur publications and offices and banning organisations.[19] This aspect will lead to further cooperation from the Central Asian governments in assisting China in dealing with its challenges in Xinjiang. China has also been supporting the efforts to contain the 'colour revolutions' of Central Asia as it harbours the apprehensions that they might spill over to China.

The stand of the Central Asian nations will also be conditioned by various other factors. To the closed space of Central Asia, the opening to one of the world's biggest markets is a huge incentive. The economic carrots that China has been offering along with this comprise an add-on. China does not try to impose democracy in the region, in any way, like the US. At the same time, it engages with the security scene here in an effective manner through fora like the SCO and joint military operations. Though this approach does not address the root of the security challenges in the region, it makes China more welcome to the region's governments. The approach of China towards the security aspect of the region can be, thus, crudely compared to the Chinese goods marketed to developing nations: not long-term, yet very attractive and very much in demand. Considering these factors, the Central Asian nations will readily cooperate with the Chinese government in tackling the presence of fundamentalist elements in Xinjiang, particularly given the fact that they face the brunt of such ethnic conflicts.[20] The few contentious issues that may slow down the Sino-Central Asian friendship include China's water sharing policies. Kazakhstan had expressed concern regarding the dam building in the Xinjiang province which led to an alarming reduction in the water levels of the Irtysh and Ili, two of the major rivers. However, China will actively observe the Central Asian geopolitics in the years to come and engage in close cooperation with them, which will strengthen its hold on Xinjiang.

Pakistan: The friendship between China and Pakistan has been hailed in terms like "higher than mountains and deeper than oceans".[21] The separatism in Xinjiang has led to varying trends in the Sino-Pak relations. Research on the subject attributes this more to the friction that has arisen in Sino-Pak relations because of the connection between the Pakistan based *jihadist* groups and Uyghur separatists. However, further study is required to analyse the facts and ascertain this.

The shift in the minority policy of the Chinese in the 1980s, aimed at the stabilisation and assimilation of the minorities, provided greater religious freedom to the Uyghurs. Islamic institutions, including the Chinese Islamic Institution, were reconstructed. Mosques and religious agencies were allowed to function freely, in what was a total shift from the earlier religious policies. This was rooted in the motive that increased religious activities would naturally reduce the space for political activities and protests. Pakistan became a major transit route for the Uyghurs who were now allowed to go for Hajj. Many of the Uyghurs settled in Pakistan instead of returning to their homeland. This period is known for the development of the Uyghurs' contacts with Pakistan. The opening of the Karakoram Highway in 1982 was another key factor that led to mobility and increased interaction of Xinjiang's Muslim population with Pakistan. Along with the normal trade, the highway has been serving as a conduit for the illicit drug trade and religion. Pakistan's religious movements—Tablighi Jamaat and Jamaat-e-Islami—are alleged to be providing education and training on *jihad* at Islamabad Islamic University and the Syed Mawdudi International Institute at Lahore.[22] The Pakistani nexus with the Uyghurs was natural if not expected, given the proximity, ideological affinity and flurry of mobility through the Karakoram Highway extending from Gilgit and Baltistan of Pakistan to Kashgar in Xinjiang. The Pakistani nexus with the Uyghur movement was exposed when, on October 2, 2003, Hasan Mahsum, the founder leader of the East Turkestan Islamic Movement (ETIM) was killed in South Waziristan, Pakistan, in a US-Pakistan joint operation. However, though it has been tolerant of the Uyghur presence on its soil, the Pakistan government has largely adopted an overtly supportive posture towards Chinese policies in Xinjiang. In 2010, Pakistan's Interior Minister Rehman Malik declared about the killing of Abdul Haq, another ETIM leader, that Pakistan treats ETIM "not only as an enemy of China but also as an enemy of Pakistan".[23]

It was a shared and reasonable concern that Xinjiang would lead to the rupturing of Sino-Pak relations. On deeper thought, given the foreign policy preferences of both nations and the trends in the relations between the two countries over the years, one would not subscribe to the view that Xinjiang has deteriorated or will deteriorate, the Sino-Pak nexus. China has rather assisted and helped the Pakistan government in various ways to break the connections between the Uyghur separatists and Pakistan's Islamist forces. As China is seeking membership in the Organisation of Islamic Conference (OIC),[24]

Pakistan's support will be crucial for it. On the other hand, China has been supporting Pakistan in crucial socio-economic and political spheres. After the US' desertion of Pakistan following the Soviet withdrawal from Afghanistan, Pakistan considers China a more reliable ally than the US. The world has been witnessing that the US' relations with Pakistan have been deteriorating in the last few years. Ever since Osama Bin Laden was found sheltered in Pakistan's backyard, US-Pak relations have had a dent of mistrust. However, the relations have been held together by strategic necessities like the US' presence in Afghanistan. Recent statements from the US have been reflecting this. US Defence Secretary of Leon Panetta, during his visit to New Delhi in June 2012, made it clear that the US and Pakistan share a "troubled relationship"[25], to which Pakistan's Ambassador to the US Sherry Rehman replied that the remarks have "reduced the space for narrowing the bilateral differences". "Just as India views the relationship with Pakistan as complicated, so do we," Mr. Panetta said. "And it is."[26] At this juncture, Pakistan is likely to look towards China rather than the US. It should be assumed that Pakistan's stance and actions on the separatist movement in Xinjiang are largely guided by its strategic needs.

China has also been providing business and trade opportunities for Pakistan in its efforts to "develop the West". Besides, factors like permanent membership in the SCO and common rivalry with India further add to Pakistan's needs from China. Perhaps it is this equation that has been averting friction between the two countries on a volatile issue like the separatist aspirations of an Islamic ethnic community. The Government of Pakistan has been extending full support to the Chinese efforts to crush the separatists. After the July 2009 crisis in Urumchi, the Pakistan government had expressed its satisfaction with the Chinese policies towards the Uyghurs. President Zardari said in the same year, "Pakistan appreciates the fact that the lives and property of Muslims in China are fully protected and their rights, including the right to worship, fully safeguarded"[27] . This was despite the fact that many mosques in Xinjiang were forcefully closed down and religious teaching outside officially approved establishments was prohibited. The Pakistan government did not raise its voice even as Amnesty International, the United Nations Committee on Economic Social and Cultural Rights (UNCESCR) and the UN Committee on Elimination of Racial Discrimination (CERD) condemned the treatment of the Uyghurs in XUAR.[28]

China and Pakistan have been conducting joint military exercises to improve their capacity and synergy in combating terrorism. These friendship exercises, that started in 2004, have boosted the ties between the nations in the non-traditional security sphere. The joint exercises aim at honing the counter-terrorism skills of both nations through sharing of professional skills and mutual experiences. The battlefield experience of the Pakistan Army is an overriding factor that China would consider important. The use of advanced weaponry, drills, live fire operations, and information exchange and the operational terrain have been highly beneficial to both armies. The Friendship 2004 exercise was conducted in Taxkorgan Tajik Autonomous county, an area bordering Jammu and Kashmir. The training here essentially helped the Pakistan Army to adapt to the terrain and the warfare methods most suitable there, a matter of crucial importance in case of a war with India. [29]On the other hand, this region is close to Xinjiang, which was beneficial to China in terms of training as well as demonstration. The Friendship 2010 exercise was conducted in the Ningxia Hui Autonomous Region jutting into Inner Mongolia, another troubled region in its northwest. Undoubtedly, these exercises have helped to increase the capability and operational efficiency of the Pakistan Army and the People's Liberation Army (PLA). The Xinjiang factor has, thus, only strengthened the already existing military cooperation between China and Pakistan in terms of arms trade and horizontal proliferation.

The building of Gwadar port in the Balochistan province of Pakistan in which China collaborated through financing and construction, is expected to be a backdoor gateway to Xinjiang. Gwadar port is also one of the important pearls in the "string of pearls strategy" of China. Though the primary objectives of China's activities in the port are to secure its oil resources in Africa and the Persian Gulf and to maintain a strategic presence in the Indian Ocean; it is also important as an alternative route to the landlocked Xinjiang. Xinjiang is 4,500 km from the east coast of China but from Gwadar it is just 2,500 km. The building of the port has led to increased cooperation and synergy between both the nations. The official website of Pakistan states that the port will catalyse projects including the trans-shipment of bulk cargo, oil storage, refinery and petrochemicals, export processing and industrial zones, tourism and export of minerals.[30] The purpose of the port has been stated as to vitalise economic growth in western and northern Pakistan, along with providing an outlet to the landlocked Central Asian countries and Afghanistan through transit trade.

The stringent measures from Beijing have been limited to the closing of road links with Pakistan for a few months or lodging protests against the Pakistani training camps that trained some of the detained Uyghur separatists. In January 2014, China's Central Bank also announced new measures to freeze the assets of the terrorist groups in China and their "overseas affiliates".[31] This move underlines China's concern over the terrorist outfits being funded by outside forces, prominently Pakistan. However, there has been cooperation between the two countries to prevent the nexus of the Uyghur separatists with Pakistan. China would need Pakistan's support and cooperation in several aspects in the years to come, combating terrorism included. If China gains membership in the OIC, it would further enhance the cooperation between the two in fighting terrorism. However, one may argue that there is nothing like all- weather friendship in international relations. Relations between any two nations are more or less like a marriage of convenience. But the counter to that is the fact is that even when viewed from this angle, the scope of Sino-Pak cooperation only increases!

Afghanistan: Known as China's "bridgehead to the West", Xinjiang is the only area where China shares a border with Afghanistan. The Afghanistan factor figures prominently when China weighs the strategic importance of Xinjiang. With the United States and the NATO forces set for a phased withdrawal from Afghanistan by December 2014, the shifting power games in the region will feature China as a major player. Raw materials and oil and other energy resources would be the luring factors for China in Afghanistan. On the other hand, China would also seek to secure its borders with Afghanistan to prevent the spread of Islamist fundamentalism to troubled Xinjiang. China which had only undertaken a small number of projects in the country before the NATO declaration of phased withdrawal, has now bolstered its ties by signing a number of agreements and projects for economic and strategic partnership. A plan for establishing direct overland trade links between Xinjiang and Afghanistan has also been floated.[32] However, this proposal is reminiscent of the opening of the Karakoram Highway, which was opened for trade, but is now infested with trans-migration of Islamist fundamentalists to Xinjiang. With the security cover of the NATO now fading, there could be an increased upsurge of Islamic fundamentalist elements in Afghanistan. These factors would prompt Beijing to be extremely cautious of the plan, if at all it is put into action. The declaration issued on June 8, 2012, after the meeting of Chinese President Hu Jintao and his Afghan counterpart, Hamid Karzai, at Beijing, calling for closer cooperation in various areas, including border security, is an indication of this.[33] The Foreign Ministry of China has also indicated that the SCO will play an increasing role in the peace and stability of the region—a clear pointer to the concerns of China regarding the influence of Islamist radicalism in Afghanistan on Xinjiang. In any case, a stable Afghanistan would be in China's interest mainly due to its concerns about Xinjiang.

Xinjiang's and China's confrontation with separatism has led to the country's engagement in many regional fora. Afghanistan has been a part of this evolving regionalism due to geographical and other situational factors. The holding of the first trilateral dialogue among Afghanistan, Pakistan and China in Beijing on February 28 to 29, 2012, has opened a new platform for cooperation between the countries to combat terrorism. Inter-connectivity, resource development and fighting the 'three evil forces' have been given focus in the first meeting. This trilateral forum will be the platform for the PRC's future plans to ensure that the radical Islamic elements of Afghanistan do not traverse to Xinjiang. Afghanistan also has observer status in the SCO, which is expected to play a vital role in the reconstruction and stabilisation of the nation. China, however, does not seem to be proactive in the international efforts to sustain and develop Afghanistan's national security forces or engage excessively with Afghanistan's politics. It would be more interested in the economic aspects of cooperation, through which it can develop strategic cooperation rather than military aid and proactive capacity building. But Afghanistan would undoubtedly gain from the PRC's concerns on Xinjiang.

Japan: Sino-Japanese relations have remained fragile, despite close cooperation in some spheres. The disputes over the Senkaku Islands and East China Sea have led to fierce rivalry between the two nations. China also views Japan's military development and defence policy as directed against China. Economic ties is the one area that has been healthy between the two powers. However, the need of the two Asian giants to establish strong economic ties has been further strained due to Japan's involvement as a major host to the Uyghur nationalist organisations.

The Uygur connections with Japan began in the 1930s when Mahmut Muhiti, the commander-in-chief of the 6th Uyghur division visited Japan, seeking aid after the fall of the First East Turkestan Republic. The Japanese emperor granted him command of a division with which he launched an attack on China in 1937. The Japanese Uyghur Solidarity Association also referred to as the Uyghur Japan Association established in 2008 by the German-based Uyghur activist Dolkun Isa, has been functioning without any hindrance in Japan. Lately, the Munich-based World Uyghur Congress (WUC), which China considers to be an "anti-China splittist organization", held its general assembly meeting at Tokyo in May 2012. This was despite fierce opposition from China. Japan also went ahead and granted a visa to the exiled Uyghur activist Rabiya Kadeer, provoking Beijing. Japan reportedly has a caucus of parliamentarians headed by the current Prime Minister Shinzo Abe to support the human rights causes of the Uyghurs.[34] Japanese parliamentarians also sent across a strong message to the PRC that pressurising the Japanese law-makers not to support the activities of the Uyghurs in Japan would be considered "interference in its internal affairs".

Japan has its fair rationales for allowing Uyghur activities in the country. The World Uyghur Congress has declared that their means of protest would be non-violent and peaceful, and would seek to promote the democratic aspirations of the Uyghurs.[35]Besides, the WUC is not a declared terrorist organisation, despite a few of the Uyghur organisations being scrutinised for terrorist activities. As an advocate and practitioner of democracy, and China's rival in the Far East, Japan's stand towards the Uyghurs is just a natural move. Yet, considering the increased pressure on Japan to revitalise the economy after the world economic meltdown, the ties with China will be crucial. Bilateral trade between the two nations has not hit a low even in times of deteriorating diplomatic relations. China's natural resources are in demand in Japan whereas Japanese technology and equipment are traded in exchange. The highly complementary nature of the trade between the two countries has helped in the growth of Japan's economy.[36] This should be further scrutinised in the light of the accusation of the Uyghur activist Rabiya Kadeer that China has been using its economic clout to soften the opposition of other countries on matters regarding the human rights violations in China. However, even as Japan went ahead and made a provocative move through allowing the WUC general assembly meeting to be held in Japan, China did not react with the expected harshness. This reflects the changing preferences in the policy choices of China, and shows that even if political relations worsen, the economic relations between the two countries are not likely to depreciate, for economic and political relations are surprisingly paradoxical in Sino-Japanese relations.

Xinjiang and the Strategic Matrix of India

India's strategic choices in Xinjiang are often highlighted as being very significant. This mainly stems from the strategic location of Xinjiang, its role as China's gateway to energy rich Central Asia and the implications that a separate Xinjiang could have on the Sino-Pak nexus. India has been taking a neutral stand on Xinjiang till now. As a nation engaged on both sides by China and Pakistan and lassoed in the synergy between the two in crucial strategic spheres, India would largely benefit from cutting off the artery between the two nations. What will be the implications of a separate Xinjiang for India? Does India have any say at all in Xinjiang's separatist struggle?

It has to be seen whether a separate Xinjiang, which at least in the next few years is a distant scenario, would be stable. The possibility of a strong and able leadership that could lead Xinjiang is also bleak, given the current circumstances. Assessing the nexus with the Islamist fundamentalists in Central Asia, Afghanistan and, most importantly, Pakistan, it would not be a wise move for a terrorism stricken country like India to support the cause of a separate Xinjiang. India is the second most affected country by terrorist activities after Iraq, as per the US State Department's Annual Report 2007.[37] Considering the picture of Xinjiang today, help and support, ideological and otherwise from Pakistani and Central Asian fundamentalists would gain momentum after its separation. In such a case, India would be at the receiving end of snow balling Islamist fundamentalism in the region.

Also, India's interference in the region will be limited if not completely absent. India's usual role of a democratic harbinger will not be viable in Xinjiang, whose credentials as an oppressed state are questioned, unlike Tibet. It is also a matter of debate whether India has the potential to affect the course of separatism in Xinjiang. Unless a nation has a firm physical presence in the region, it is difficult to involve and guide the course of a separatist movement. This involves a number of both minor and major factors like ideological affinity, similarity in physical features, political and diplomatic support, and assistance in capacity building and promoting the cause in international fora.[38] None of these seems to be India's forte in Xinjiang.

India's aspirations in the SCO should also limit any support from it to the Uyghur nationalists. With India having expressed its keen interest in playing an active role in the counter-terrorism efforts under the SCO and with the SCO's Tashkent-based Regional Anti-Terrorism Structure (RATS)[39], its moves on Xinjiang will not be overtly supportive. At present, Russia has been supportive of India's permanent membership in the SCO, while Beijing has been sceptical, insisting that India should first fulfill the criteria of membership.

Conclusion

China has been successful in assembling many of the member countries under the banner of "fight against the three evils" to counter separatism in Xinjiang. Kazakhstan, Uzbekistan and Pakistan have put restrictions on, and also disbanded, many Uyghur political parties[40]. This will considerably reduce the support base for the Uyghurs in Xinjiang. As China seeks to increase its multilateral participation and cooperation in the security domain, Xinjiang will serve as a bait in its hands to garner support and cooperation in combating non-traditional security challenges through various security fora. At the same time, the reaction of the PRC towards the separatists will have to be wisely crafted. It will constantly pose a challenge to China's desire of projecting its image as a harmony seeking and responsible global actor. This becomes especially significant in the contemporary scenario where, in spite of press censorship, news and reports about Xinjiang are widely spread through Uyghur websites and other platforms of the new media. [Now, the US-based Radio Free Asia (RFA) is assisting in the broadcasting services of the Uyghurs]. This ensures that the incidents censored and unreported in the state controlled media are made known to the outside world. These factors make China's human rights diplomacy weak at a time when China needs it the most. There is an equally strong opinion that China would use an iron fist to stifle its domestic turmoil under the established belief that the world may protest at first, but later, will come to accept it.[41] However, China views the next twenty years as the ideal time for its growth and development, as it does not foresee a major power war in this time period. This view of China is often expressed in many fora by important Chinese officials. China will seek to make use of all diplomatic moves to establish its status as a benign and benevolent power in this crucial time period, and is not likely to risk deterioration of diplomatic ties with other nations. It would rather adopt a policy of cooperation with the regional actors in combating this issue. A popular hope was that the leadership changes in China would influence its minority policies, thus, transforming its treatment of the Uyghurs. However, even with the new leadership, it will take years for the policies to transform completely.

Predictions on Xinjiang's future status would be dicey. However, one can say with firm conviction that Xinjiang will shape many of the important policies and the diplomatic posturing of China in the years to come. China would employ every possible strategy to win over Xinjiang, considering that the national goal of safeguarding national sovereignty and security is primary for its development. The increasing domestic security budget of China has already been reflecting this contingency. Since maintaining domestic stability in China is firmly linked to maintenance of regional stability, the regional states will see China increasingly play a dominant role in the multilateral fora and regional organisations. This will make it cumbersome for the Uyghur organisations to garner support from the regional states. The fears of China shedding its long held dictum "observe calmly; secure our position; cope with affairs calmly; hide our capabilities and bide our time; be good at maintaining a low profile; and never claim leadership" will further reduce the international space and opportunity for the Uyghur separatists to get a support base. In other words, the PRC's success in Xinjiang will reflect, to a large extent, its success as an approved regional leader and vice-versa.

Notes

1. Evan S Medeiros, *China's International Behavior* (Santa Monica: RAND Corporation, 2009), p. 47.
2. William A Joseph, *Politics in China: An Introduction* (New York: Oxford University Press, 2010), p. 342.
3. Edward Burman, *China, the Stealth Empire* (Gloucestershire: The History Press Ltd, 2008), p. 57.
4. K. Warikoo, "China and Central Asia: Review of Ching Policy in Xinjiang, 1755-1884" in K.Warikoo and Dawa Norbu, eds., *Ethnicity and Politics in Central Asia* (New Delhi: South Asian Publishers, 1992).
5. "Justice, Justice", the July 2009 protests in Xinjiang, China, 2010, Amnesty International

Publications, United Kingdom, see http://www.observatori.org/paises/pais_81/documentos/asa17027201 0en.pdf, accessed on July 2, 2012.

6. "Jobs, Education Highlighted in Xinjiang Development", Xinhuanet, see http://news.xinhuanet.com/english/china/2013-09/24/c_132747142.htm
7. Virendra Sahai Verma, "The Karakoram Highway", in Swaran Singh, ed., *China-Pakistan Strategic Cooperation: Indian Perspectives* (New Delhi: Manohar Publishers, 2007), p. 340.
8. Monika Chansoria, "India and China: Assessing the Need to Strengthen Bilateral CBMs", Sandia National Laboratories Albuquerque, 2012, p. 10, see http://prod.sandia.gov/techlib/access-control.cgi/2012/1210041.pdf, accessed on January 19, 2014.
9. Joseph, n. 2, p. 47.
10. 1989 - Formation of the Nevada Semipalatinsk Movement, International Campaign to Abolish Nuclear Weapons, see, http://www.icanw.org/1989, accessed on July 15, 2012
11. "Chinese Nuclear Tests Allegedly Caused 750,000 Deaths", *The Epoch Times*, see http://www.theepochtimes.com/n2/china-news/chinese-nuclear-tests-allegedly-cause-750000-deaths-14535.html, accessed on July 17, 2012.
12. George Gavrilis, "Beyond the Border Management Programme for Central Asia (BOMCA)", November 2009, see http://www.eucentralasia.eu/fileadmin/user_upload/PDF/Policy_Briefs/PB11.pdf, accessed on June 13, 2012.
13. Segey Rasov, "Kazhak Aspect of Uygur Problem, European Dialogue", see http://eurodialogue.org/eu-central-asia/Kazakh-Aspect-Of-Uyghur-Problem, accessed on July 15, 2012.
14. Lillian Craig Harris, "China's Policy in the Islamic World", *The China Quarterly*, March 1993, no. 133, pp.118-119, see http://www.clas.ufl.edu/users/ckshih/ANG6360/1119/Harris%20 1993.pdf, accessed on June 13, 2012.
15. Yitzhak Shichor, "China's Central Asian Strategy and the Xinjiang Connection: Predicaments and Medicaments in a Contemporary Perspective", *China and Eurasian Forum Quarterly*, (Washington DC: Central Asia Caucus Institute, 2008), vol. 6, no. 2.
16. Hongyi Harry Lai, "China's Oil Diplomacy: Is it a Global Security Threat?", *Third World Quarterly* (London: Routledge Taylor and Francis Group, 2007), vol. 28, no. 3, p. 522, see http://myweb.rollins.edu/tlairson/asiabus/chioildipl.pdf, accessed on January 7, 2013.
17. "China Launches Landmark Central Asia Gas Pipeline", *The Hindu*, see http://www.thehindu.com/news/international/article64979.ece, accessed on June 18, 2012.
18. Christinelu, "Chinese Interest in Central Asia", War Eye, 2011, see, http://wareye.com/chinese-interest-in-central-asia, accessed on January 15, 2013.
19. Niklas Swanstro, "China and Central Asia: A New Great Game or Traditional Vassal Relations?", *Journal of Contemporary China* (Abingdon: Taylor & Francis, 2005), p. 573, see http://www.silkroadstudies.org/docs/publications/2005/JCC_Swanstrom.pdf, accessed on January 7, 2013.
20. Bhagaban Behra, *Central Asia- China Relations Since 1991* (New Delhi:Vista International Publishing House, 2006), p. 194.
21. Rajshree Jetly, "Sino-Pakistan Strategic Entente: Implications for Regional Security", ISAS Working Paper (Singapore: National University of Singapore, February 2012) , see, http://www.isas.nus.edu.sg/Attachments/PublisherAttachment/ISAS_Working_Paper_143_-_Email_-_Sino_Pakistan_Strategic_Entente_14022012160926.pdf, accessed on July 17, 2012.
22. K. Warikoo, "The Xinjiang Issue: Indian Perspectives on Chinese, Strategies in the Far West", in Marlène Laruelle and Sébastien Peyrouse, eds., *Mapping Central Asia: Indian Perceptions and Strategies* (Johns Hopkins University: 2011), p. 227.
23. "Pakistan Tells 'Chinese Brothers', Uighur Leader Killed", May 7, 2010, see http://www.worldbulletin.net/index.php?aType=haber&ArticleID=58193, accessed on June 13, 2012.
24. Abanthi Bhattacharya, "The Xinjiang Factor", in Singh, ed., n. 7, p. 357.

25. Gardiner Harris, "Defence Chief Shrugs off Objections to Drones", *The New York Times*, see http://www.nytimes.com/2012/06/07/world/asia/in-new-delhi-leon-e-panetta-defends-drone-strikes-in-pakistan.html, accessed on July 15, 2012.
26. Ibid.
27. Gunjan Singh, "China in Pakistan: The Xinjiang and Kashgar Factors" (New Delhi: Institute of Peace and Conflict Studies, August 10, 2010), see http://www.ipcs.org/article/china/china-in-pakistan-the-xinjiang-and-kashgar-factors-3209.html, accessed on June 20, 2012.
28. Joseph, n.2 , p. 10
29. Ajay Lele, "Friendship 2004: Sino-Pak Military Diplomacy Coming of Age", *Opinion* (New Delhi: Society for the Study of Peace and Conflict, September 11, 2004), see http://www.sspconline.org/opinion/Friendship2004Sino-PakMilitaryDiplomacyComingofAge_AjeyLele_110904, accessed on June 28, 2012.
30. Gwadar Port, Thursday, June 21, 2012, see http://www.gwadarport.gov.pk/Home.aspx, accessed on June 21, 2012.
31. Ananth Krishnan, "China Moves to Choke Funding of Terror Outfits in Xinjiang", *The Hindu* (Bangalore), January 18, 2014.
32. Ananth Krishnan, "Xinjiang Eyes Direct Land Trade with India, Afghanistan", *The Hindu*, June 5, 2012, see http://www.thehindu.com/business/Economy/article3493966.ece, accessed on June 28, 2012.
33. China "Gets Ready for Bigger Role in Afghanistan", CBC news, see, http://www.cbc.ca/news/world/story/2012/06/08/china-afghan.html, accessed on June 28, 2012.
34. "Japan Backs Uyghur Rights", The Uyghur American Association, see http://uyghuramerican.org/article/japan-backs-uyghur-rights.html, accessed on July 2, 2012.
35. "HRH Bergen, Rafto Prize Laureate Reelected as President of Uyghur Congress", June 3, 2012, Human Rights House Network, see, http://humanrightshouse.org/Articles/18136.html, accessed on July 10, 2012.
36. Chu-yan Cheng, "Sino-Japanese Economic Relations: Interdependence and Conflict" in James C Hsiung, ed., *China and Japan at Odds* (New York: Palgrave Macmillan, 2007), p. 83.
37. Devyani Srivastava, "Terrorism & Armed Violence in India IPCS Special Report: An Analysis of Events in 2008" (New Delhi: Institute of Peace and Conflict Studies, May 2009), p.1, see http://www.ipcs.org/pdf_file/issue/SR71-Final.pdf, accessed on June 11, 2012.
38. Interaction with Capt.A.V. Chandrashekaran, Senior Fellow, Centre for Air Power Studies) at CAPS, Delhi, on July 12, 2012.
39. "SM Krishna Arrives in China for SCO Summit", *Jagran Post*, June 6, 2012, see http://post.jagran.com/SM-Krishna-arrives-in-China-for-SCO-summit-1338959238, accessed on June 19, 2012.
40. Ariel Pablo Sznajder, "China's Shanghai Cooperation Organization Strategy", *Journal of IPS* (International Studies Association: Wiley, 2006), vol .5, p. 93, see http://irps.ucsd.edu/assets/004/5367.pdf, accessed on October 2, 2012.
41. The interaction with Mr Jayadev Ranade (Distinguished Fellow, Centre for Air Power Studies), at CAPS, New Delhi, on July 12, 2012.

12

The Emerging Sea-Based Nuclear Deterrence Capabilities of China and India

Arjun Subramanian P

The need to build deterrence arises from the fear of being harmed by another nation state with superior capability. This may be harm by way of physical damage or coercion or blackmail to constrain one's ability to pursue foreign policy objectives. This fear forces a nation to acquire the capability to neutralise the threat by building a deterrent force. The Cold War introduced deterrence at the nuclear level, and for the next 50 years, the game of deterrence was aggressively followed with every move at improving nuclear strike capability by the opposite camp being perceived as a threat, and counter-capability being developed as a result. The resultant nuclear deterrence prevented large scale wars for fear of crossing the nuclear threshold.

In the 21st century, two decades after the end of the Cold War, signs can be seen of a new game of nuclear deterrence emerging in a different region—in Asia. This can be seen in the context of the rapid emergence of some countries in Asia like China, India, Pakistan and Iran. Though there are, at present, five declared nuclear weapon possessing countries, only three have advanced and mature capabilities in terms of weapons, delivery systems, and command and control establishment, and they are: China, India and Pakistan. Among these three, China and India are in the process of acquiring a workable third leg i.e. sea-based nuclear delivery system. This paper attempts to study the emerging sea-based deterrence capability of China and India.

The Logic of Sea-Based Deterrence

The development of efficient delivery vectors for nuclear weapons has added tremendous value to it. Without the delivery systems, the utility of nuclear weapons as a deterrence tool would be negligible or zero. An example being the Soviet Union which attained nuclear weapon capability in 1949—ending the US' nuclear monopoly—but had no means to deliver it, hence, the Soviet nuclear bombs were not operationally deployed until 1953, when they managed to deploy their first strategic nuclear bomber, the TU-4 Bull.[1] So far, three primary modes of delivery have been developed: aircraft, land-based missiles and submarine launched missiles. The developmental progression of delivery vectors from aircraft-based to land-based missiles to undersea platforms was backed by concerns over the degree of the platforms' penetrating capacity into enemy air space, and survivability. These three modes of delivery have continued to evolve and improve, which, as a result, increased the value of nuclear weapons. A notable fact is that, even today, all three modes of delivery continue to be maintained by the nuclear weapon states.

By the time nuclear weapons were developed, the first mode of the delivery vector was already in place in the form of the B-29 'Superfortress' which was used to deliver the weapons on the two Japanese cities of Hiroshima and Nagasaki. Over more than a decade after World War II, long range bomber aircraft remained the only mode for long range delivery of nuclear weapons until the arrival of nuclear capable ballistic missiles. However, even after the deployment of missiles for nuclear delivery, nuclear capable aircraft continue to be deployed for the nuclear deterrence role. Nuclear weapon states still maintain nuclear capable aircraft in service like the US B-2 stealth bombers, Russian Tupolev TU-95 "Bear", Chinese H-6, and India's Jaguars and SU-30MKIs. Advancement in technology has led to tremendous improvement in nuclear strike aircraft in terms of penetrating capacity and standoff weapon launch capacity (with the development of long range air launched and nuclear capable cruise missiles). Despite these improvements, a bomber has drawbacks compared to ballistic missiles. A bomber is comparatively slower and relatively easier to intercept. The pre-launch survivability of a bomber is very low as the bomber bases are fixed assets and, hence, are easy targets. A bomber aircraft, unless it is a stealth aircraft, needs support aircraft to penetrate defended enemy air space to deliver the nuclear payload. Moreover, the ongoing research and development of counter-stelth radars will nullify the advantage of the stealth aircraft in the future.

Modern land-based ballistic missiles are far more efficient as a nuclear delivery platform than aircraft in terms of pre-launch survivability and penetrating capacity. A ballistic missile travels at hypersonic velocity and, hence, is extremely hard to intercept. Earlier, ballistic missiles were liquid fuelled and lacked mobility; they were stored in hardened silos to enhance survivability. Over the years, several improvements were made in ballistic missile technology which has made defence against it extremely complicated. Most of the modern missiles are solid fuelled and, hence, have the advantage of better mobility and less launch preparation time. Penetrating capacity is further enhanced with the use of the Manoeuvrable Reentry Vehicle (MARV), Multiple Independently Targetable

Reentry Vehicle (MIRV) technology and employment of pen-aids. The Gulf War was one rare case which demonstrated the pre-launch survivability of ballistic missiles. Despite the sophisticated and extensive surveillance and reconnaissance capability of the United States armed forces, the success rate in hunting down Iraqi mobile Scud launchers was very poor. The Iraqis employed a variety of tactics to prevent the US forces from locating and targeting their Scud missiles and launchers. "The elusive nature of the Iraqi targets (Scuds) is illustrated dramatically by the fact that on the 42 occasions during the war, when orbiting strikers visually sighted mobile TELs, in only eight instances were they able to acquire the targets sufficiently well to release ordnance."[2]

Nevertheless, even mobile land-based missiles could still be seen and could be targeted. In the Gulf War Scud hunt operations, the US military attempted to destroy the Scud targets by means of conventional precision targeting. Now, assuming the same scenario in the above example where 42 Transporter, Erector, Launchers (TELs) were visually sighted, and if Tactical Nuclear Weapons (TNWs) were used in the target area instead of Precision Guided Munitions (PGMs), the chances of complete destruction of all the sighted TELs is a near certain possibility. Hence, as a nuclear deterrence weapon, the land-based missile is still vulnerable to being targeted. This vulnerability factor served the logic for graduating towards deploying a sea-based nuclear deterrence force. Over the years, the submarine became the primary platform for deploying nuclear tipped ballistic missiles because of its extreme stealth characteristics. Particularly, a nuclear powered submarine with its tremendous endurance can patrol vast ocean areas, thereby extremely complicating Anti-Submarine Warfare (ASW) operations. "The concept of launching strategic ballistic missiles from submarines was first studied by the German Navy as a possible means of attacking American coastal facilities during the Second World War." In the post-war period, these German studies were used in US naval research to determine the feasibility of launching ballistic missiles from both surface and sub-surface combatants. While these studies became the source of technological development of submarine-based ballistic missile systems, the doctrine governing employment of these weapons in a strategic nuclear warfare context had another source.[3] Oskar Morgenstern, in his book *The Question of National Defense* (1959), recommended moving the main strategic retaliatory force out of the continental United States into the sea.[4]

Nuclear weapon states with only one leg of the nuclear deterrent have chosen the undersea arm of deterrence. The United Kingdom, at present, maintains only its sea-based nuclear deterrent force which consists of a couple of Vanguard SSBNs (nuclear powered ballistic missile submarines). Earlier, the UK maintained an air vector too in addition to SSBNs. "The July 1998 Strategic Defence Review precipitated major changes to the

British nuclear weapons programme, including the removal of air-delivered weapons from service and exclusive reliance on SSBNs for nuclear deterrence."[5] However, the UK never deployed land-based nuclear missiles for nuclear deterrence. The logic for this choice could be that the UK does not have a huge landmass and, hence, lacks strategic depth. Even with mobile nuclear forces, its mobility would have been restricted within its limited landmass. This reduces the survivability of the nuclear force. However, countries with a huge landmass and strategic depth have also deployed strong sea-based deterrence. This is due to concern over the survivability of their land-based nuclear forces and because sea-based deterrence is more survivable and would require enormous resources of the enemy to eliminate. Moreover, the enemy has a very small time window to eliminate all the SSBNs and, hence, this is a time critical task, which, if missed, might most possibly result in a nuclear strike from the remaining forces. And this is why nuclear armed states strive hard, despite enormous challenges, to have an effective undersea deterrence arm.

Chinese Sea-Based Deterrence

China's decision to develop and deploy a credible sea-based nuclear deterrent was a natural progression of its nuclear policy. Since China claims to continue and maintain a minimum deterrence posture, the primary emphasis is laid on the survivability of its nuclear assets from possible enemy strikes. One element of this survivable nuclear force is the underwater nuclear ballistic missile submarine force. Work on building a nuclear ballistic missile began during the Mao era, and on October 12, 1982, the People's Liberation Army (PLA) conducted its first successful test of a 1,700 km range Submarine Launched Ballistic Missile (SLBM), the JL-1, which carried a 600 kg payload. "A year before China had launched the Xia-class (Type -092) SSBN, derived from the Han-class SSN, with the hull lengthened to accommodate the missile tubes. The Type-092 became operational in 1983, though missile firings conducted in 1984 and 1985 were unsatisfactory due to fire control problems which were not resolved until 1988."[6] Even after two decades since it was deployed, it has not undertaken a single nuclear deterrence patrol. "In 2007, it completed a multi-year overhaul but did not sail on patrol."[7] The Type 092 vessel is said to suffer from major design problems, particularly with the nuclear propulsion system. The Xia class is slow, noisy and its reactor is unreliable.[8]

A new design (Type-094) has been planned since the late 1980s. This was based on the Type-093 (Shang class) nuclear-powered attack submarine, utilising the same power plant.[9] There were speculations that the development of the Type-094 class was assisted by the Russian Rubin Design Bureau. However, this information has not been confirmed.[10] This submarine is to be equipped with 16 JL-2 SLBMs, with a range of 8,000 km, and with an improved Circular Error Probable (CEP) compared to its predecessor, the JL-1. This improved system gives China the ability to launch nuclear strikes from a longer distance. However, though there were some reports on the successful test firing of the JL-2 missile, till date it has not been confirmed and even if it was test fired, the launch platform is not known.

Breaking out from its tradition of secrecy about its nuclear force, China this year made public its SSBN fleet capability. On this occasion, it was decommissioning its Xia class submarines after more than 30 years.[11] This event was followed by tremendous advertisement of the capability of its Jin class submarine to strike the United States. A number of state run Chinese newspapers carried articles boasting about China's ability to launch nuclear attacks against the United States. Estimates were made in the *Global Times* on the scale of damage the JL-2 could cause to the US. It said, "Because the Midwest states of the US are sparsely populated, in order to increase the lethality [our] nuclear attacks should mainly target the key cities on the West Coast of the United States, such as Seattle, Los Angeles, San Francisco and San Diego." It further said "The 12 JL-2 nuclear warheads carried by one single Type 094 SSBN can kill and wound 5 million to 12 million Americans".[12] Various Chinese newspapers gave out varying range estimates of the JL-2 SLBM. For example, the *Daily Mail* article reported that "JL-2 missiles have a range of about 8,700 miles and could hit almost the entire continental US with independently targetable reentry vehicle (MIRV) warheads."[13] However, in their "annual overview of China's nuclear forces" in the *Bulletin of Atomic Scientists*, Hans M. Kristensen and Robert S. Norris report that the JL-2, which is nearing initial operational capability, is only capable of carrying one nuclear warhead. Kristensen and Norris also put the JL-2's range at 7,000-plus km, while noting that the missile has never been flight tested at that range. If the range is 7,000-plus km, it is not capable of hitting the continental United States unless it is far from China's waters, Kristensen and Norris note.[14]

Employment Constraints and Vulnerability

The current Chinese nuclear submarine force comprises the Jin class (yet to be operational) submarine. The main asset of any submarine, particularly for a nuclear submarine, is its stealth, and that is the reason why nuclear submarines do not operate in groups; also, they operate at very low speeds, mostly four to five knots[15]. Though the Jin class submarine incorporates a lot of improvements over its predecessor in terms of stealth and other aspects, it still does not match or even come close to its US counterparts.

A 2009 report from the US Navy's Office of Naval Intelligence indicates that the Type 094 is louder than the Russian Delta III-class submarine developed in the 1970s. This means that the new Type-094 boats are more detectable than Russian technology nearly forty years old.[16] China is reportedly working on another SSBN design, namely, the Tang class, but it is unlikely to be operational in the near future. Hence, the Chinese might not press their SSBN fleet into long range nuclear deterrence patrols. Moreover, the US Navy, throughout the Cold War period had the practice of finding and trailing the Soviet boomers. The mission of these ASW forces was to detect, trail and if needed sink them. Therefore, it can be assumed that the Chinese will not risk sending their SSBNs on long range patrols, instead, as discussed by James. R Holmes and Tashi Yoshihara in their book *Red Star over the Pacific*, the Chinese might adopt the Soviet Union's bastion strategy, where the boomers would be operating under the protective cover of land-based and sea-based defences. They further argue that authoritarian regimes and particularly those driven by ideologies like Communism, which prize military officers' loyalty to the regime—and go to extraordinary lengths to enforce it—are ill-disposed to permit naval commanders this degree of control over strategic assets.[17] According to the US Department of Defence (DoD), the PLA has only limited capacity to communicate with submarines at sea, and the PLA Navy (PLAN) has no experience in managing an SSBN fleet that performs strategic patrols with live nuclear warheads mated to missiles.[18] Already, the Chinese have made an impressive advance in enhancing their anti-access and area denial strategy, so the possibility of them adopting this 'bastion strategy' is quite high.

However, the Chinese undersea deterrence force still suffers from serious vulnerabilities even within the bastion. Firstly, as discussed above, it radiates more noise and, hence, might be easily detected by the enemy ASW force. Secondly, the range of the missile deployed in this boat restricts the freedom of operation even within protective shore-based defences. The JL-2 has a range of 8,000 km; with this range, the submarine has to operate beyond the first island chain and away from the protective envelope of land-based defences to target the US mainland. Otherwise, operating within the first island chain, the submarine can target Alaska and hit the extreme eastern fringes of the US mainland from the Sea of Japan and, operating from the northeastern areas of the South China Sea, Bohai Sea and Yellow Sea, it can target Alaska.[19] Hence, the range, constraint of the missile restricts the submarine to certain geographical areas even within the protective bastion. During times of crisis, the adversary could concentrate some of his ASW forces in these areas. Thirdly, the number of Jin class SSBNs that China deploys will also determine the effectiveness of its underwater deterrence.

According to *Jane's Underwater Warfare Systems*, four boats have been laid down[20] and with four boats, approximately two submarines can be on patrol at any given time. Therefore, in quantitative terms, the US would need to deploy less ASW resources for these two boats. Even if the submarines are operating within the protective bastion of land-based defences, the underwater ASW component of the US Navy, which is known to be quite advanced in terms of stealth and other aspects is certain to restrict the freedom of operation of the Chinese boomers. Above all, it is unlikely that China's Central Military Commission (CMC), which controls the country's nuclear arsenal, would hand over custody of the nuclear warheads to the navy during peace-time, which means that China would not deploy a fully functional sea-based deterrent like that of the United Kingdom or the United States. In a crisis, the SSBNs would have to be first outfitted with warheads and then deployed, and this being the case, the Chinese SSBN fleet would have no experience of operating an SSBN during a realistic military operation.[21]

Another factor affecting the Chinese deterrence in a major way would be the vulnerability of shore-based defences. The core elements of the Chinese shore-based defences are their anti-ship capability and air defence systems. The key components of their anti-ship capability are air-launched anti-ship cruise missiles and land-based cruise missiles and, possibly in the future, anti-ship ballistic missiles. The effectiveness of arrays of anti-ship missiles is based on the ability of the surveillance systems to detect, track, locate and cue target information to missile units or platforms. In a possible conflict, the surveillance systems along with air bases from where attack sorties could be launched, would be one of the primary targets of the US forces. Surface forces might find it difficult to enter the zone protected by land-based defences: hence, the underwater forces might deliver the initial blows on these targets along with US stealth aircraft. With the end of the Cold War, most of the US Navy SSBNs have been converted to SSGNs (nuclear powered guided missiles submarines) equipped with Tomahawk cruise missiles for the land attack role. Almost all of the US Navy's SSN fleet has also been optimised for the land attack role, equipped with Tomahawk cruise missiles, with a range of over 1,800 km.[22] The long range of the missile enables the submarine to operate outside the Chinese bastion (immediately out of the first island chain to the east of Japan and from the northern Philippine Sea[23]) to strike the shore-based defences, and the stealth of the submarine permits it to penetrate the defended waters, considering the relative weakness of the Chinese ASW capability. "China has very limited ASW capabilities and appears not to be making major investments to improve them," explains Owen Cote, Jr. , an analyst at the Massachusetts Institute of Technology. "The ASW capabilities it does have appear focused on coastal defence, and on the threat posed by the diesel submarines of potential regional adversaries as opposed to American nuclear attack submarines (SSNs)."[24] The PLAN has deployed a large number of diesel-electric and nuclear powered attack submarines primarily for coastal defence. But the submarine crew suffer from lack of operational experience which is evident from the number of patrols the total submarine force has undertaken, which is just 55 from 1981 to 2007.[25] Recently, there were reports of increased Chinese submarine patrols.[26] After the year 2000, which saw the highest number of submarine patrols (6 patrols) since 1981, the year 2007 witnessed the same number of submarine patrols. The 12 patrols conducted in 2008 constitute the highest number of patrols ever for the Chinese submarine fleet.[27] This might have imparted some operational experience, however little, to the submarine crew. On the other hand, the flurry of undersea activity gives US forces more opportunities to tail and examine the Chinese submarines.[28]

Technological Bottlenecks and Options

The Chinese sea-based deterrence has a long way to go to be effective and credible. For the PLAN SSBNs to perfectly fit in their bastion strategy i.e. for their SLBMs to strike most part of the continental United States, staying within protected waters, the range of their SLBMs needs to be improved. A significant hurdle in this is that China may have to adopt a new SSBN design and build it to accommodate any new SLBM with increased ranges. Observing the pictures of the Jin class submarines available in the public domain, it can be observed that the missile section of the boat is raised in order accommodate the JL-2 missile as its length is longer than the height of the submarine's hull. Though the Chinese have made tremendous advances in ballistic missile technology, their solid rocket motor technology is not yet advanced enough to provide better burn rate performance comparable to the United States to enable reducing the size of their missiles for a given range. Hence, the Chinese may have to build a new submarine and new ballistic missiles with improved range to have the capability to launch strikes on the US from within the bastion. The other option is that their submarine technology has to reach a certain mark in reducing the acoustic signature for the SSBNs to venture out of the protected waters to operate autonomously and strike the US mainland with the current JL-2 missile.

Indian Undersea Nuclear Deterrence

The Logic of India's Sea-Based Deterrence

Having adopted a minimum deterrence doctrine which means that India's nuclear force structure will be minimal, with the assets required to just cause unacceptable damage so as to deter the adversary from launching a first strike, the primary focus would be on continuously enhancing the survivability of its nuclear strike force. The forces that are capable of surviving a disarming first strike should be enough to cause unacceptable damage to the state that launched the first attack, or to put it another way, the surviving forces should be capable of causing damage beyond what the aggressor thinks he can absorb. The survivability of the land-based nuclear force is a sum of several factors such as the mobility of the delivery systems, the hardening of the command and control system and the redundancy in place, the extent of knowledge of the enemy on the location of the nuclear assets and its vulnerability and its capability (force levels) to neutralise the adversary's assets. These are the factors that need to be known to measure the survivability of own nuclear force. Unfortunately, the last two factors cannot be known in full detail and even if known, the element of doubt always remains. And this element of doubt leads to the quest for a better delivery platform that is hard to detect and destroy. One platform that is very hard to detect, track and destroy is the submarine. And this is the reason why India too, following in the footsteps of other nuclear weapon states, has opted for deploying a sea-based deterrent force.

The Indian ATV Programme

Prime Minister Manmohan Singh on July 26, 2009, dedicated the indigenously built nuclear submarine INS *Arihant* to the nation. Plans to build an indigenous SSBN started in 1974[29] and the Advance Technological Vessel (ATV) project was launched in 1983 under the guidance of Dr Raja Ramanna, with Vice Adm Mihir K Roy as the director general of the project.[30] To train the naval personnel in operating a nuclear submarine and to familiarise the scientists with nuclear submarines, India leased a Charlie class submarine (INS *Chakra*) from the Soviet Union for the period 1987 to 1991. However, most of the experience gained in operating the SSN was lost by 2009 when the indigenous SSBN was launched as many senior commanders who were involved in it had already retired. To address this, India again leased a Russian Akula II class nuclear attack submarine (SSN) in 2010 for a ten-year period to impart training to naval personnel in operating a nuclear submarine.

In 1998, India declared itself a nuclear weapon state with a No First Use (NFU) policy, after testing five nuclear devices in the deserts of Rajasthan. "After the Kargil conflict in 1999, the Indian government announced its intention to put in place a nuclear triad. The ATV project got a big boost at this time, when, in November 2003, the miniaturised nuclear reactor went critical inside a simulated submarine hull (seeking to replicate *Arihant* conditions) on land at Kalpakkam. In 2006, the land-based prototype nuclear reactor at Kalpakkam was declared operational, and in January 2008, it was integrated into the *Arihant*."[31] The INS *Arihant's* 80MW reactor achieved criticality in August 2013 and is undergoing sea trials. Several agencies, both public and private, are reported to have taken part in the design and fabrication of the vessel. Those agencies are the Department of Atomic Energy (DAE), Defence Research and Development Organisation (DRDO), Indian naval engineers, and among the private participants, Larsen & Toubro (L&T) played a major part in fabricating the hull of the submarine.[32] At present, it is reported that two more vessels of the same class are under construction.

Design of INS Arihant

The design is said to be based on the Russian Akula-1 class SSN. However, it can be observed from the pictures of the INS *Arihant* available in the public domain that the coning tower is different from the Akula class. Unlike the Akula class, the coning tower looks taller and rectangular and is located near the bow and not at the centre. It suggests that the four Vertical Launch Stations (VLS) (tubes) are located behind the tower. Each VLS can carry a maximum of three K-15 Sagarika (B05) missiles or one long range K-4 missile, which is under development. Since the INS *Arihant* is said to be based on the Russian submarine, it should most probably be a double hulled design. All the Soviet submarines, except the latest Lada class boats are double hulled.[33] The two-hull construction of military submarines is based on the fact that the optimal shape for a deep-diving pressure hull and the optimal shape for a high speed hull are different. The outer hull does not support the external water pressure; since the space between the pressure hull and the outer hull is flooded, the outer hull provides a hydro-dynamically smooth surface over the main ballast tanks, hull-mounted hydro-phone arrays, and external frames. US submarines have two hulls in the bow, stern, and over the missile tubes, and a single hull along the rest of the ship. A double hull would protect the inner pressure hull from the initial high, peak overpressure of an underwater explosion, although it would not attenuate the aftershocks associated with such an explosion. The advantage of a double hull is that less space is used for structural support in the cramped pressure hull, and that "considerable eccentricity or non-circularity of the hull can be tolerated," whereas single hulls must be very nearly circular to withstand high pressures.[34]

The other important factor is the reactor design. India has built an 80MW reactor to power the INS *Arihant*. The life of a reactor can be guessed to an extent by knowing the level of enrichment of the fuel. US SSBN reactors use highly enriched uranium and, hence, the reactor life is equal to the operational life of the boat. The Russian SSBN reactors which used low enriched uranium, had a shorter life. The Indian reactor is said to be built with Russian assistance and, hence, the reactor life could be shorter.

Command, Control and Communication

Having a sea-based deterrent force is a complex task in every aspect from design of the submarine, testing of the delivery vehicle to operating it. Operating a SSBN fleet is a long and complicated task. Better Command, Control, Communication (C3) is indispensible for war-fighting, and to have an efficient system in place that will work under a restricted environment, is a major challenge. Submarine operations, particularly SSBN operations, present major challenges in maintaining an efficient C3. The primary problem is that sea water heavily attenuates radio signals and this complicates communicating with a submarine. Certain low frequency waves penetrate up to a few metres, for example, Very Low Frequency (VLF) and Extremely Low Frequency (ELF) are mostly used for submarine communication. VLF penetrates up to a certain depth, say 40 to 50 metres (m) and ELF, due to its lower frequency, penetrates still deeper.

The Indian Navy is using VLF to communicate with its submarine fleet. A huge VLF transmission station was set up some 23 km north of Kudankulam in Tamil Nadu, named INS *Kattabomman* and was commissioned in 1990.[35] The primary role of the base is to provide a continuous global communication link in the VLF spectrum to ships and submarines in the country's areas of interest. The 3,000 acre base enclosed in a 22 km perimeter wall hosts the VLF transmitting grid, which is the only one of its kind in the country. The antenna structure consists of 13 high raised cable-stayed steel masts in the form of a 6-pointed star.[36] VLF has its advantage as well as disadvantages, for instance, the VLF can be used over long distances for communication and can penetrate up to a certain depth. However, due to its low frequency, the bandwidth is limited and can transfer at the rate of 67 words per minute.[37] To receive the transmitted data, the submarine needs to rise up to a shallower depth and has to move at a slower speed for better reception. ELF has some similar kinds of advantages and disadvantages with deeper penetration than VLF and longer range transmission, but much lower bandwidth. Another big disadvantage is that the transmitting stations are huge; the transmitting antenna runs into several kilometres (the length of the antenna is inversely proportional to the frequency of the transmitted wave), making it a huge target. Hence, to build redundancy in the submarine communication system, India needs to look at several methods and multiple transmission systems.

The Defence Electronics Applications Laboratory, Dehra Dun, conducted a study on the applicability of ELF and concluded that ELF radio communications is the most reliable means of withstanding a nuclear explosion.[38]It is to be noted that the former Navy Chief, Adm Nirmal Kumar Verma, in 2008, as flag officer commanding-in-chief, Eastern Naval Command, visited the INS *Kattaboman* just a year before the INS *Arihant* was launched. On February 28, 2013, *Jane's* reported that India was setting up an ELF transmission facility very close to the VLF station. The construction began in March 2012, when Adm Nirmal Verma laid the cornerstone for the ELF facility near the village of Vijaya Narayanam.[39] So the ELF will be used for communicating with the Indian SSBN force in the future. This might also indicate that India has plans to put its SSBNs on patrol over longer distances. There is also a possibility that the navy might use high frequency satellite communication. It has to be noted that this year, a military satellite dedicated to the Indian Navy was launched, which could be used for communicating with its SSBN fleet.

Apart from this, the Strategic Forces Command (SFC) could also look at the US Take Charge And Move Out (TACAMO) systems. These are airborne command posts and these aircraft are linked to airborne VLF transmitters directly, through relay aircraft, ground stations, satellites, and even the emergency rocket communication system on some Minuteman II Intercontinental Ballistic Missiles (ICBMs). During a war, it is expected that the land-based VLF and LF transmitters will be destroyed, and, therefore, they are relegated to a support role in the joint chiefs' war-time Minimum Essential Emergency Communication Network. TACAMO aircraft transmit VLF signals at a power of 200 kilowatts through a pair of wires, one 30,000 ft long that hangs downwards, and one 4,000 ft long that trails behind the plane as it executes a slow, continuous turn. The antenna configuration resulting from this manoeuvre generates a signal that efficiently penetrates sea water to depths of 30-50 ft.[40]

The navy should also invest in R&D for future submarine communication systems. Submarines very rarely transmit messages, as transmission of radio energy makes it vulnerable to detection. Moreover, submarines cannot transmit in low frequency as that will require large antennas which cannot be incorporated in a submarine. However, two-way communications will enable better command and control of the SSBN fleet. One fact which might be of interest to the Indian Strategic Forces Command (SFC) is the High Frequency Active Auroral Research Programme in the US which investigated using the ionosphere as an antenna for communication. The idea was to excite the upper atmosphere with high frequency radio waves, and it would then emit the ELF bands required for one-way communication with submerged submarines. The new system is the first two-way communication method for submarines at depth. The actual depth is classified, but according to Reints, the cables attached to the tethered buoys are "measured in miles" and would allow them to be launched from "a significant depth." The submarine could continue normal operations at its normal speed while communicating.[41]

As far as command and control is concerned, it will be centralised and launch orders will flow from the political authority to the SFC, which will then communicate it to the SSBNs. For SSBN operations, a centralised C3 is preferable. During the Cold War, both the United States and the Soviet Union maintained constant centralised control over their submarine forces.[42] A centralised C3 system seeks to empower a central commander to collect and process enormous amounts of information, and issue orders to guide the actions of subordinate command units. Centralised C3 requires a reliable communication system so that the central commander can remain in constant contact with his subordinates. The system requires training, consisting of rote drills and scripted exercises designed to get officers at the tactical level to follow orders.[43] It would take several years for all this to be perfected and, hence, it would take a long time for the completion of the Indian nuclear triad in the real sense.

Present Capability and Limitations

Some analysts believe that the INS *Arihant* is just a prototype and will not be deployed on strategic deterrence patrols but will remain as a test and training platform. On the other side, reports claim that the boat will be deployed and will be operationalised by 2014.[44] However, looking at various aspects, it appears that it will take much longer than what is claimed to push this first vessel into a deterrence patrol and even longer to attain a credible sea-based nuclear deterrent force in the real sense. The primary problem is with the range of the K-15. The missile is reported to have a range of 700 km when launched in the conditions under which it has been tested so far. This limited range becomes a serious constraint. For example, this missile cannot reach Islamabad or Lahore even when the boat positions itself close to the Pakistani shore. The only major city that the boat can threaten from a safe distance is the port city of Karachi.

For strikes against China, the boat has to position itself inside the first island chain to get within striking distance of Shanghai. Worse, to reach within striking distance of Beijing, it has to operate in the Yellow Sea or Bohai Sea, which is close to one of the PLAN bases, which is also a base for its submarine fleet. This will be a highly risky endeavour as the boat has to operate in a tactically live area, making it highly vulnerable to detection. Hence, as a sea-based deterrent, this missile has relatively very limited value. The DRDO is also developing the K-4 SLBM that reportedly will have a maximum range of 3,500km, which, when deployed, will enable the submarine to operate from a longer distance to be within striking distance of the target and complete the triad in the real sense.

As mentioned earlier, the INS *Arihant* has four VLS which can house 12 K-15 SLBMs i.e. three in each tube or each tube can be fitted with one 3,500 km K-4 SLBM. However, the size and weight of the K-4 might necessitate some modification to be made to the submarine like adjustment in the Centre of Gravity (CG), centre of buoyancy, acoustic signature and power. The length of the missile is reported to be 12 m and according to *Jane's Fighting Ship* (2011), the height of the submarine is 14 m. Now considering the launch tube, gas generator and the space that will be left from the hull to the beginning of the launch tube from below, it appears that a portion of the missile might be popping out of the present hull. If this is the case, then a hydrodynamic outer envelope might be needed. Almost all of the Russian and Chinese SSBNs have this outer envelope due to the extra length of the missile. In the Jin class submarine (Fig 12.1), for example, the outer cover can be observed. India should work towards reducing the length of the missile by increasing the burn rate performance of solid booster stages and make other improvements.

Fig 12.1

Source: http://www.military-today.com/navy/jin_class.jpg

Operation Strategy

A country's SSBN operation philosophy depends on the capability of its platform, technological sophistication compared to its potential adversaries and the capability of its SLBM. The Soviet Union adopted the bastion strategy because of the technological inferiority of its submarines and SLBMs. The Soviet SSBNs were noisy and at one stage of the Cold War, had SLBMs with sufficient range to target the entire continental

United States. So these boats were operated close to the Soviet coastal waters under the protective envelope of its land-based and sea-based forces. The Chinese too, as explained above, have adopted the bastion strategy due to similar reasons. Now what will be the operational philosophy of the Indian SSBN fleet?

The limitations as discussed above, are two: firstly, the range of its SLBM and the limitation of its design, more specifically, its acoustic signature. Being based on a Russian design, it can be said that the acoustic profile cannot be as good as the US and other Western SSBNs. As far as Pakistan is concerned, the boat has tremendous deterrence value as the range is sufficient and the boat can remain within the protected envelope. However, its deterrence value against China has some limitations. Considering the second limitation, the best strategy for India would be to adopt the bastion strategy, i.e. to operate the SSBN close to its home waters within the protective envelope of its land-based and sea-based firepower. The waters surrounding India are, to some extent advantageous for submarine operations as a tropical climate is favourable for submarine operation in terms of temperature and other bathymetric profile which complicate ASW operation. However, the first limitation i.e. the limited range of the SLBM, puts a question mark on the possibility of adopting such a strategy. Even with the K-4, the boat has to operate on the extreme northeastern zone of the Bay of Bengal, close to the coast of Bangladesh and Myanmar to target the political and economic hubs of China. It is to be noted that Bangladesh is reportedly buying two Chinese submarines.[45] However, if operated outside the protected waters, the K-4 offers the luxury of operating far away from the Chinese coast. It can operate in the Pacific Ocean to a considerable extent across Japan and a little beyond the Philippines Sea and the South China Sea (the littoral environment offers a perfect zone for submarine operations). However, considering the current and near future state of the INS *Arihant*, it cannot perform truly autonomous operations.[46]

Reactions from Pakistan

India establishing a nuclear triad is a cause of concern for Pakistan as it shakes the very foundation of Pakistan's strategic policy. Pakistan's security policy is primarily India focussed and it uses its nuclear capability as an umbrella for continuing its anti-India activities, and also to deter even a major conventional offensive by India in retaliation to any of its anti-India activities. By deploying an effective sea-based deterrent, India is strengthening its retaliatory capability against Pakistan. As a response to this move, Pakistan is planning to deploy its own sea-based deterrence force.

Pakistan is planning to deploy its indigenously built nuclear capable cruise missile, the Babur, on conventional submarines. Also, it can arm its Harpoon missile with a nuclear payload.[47] However, it has to overcome the hurdle of miniaturising the nuclear warheads to fit into the missiles. Pakistan has acknowledged the existence of a sea-based nuclear deterrent with the recent inauguration of the Headquarters of the Naval Strategic Force Command (NSFC) by the head of the Navy, Adm. Asif Sandhila. A May 19 press release by the military's Inter-Services Public Relations stated that the NSFC "will perform a pivotal role in development and employment of the Naval Strategic Force," and was "the custodian of the nation's 2nd strike capability."[48] Pakistan has been working to integrate the French-built Khalid class submarines into its strategic forces for several years, but significant hurdles remain. Specifically, missile tubes have to be modified to handle nuclear-capable missiles like the Babur cruise missile, and the navy needs to be integrated into the country's existing nuclear command and control architecture, which is currently dominated by the army. [49] A Pakistani sea-based deterrent based on conventional submarines would, as a platform, be very effective against India. Conventional submarines emit very little noise compared to nuclear submarines. Moreover, some of Pakistan's submarines are Air-Independent Propulsion (AIP) equipped making them even more quiet, and all vital targets, from political to economic centres, are within the range of the Babur cruise missile.

Apart from deploying its own sea-based deterrent, it might push Pakistan closer to China. The 'all weather friends' might increase their strategic cooperation with an aim to offset India's nuclear lead. China is known to have supplied nuclear materials to assist Pakistan in its nuclear weapons programme. China is also building two nuclear reactors in Chashma, which will enable Pakistan to produce more plutonium to shift from uranium to plutonium fuel used in the bomb core, resulting in miniaturisation of its nuclear warheads. There is also a possibility of China providing Pakistan the knowhow of SSBN technology. However, it is doubtful if Pakistan can venture into this costly programme, given the poor state of its economy.

Conclusion

The Chinese and Indian sea-based nuclear programmes might best be stated as being at a nascent stage. While China has made considerable progress on this front during the past 30 years, India is just starting off with its first SSBN, which, in practical terms, can be called a technology demonstrator and a test-bed for building future platforms. China, though with considerable lead over India, has not, till date been able to operationalise its SSBN. The type 094 vessel has not undertaken even a single deterrence patrol though it is operational, but without a missile.[50] An enormous challenge lies ahead for both countries to deploy an operational undersea deterrent force. The first step, for both, would be to deploy a workable platform at sea which can at least perform the basic functions of an SSBN like sailing on a long distance mission, and test launching SLBMs from the platform. After this, there will be other tasks that have to be learned and perfected like setting up an efficient command, control and communication system with redundancy built into it, and a proper set of procedures during communication cut-off, and deploying sufficient numbers to enable having or two SSBNs on patrol at any given time. This process to put in place an undersea deterrence force of considerable effectiveness will take a long time.

In future, the importance of sea-based deterrence would only grow as the advancement of technology has enabled the possibility of high precision strikes using conventional means within a limited time window. The improving efficiency and precision of C4ISR networks in locating targets and the speed of strike platforms has reduced the sensor-to-shooter time. The US has been working on a project named Prompt Global Precision Strike which intends to strike any target across the globe within one hour of it being detected. Such advances in conventional precision strike technology will continue to reduce the degree of survivability of even mobile missile units. So, in the future, undersea platforms will continue to be the most survivable assets. Hence, India and China would only push further towards deploying an effective sea-based deterrent force.

Notes

1. George J. Refuto, *Evolution of the US Sea-based Nuclear Missile Deterrent: Warfighting Capabilities* (USA: Xlibris Corporation, 2011), p. 76 (pp 75-110).
2. William Rosenau, "Special Operations Forces and Elusive Enemy Ground Targets: Lessons from Vietnam and the Persian Gulf War", Monograph reports series, Document number MR-1408-AF, RAND Corporation, 2001, p.34.
3. Refuto, n.1, p.129 (pp 126-169).
4. Ibid., pp.129, 131.
5. "Overview", http://www.nti.org/country-profiles/united-kingdom/, July 2013, accessed on January 12, 2014.
6. "Type 92 Xia", http://www.fas.org/nuke/guide/china/slbm/type_92.htm, accessed on December 19, 2013.
7. Hans M. Kristensen, "Chinese Submarine Patrols Doubled in 2008", http://www.fas.org/blog/ssp/2009/02/patrols.php, February 3, 2009, accessed on December 21, 2013.
8. "Xia Class:Ballistic Missile Submarine", http://www.military-today.com/navy/xia_class.htm, accessed on December 21, 2013.
9. "Type 094 Jin-Class Ballistic Missile Submarine", http://www.globalsecurity.org/wmd/world/china/type_94.htm, accessed on December 19, 2013.
10. "Jin Class: Ballistic Missile Submarine", http://www.military-today.com/navy/jin_class.htm, accessed on December 20, 2013.
11. "China Unveils Nuclear Submarines That Could Reportedly Reach US", http://www.theblaze.com/stories/2013/11/01/china-unveils-nuclear-submarines-that-could-reportedly-reach-U-S/, November 1, 2013, accessed on December 18, 2013.

12. Ibid.
13. "State Media Boasts of China's Ability to Nuke US Cities", http://thediplomat.com/2013/11/state-media-boasts-of-chinas-ability-to-nuke-us-cities/, November 5, 2013, accessed on December 20, 2013.
14. Ibid.
15. Capt P Ashokan, " Nuclear Submarine For the Indian Navy –Roles and Concepts", *College of Naval Warfare (CNW) Journal*, annual issue, 2008, p. 109.
16. Thomas M. Skypek, "China's Sea-Based Nuclear Deterrent in 2020: Four Alternative Futures for China's SSBN Fleet", Centre for Strategic & International Studies, p. 110.
17. Toshi Yoshihara and James R Holmes, *Red Star Over The Pacific* (Annapolis, Maryland: Naval Institute Press, 2010), p. 131 (pp. 125-148).
18. US DoD, "Annual Report to Congress, Military and Security Developments Involving the People's Republic of China 2010.", http://www.defense.gov/pubs/pdfs/2010_cmpr_final.pdf, accessed on November 18, 2013.
19. The reach of the missile was measured with the help of the Google earth ruler tool.
20. Skypek, n. 16, p. 109.
21. Hans M. Kristensen and Robert S. Norris, "Chinese Nuclear Forces", *Bulletin of the Atomic Scientists*, 2011.
22. The inference was made from studying the details on the US SSN force from Cmde Stephen Saunders RN, *Jane's Fighting Ships* (Surrey, UK), 2011
23. Range measurements done by using Google earth application.
24. David Axe, "China's US Sub Hunter?", http://thediplomat.com/flashpoints-blog/2011/11/28/china%E2%80%99s-u-s-sub-hunter/, November 28, 2011, accessed on December 18, 2013.
25. Hans M Kristensen, "Chinese Submarine Patrols Rebound in 2007, but Remain Limited", ww,fas.org/blog/ssp/2008/01/Chinese_submarine_patrols_rebo.php, January 7, 2013, accessed on December 20, 2013.
26. David Axe, "China's Noisy Subs Get Busier --- And Easier to Track," http://www.wired.com/dangerroom/2011/12/china-submarines/, December 27, 2011, accessed on December 17, 2013.
27. Kristensen, n. 7.
28. Axe, n. 26.
29. "Why India Needs to Opt for Nuclear Submarines", http://www.indiastrategic.in/topstories765.htm , October 2010, accessed on January 10, 2014.
30. "How India's Pride INS *Arihant* was Built: A Look at How India's First Nuclear Powered Missile Submarine Came Into Existence", http://www.business-standard.com/article/specials/how-india-s-pride-ins-arihant-was-built-113081100745_1.html , August 12, 2013, accessed on January 11, 2014.
31. Ibid.
32. "Analysis: Now to Build Two More Nuclear-Submarines Quickly", http://www.ndtv.com/article/india/analysis-now-to-build-two-more-nuclear-submarines-quickly-403821, August 10, 2013, accessed on January 11, 2014.
33. Saunders n. 22, p. 663.
34. Tom Stefanick, *Strategic Antisubmarine Warfare and Naval Strategy* (Massachusetts: Lexington Books, 1987), p. 133 (pp 131-154).
35. "The Indian SSN Project: An Open Literature Analysis", http://www.fas.org/nuke/guide/india/sub/ssn/part01.htm, accessed on December 12, 2013.
36. "INS Kattabomman", http://indiannavy.nic.in/about-indian-navy/ins-kattabomman, accessed on December 20, 2013.
37. Stefanick, n.34, p. 146.
38. n. 35.

39. James Hardy, "India Makes Headway with ELF Site Construction", http://www.janes.com/article/11147/india-makes-headway-with-elf-site-construction, February 28, 2013, accessed on December 21, 2013.
40. Stefanick, n.34, p. 147.
41. Lin Edwards, "New Buoys Enable Submerged Subs to Communicate", http://phys.org/news198219967.html, July 13, 2010, accessed on December 19, 2013.
42. Andrew S. Erickson, Lyle J. Goldstein, Willian S. Murray, and Andrew R. Wilson, eds., *China's Future Nuclear Submarine Force* (Annapolis, Maryland: Naval Institute Press, 2007), p. 215 (pp. 212-228).
43. Ibid., p. 213
44. Compiled by Atul Chandra, "Indian Navy Procurement Plan", http://www.forceindia.net/newsyoucanuse_indian_navy_procurement_plan.aspx, accessed on December 20, 2013.
45. "Bangladesh Finalises Deals with China for 2 Submarines", http://zeenews.india.com/news/world/bangladesh-finalises-deals-with-china-for-2-submarines_898189.html, December 20, 2013, accessed on December 20, 2013
46. The analysis done here is based on the current available in the public domain.
47. Usman Ansari, "Pakistan Acknowledges Sea-Based Nuclear Deterrent", http://www.defensenews.com/article/20120523/DEFREG03/305230004/Pakistan-Acknowledges-Sea-Based-Nuclear-Deterrent, May 23, 2012, accessed on December 19, 2013.
48. Ibid
49. Shane Mason for James Martin, "From Dyad to Triad: What India's Nuclear Developments Mean for Pakistan", http://www.isn.ethz.ch/Digital-Library/Articles/Detail/?id=152229, September 14, 2012, accessed on December 17, 2013.
50. Kristensen and Norris, n. 21.